Grade 8

Grammar for Writing

Senior Series Consultant
Beverly Ann Chin
Professor of English
University of Montana
Missoula, MT

Series Consultant
Frederick J. Panzer, Sr.
English Dept. Chair, Emeritus
Christopher Columbus High School
Miami, FL

Series Consultant
Anthony Bucco
Language Arts Literacy Teacher
Pierrepont Middle School
Rutherford, NJ

Series Editor
Phyllis Goldenberg

Valerie T. 8A

Reviewers

Maria Davis Baisier
English Teacher
Holy Cross School
New Orleans, LA

Joan Borrasso
English Teacher
Aquinas Academy
Gibsonia, PA

Melissa Churchwell
Language Arts Teacher
Brooklawn Middle School
Parsippany, NJ

Jay Falls
Language Arts Teacher
Solon Middle School
Solon, OH

Stephanie Jones
Sixth Grade Teacher
Saint Francis of Assisi
Cordova, TN

Sister Rita Ann Keller, IHM
Language Arts Teacher
St. Gregory the Great
Virginia Beach, VA

Cheryl Kordes
Language Arts Teacher
St. Peter in Chains
Hamilton, OH

John T. Ludwig
Language Arts Teacher
Our Lady of Lourdes
Melbourne, FL

Darbie Dallman Safford
Language Arts Teacher
St. Monica School
Dallas, TX

Joan Sieja
Language Arts/Reading Teacher
Mary Queen of Heaven
Brooklyn, NY

Sister June Clare Tracy, O.P., Ed.D.
District Superintendent
Manhattan Catholic Schools
New York, NY

Mollie Mumau Williams
Language Arts Teacher
James W. Parker Middle School
Edinboro, PA

Acknowledgments

Every good faith effort has been made to locate the owners of copyrighted material to arrange permission to reprint selections. In several cases this has proved impossible. Thanks to the following for permission to reprint copyrighted material.

Excerpt from "Arctic Explorer: The Story of Matthew Henson" by Jeri Ferris. Text copyright © 1989 by Jeri Ferris. Reprinted with the permission of Carolrhoda Books, a division of Lerner Publishing Group, Inc. All rights reserved. No part of this text excerpt may be used or reproduced in any manner whatsoever without the prior written permission of Lerner Publishing Group, Inc.

Excerpt from BABE DIDRIKSON ZAHARIAS: THE MAKING OF A CHAMPION by Russell Freedman. Copyright © 1999 by Russell Freedman. Reprinted by permission of Clarion Books, an imprint of Houghton Mifflin Harcourt Publishing Company. All rights reserved.

Excerpt from *Chinese Cinderella and the Secret Dragon Society* by Adeline Yen Mah. Used by permission of HarperCollins Publishers.

Excerpt from *Elements of Style*. Copyright © Pearson Education.

Flight to Freedom. Copyright © 2002 by Ana Veciana-Suarez. All rights reserved. Published by Orchard Books, an imprint of Scholastic Inc.

Excerpt from *Freedom Rides: Journey for Justice* by James Haskins. Copyright © 1995 James Haskins.

Reprinted with the permission of Simon & Schuster Books for Young Readers, an imprint of Simon & Schuster Children's Publishing Division from HABIBI by Naomi Shihab Nye. Copyright © 1997 Naomi Shihab Nye.

From HOOT by Carl Hiaasen, copyright © 2002 by Carl Hiaasen. Used by permission of Alfred A. Knopf, an imprint of Random House Children's Books, a division of Random House, Inc.

From HUSH by Jacqueline Woodson, copyright © 2002 by Jacqueline Woodson. Used by permission of G. P. Putnam's Sons, a division of Penguin Putnam Books for Young Readers, 345 Hudson Street, New York, NY 10014. All rights reserved.

Reprinted by arrangement with The Heirs to the Estate of Martin Luther King Jr., c/o Writers House as agent for the proprietor New York, NY. *Copyright 1963 Dr. Martin Luther King Jr.; copyright renewed 1991 Coretta Scott King*

From IN MY HANDS: MEMORIES OF A HOLOCAUST RESCUER by Irene Gut Opdyke and with Jennifer Armstrong, copyright © 1999 by Irene Gut Opdyke with Jennifer Armstrong. Used by permission of Alfred A. Knopf, an imprint of Random House Children's Books, a division of Random House, Inc.

Excerpt from *M.C. Higgins, the Great*. Reprinted with the permission of Simon & Schuster Books for Young Readers, an imprint of Simon & Schuster Children's Publishing Division from M.C. HIGGINS, THE GREAT by Virginia Hamilton. Copyright © 1974, 1999 Virginia Hamilton. Copyright renewed © 2002 Arnold Adoff.

From MY SIDE OF THE MOUNTAIN by Jean Craighead George, copyright © 1959, renewed © 1987 by Jean Craighead George. Used by permission of Dutton Children's Books, A Division of Penguin Young Readers Group, A Member of Penguin Group (USA) Inc., 345 Hudson Street, New York, NY 10014. All rights reserved.

Excerpt from *Red Scarf Girl: A Memoir of the Cultural Revolution* by Ji Li Jiang. COPYRIGHT © 1997 BY JI LI JIANG. FOREWARD COPYRIGHT © 1997 BY HARPERCOLLINS PUBLISHERS. Used by permission of HarperCollins Publishers.

From *Rescue Josh McGuire* by Ben Mikaelsen. Copyright © 1991 by Ben Mikaelsen. Reprinted by permission of Disney • Hyperion Books, an imprint of Disney Book Group, LLC. All rights reserved.

Copyright © 2003 by Houghton Mifflin Company. Reproduced by permission from *Roget's II: The New Thesaurus, Third Edition*.

Somewhere in the Darkness. Copyright © 1992 by Walter Dean Myers. All rights reserved. Published by Scholastic Inc.

Excerpt from *The Century for Young People* by Peter Jennings and Todd Brewster. Copyright © ABC 1999. Published by Doubleday, an imprint of Random House, Inc.

From THE ROAD TO PARIS by Nikki Grimes, copyright © 2006 by Nikki Grimes. Used by permission of G.P. Putnam's Sons, A Division of Penguin Young Readers Group, A Member of Penguin Group (USA) Inc., 345 Hudson Street, New York, NY 10014. All rights reserved.

Credits

Cover Art and Design
Quarasan, Inc.

Interior Photos
Alamy/Image Source Aurora: 8 background; PhotoAlto sas: 300. Mark Anderson, www.Andertoons.com: 251. Jane Bernard: 224 right. CALVIN AND HOBBES © 1992 Watterson. Dist. by UNIVERSAL PRESS SYNDICATE. Reprinted with permission. All rights reserved.: 55. CALVIN AND HOBBES © 1994 Watterson. Dist. By UNIVERSAL PRESS SYNDICATE. Reprinted with permission. All rights reserved.: 185. CartoonStock/© Jason Love, www.CartoonStock.com: 180 bottom, 229; © Royston Robertson, www.CartoonStock.com: 283. Corbis/Blend Images/Erik Isakson: 99 bottom; Robert Llewellyn: 268 background. Getty Images/David Buffington: 126; Connie Coleman: 250 background; Color Day Production: 250; Jonathan Daniel: 286; Reza Estakhrian: 32 background; Arvind Gang: 64 background; Annie Griffith Belt: 224 background; Hulton Archive: 213; Dorothea Lange: 111; Bruce Laurance: 32; Liquorice: 8; Wallace Marly: 180 top; Patti McConville: 198; NASA: 276; Steve Snowden: 301; Stockbyte: 300 background; Siri Strafford: 224 left; Time & Life Pictures: 292; Transcendental Graphics: 178; Kevin Winter: 162. Copyright © Randy Glasbergen; www.glassbergen.com: 76. International Surrey Company Ltd.: 97 right. iStockphoto.com/Ana Abejon: 163; Martin Adams: 13; AzureLaRoux: 187; James Colin: 182; FreezeFrameStudio: 37; Jamie Garrison: 181; Christian Johnson: 253; Sergey Lavrentev: 274; Robert Linton: 113; Oleg Mitiukhin: 207; Andreas Rodriguez: 118; Spiderstock: 317; Luis Carlos Torres: 115. Jupiter Images/AbleStock.com: 152; BananaStock: 52, 239; Brand X Pictures: 11, 56, 64, 150, 186, 215, 261; Comstock: 41, 130, 204, 217, 258, 284, 287, 310; Photos.com: 18, 22, 70, 128, 156. Library of Congress/Prints and Photographs Division, LC-USZ62-108565: 77; LC-USZ62-111147: 210; LC-USZ62-25812: 234; LC-USZ62-43605: 206. NASA: 99 top. Picture History: 160. Punchstock/Brand X Pictures: 150 background, 170 background; Digital Vision: 97 background; Photodisc: 97 left, 170; Pixtal: 198 background; Stockbyte: 268. Used under license from Shutterstock.com/aceshot1: 209; Galyna Andrushko: 256; Annetje: 136; Cristi Bastian: 252; Christian Delbert: 126 background; Christa DeRidder: 184; Digitalskillet: 272; enote: 67; FloridaStock: 16; Joe Gough: 102; Laurence Gough: 315; Margie Hurwich: 75; iofoto: 51; Marcel Jancovic: 228; Jim Lopes: 81; manzrussali: 216; Andrew McDonough: 154; Stephen Meese: 71; MWProductions: 86; Richard L. Paul: 176; Elisei Shafer: 133; Floris Slooff: 200; Christophe Testi: 34; Tomasz Trojanowski: 278; Olga Tropinina: 308; Suzanne Tucker: 49, 312; Marcus Turner: 46; Bruce Wheadon: 85.

Copyright © 2014 by William H. Sadlier, Inc. All rights reserved.

This publication, or any part thereof, may not be reproduced, in any form, or by any means, including electronic, photographic, or mechanical, or by any sound recording system, or by any device for storage and retrieval of information, without the written permission of the publisher. Address inquiries to Permissions Department, William H. Sadlier, Inc., 9 Pine Street, New York, NY 10005-4700.

is a registered trademark of William H. Sadlier, Inc.

Printed in the United States of America
Student Edition: ISBN: 978-1-4217-1118-8
8 9 LSCW 19 18

Dear Student:

As a student, you are constantly being challenged to write correctly and effectively in a variety of subjects. From homework to standardized tests, more and more assignments require that you write in a clear, correct, and interesting way.

Grammar for Writing, Enriched Edition, teaches you the writing and language skills you'll need to be an effective writer and speaker, and prepares you to build on those skills in high school, college, and beyond. The first half of the book focuses on writing. In this section, you'll learn how to write correct and effective sentences, choose the best words to get your message across, and write strong paragraphs and essays. The second half of the book presents grammar lessons in a clear and entertaining way. You'll learn how grammar is used in everyday writing and how grammar mistakes can lead to misinterpretations that you'll want to avoid. Also, **Writer's Workshops** show you how to craft different types of writing, such as essays and stories.

Writing and grammar are subjects that you use every day. Whether you are writing a paper for class or e-mailing your friend, you can express yourself best if you know how to write effectively. *Grammar for Writing* was created with you in mind, and it includes topics that will inspire you and spark your curiosity.

While no textbook can make writing easy, *Grammar for Writing* breaks down the essential steps of writing in a way that makes sense. Throughout the book, there is a **Write What You Think** feature that helps you think critically to develop clear arguments. **Literary Models** draw examples from popular literature. Exercises in each lesson are interesting and easy to understand. If you need help, **Hint** features point you in the right direction and ensure that you get the most out of the practice.

The point of *Grammar for Writing, Enriched Edition,* is to sharpen the way you speak and write. By explaining grammar rules and writing techniques in a simple way, this book will help you become a better writer and more successful student.

Good luck!
The Authors

CONTENTS

Part I: Composition

Part II: Grammar, Usage, and Mechanics

CHAPTER 1

The Writing Process

Copyright © 2014 by William H. Sadlier, Inc. All rights reserved.

LESSON 1.1

Prewriting

You should always begin a writing task by planning, or **prewriting.** Prewriting includes the following steps: exploring possible topics, choosing and narrowing a topic, identifying a purpose and an audience, and collecting and organizing details.

Use these techniques to generate a list of possible topics.

Writer's Notebook	Keep a notebook to write about things you experience and observe, ideas you have, and people you meet.
Freewrite	Focus on a word or topic, read an article or passage, or study a picture. Then write down every thought that occurs to you. Be specific, but don't stop to think or to correct errors. Write for three to five minutes.
Brainstorm	Think of a broad topic. Then generate ideas related to this topic. Instead of writing sentences, make a list, or jot your ideas in a Web or other graphic organizer.
Discuss	Talk with friends and family members about common interests and experiences.

Remember

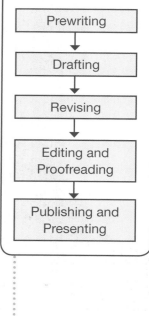

The **writing process** consists of five stages.

Prewriting → Drafting → Revising → Editing and Proofreading → Publishing and Presenting

Review your ideas to **choose** and **narrow** your topic.

- How interested am I in this topic?
- Is it narrow enough to write about?
- Can I easily gather details about it?

Check that your topic fits the length and specifics of the assignment. Ask ***5-W and How? questions*** to divide a big topic into smaller parts. Here are one writer's questions about the astronomer Galileo.

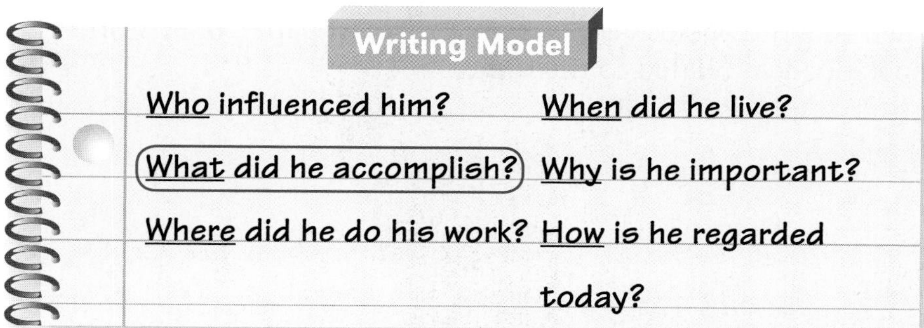

Writing Model
Who influenced him?
When did he live?
What did he accomplish?
Why is he important?
Where did he do his work?
How is he regarded today?

Circle the part of the topic that you will write about.

Now, think about *why* you are writing and *who* your readers are. Determine your **purpose,** and analyze your **audience** by asking yourself these questions:

- Do I want to explain a topic, describe an experience, or persuade someone about an issue?
- What is the main thing I want my readers to learn?
- Who will read my paper? How much does my audience know about the topic?
- How can I help my readers connect to the topic?

Next, use a graphic organizer, such as a Web, to help you collect details. Consider how best to organize them.

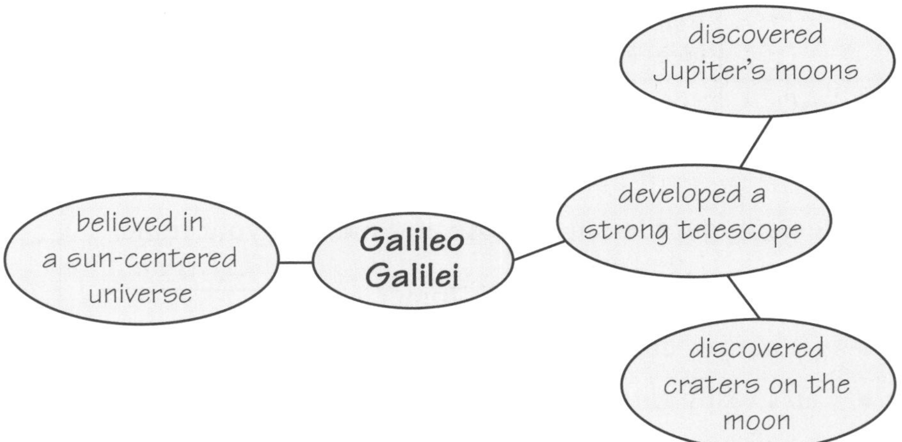

Exercise 1 Generating Topic Ideas

Select one topic from the list below, or choose a topic of your own to write about. On a separate sheet of paper, brainstorm specific ideas related to the topic.

sports	history	travel	animals
music	technology	foods	books

Copyright © 2014 by William H. Sadlier, Inc. All rights reserved.

Exercise 2 Narrowing a Topic

Review your list from Exercise 1. Choose the topic you most want to write about in a three-page paper. List three narrow topics that relate to that topic.

Unusual birds: my uncle's parakeet
the time I saw a bald eagle
ostriches

Exercise 3 Deciding on Purpose and Audience

Return to the narrowed topics you listed in Exercise 2.

1. On a separate sheet of paper, create a two-column chart, like the one below.
2. Choose one topic, and list two different purposes and possible audiences.

Topic: the time I saw a bald eagle

Purpose	Audience
to explain what a bald eagle looks like	younger children
to describe the excitement of seeing a bald eagle up close	friends and classmates

Exercise 4 Collecting Details

Choose one of the purposes and audiences you listed in Exercise 3.

1. Develop your thoughts about your topic by doing research or freewriting about it.
2. To collect specific details to use in your paper, use a Web or make a list. Number the details to show the order in which you will present them.

LESSON 1.2

Drafting

During the **drafting** stage, you express the ideas you developed during prewriting in complete sentences and paragraphs.

➡ Use the notes and organizers you created during prewriting, but feel free to make changes as you write. Keep your purpose and audience in mind as you draft.

➡ Follow these guidelines to keep moving through your draft:

1. Focus on putting all of your ideas on the page without interruption.
2. Don't worry about neatness or errors, such as missing commas, incorrect capital letters, or misspelled words. You will make corrections later.

➡ As you draft, **organize** your writing into the three parts of an essay: the introduction, body, and conclusion.

For more information about the parts of an essay, see the lessons in **Chapter 5.**

Introduction	Your **introduction** should include your essay's thesis statement, or claim, which is the main idea the rest of your essay will defend. It should also grab your readers' attention.
Body	Put all of the main points and details that support your thesis into **body** paragraphs.
Conclusion	Your **conclusion** should restate your thesis in new words and be memorable. It should give your readers a sense of completeness.

To help you organize your draft, refer to any lists or **outlines** you made during prewriting. Add or rearrange details as needed. Use them to help you group together related ideas into paragraphs and to arrange your paragraphs in an easy-to-follow order. Remember to use a style that is appropriate to the kind of writing you are drafting. For example, you might use a formal style for a research report or business letter but an informal style for a short story.

On the next page is part of a first draft about Galileo.

Copyright © 2014 by William H. Sadlier, Inc. All rights reserved.

Writing Model

Before Galileo, telescopes were mostly used to look at things here on Earth. The reason for this was that the telescopes were not very good. Galileo was able to improve the telescope so that it had a much stronger magnifacation. sp? He soon discovered that the moon was covered with mountains and craters. With his improved telescope, Galileo could look up at objects in the sky. He could see things that no other human had ever seen before in all of humanity. ~~Galileo also invented the thermometer.~~

Reminder to check spelling

Detail moved to improve organization

Unrelated idea crossed out

Exercise Writing a Draft

On a separate sheet of paper, write your first draft.

1. Use any outlines or prewriting notes to help you organize your ideas.
2. Include an introduction, at least two body paragraphs, and a conclusion.

HiNT

Give yourself space to make changes later. If you type your draft on the computer, double-space.

LESSON 1.3

Revising

When you **revise,** you evaluate your draft and make changes to improve it.

➡ Between the drafting and revising stages, set your work aside for a short period. Giving yourself a little break will help you decide what ideas, words, and sentences to add, delete, replace, or rearrange.

➡ Evaluate your essay by answering questions related to five of the six **traits of good writing.**

1. **Ideas and Content** How clearly did you express your ideas? Which details should be added or deleted? What else do readers need to know?
2. **Organization** How logically did you organize your ideas? Where should you add transitional words and phrases to connect sentences and paragraphs? How effective are your introduction and conclusion?
3. **Sentence Fluency** How smoothly does one sentence flow to the next when you read your draft aloud? How could varying sentence lengths or sentence beginnings improve the sound of your essay?
4. **Word Choice** Which nouns, adjectives, verbs, and adverbs need to be replaced with more precise words? Which words have been used too often? Where could you add more vivid description or eliminate unnecessary words or phrases?
5. **Voice** How natural and sincere does your essay sound? How well have you communicated your interest in the topic?

The sixth trait of good writing is **conventions,** or correct grammar, spelling, usage, punctuation, and mechanics. In **Lesson 1.4,** you will look for and fix these kinds of errors.

Read your essay several times. Each time you read, focus on a different trait. Depending on the kinds of changes you make, your final paper may not look much like your first draft. Major changes might require that you reorder, delete, or add ideas.

➡ Have a classmate review your paper. Exchange drafts, and use the traits of good writing to check each other's work. **Peer reviewers** should follow the tips on the next page.

Copyright © 2014 by William H. Sadlier, Inc. All rights reserved.

Do	Don't
• Do begin a review with positive feedback. Describe what works and why.	• Don't be overly negative or harsh.
• Do ask questions about things you don't understand.	• Don't make vague comments. Avoid broad statements like "This needs work," "This is confusing," or "This is great."
• Do be specific when you identify problems and make suggestions.	• Don't identify problems without offering solutions.

The passage below shows one writer's revision of a body paragraph. What other revisions would you suggest? Why?

Writing Model

Before Galileo, telescopes were mostly used to look at things ~~here~~ on Earth~~. The reason for this was that the telescopes were not very good.~~ because they were too weak to observe objects miles away. Galileo was able to ~~improve~~ strengthen the telescope's ~~so that it had a much stronger~~ magnification. With his improved telescope, Galileo could look up at objects in the sky~~. He could~~ and see things that no other human had ever seen before ~~in all of humanity~~. For example, ~~He~~ he soon discovered that the moon was covered with mountains and craters.

Add details.

Eliminate unnecessary words.

Combine short sentences.

Add transitions.

Exercise 1 Revising a Paragraph

On a separate sheet of paper, rewrite the paragraph below. Use the questions on page 14 to guide your revision.

[1]In my opinion, my most exciting experience this year was watching a bald eagle in the wild. [2]Some people see bald eagles in zoos, but that's not nearly as cool. [3]My brother thinks I'm lying about the whole thing. [4]My chance came during a family trip. [5]We were in Alaska. [6]They had returned to our campsite to eat, but I stayed behind. [7]I saw movement in the branches above my head. [8]I didn't think much of it until I heard a strange sound. [9]A bald eagle appeared. [10]It swooped down. [11]It took a fish out of the river. [12]It flew back into the tree. [13]It all happened in the blink of an eye, but I will remember it always.

Exercise 2 Revising with a Peer

Exchange the draft you wrote in Lesson 1.2 with a partner. Use the questions about the traits of good writing and the peer review tips to guide your review.

1. Meet with your partner to discuss his or her suggestions.
2. On a separate sheet of paper, revise your draft. Use suggestions from the peer review and your own evaluation.

Copyright © 2014 by William H. Sadlier, Inc. All rights reserved.

Editing and Proofreading

LESSON 1.4

When you **edit and proofread,** you focus on the sixth trait of good writing, **conventions.** Carefully read and reread to find and fix errors in grammar, usage, spelling, mechanics, and punctuation. Note the tips below.

1. Treat each line as if it were alone on the page. Pay attention to every word and punctuation mark. Don't skip anything.
2. Read your work slowly, sentence by sentence. Ask yourself, "Do any parts sound awkward or incorrect?" If so, identify the problem, and fix it.
3. Create a list of common errors like the one below. With each reading, focus on just one item. If you check for too many items at once, you may miss errors. If you find yourself making the same error repeatedly, add it to the checklist.

Editing and Proofreading Checklist

- ❑ Are all words spelled correctly?
- ❑ Have I fixed all fragments and run-on sentences?
- ❑ Have I checked that all commas are used correctly?
- ❑ Does every sentence end with the correct punctuation mark?
- ❑ Do all subjects and verbs agree?
- ❑ Have I capitalized proper nouns and the first word of every sentence?
- ❑ Did I check that all words are used correctly and that I have not mixed up easily confused words, such as effect and affect?

Remember

Ask a friend or family member to proofread your writing. He or she may discover errors that you have missed.

➡ Follow these tips for editing and proofreading while using a **computer:**

1. Use an online dictionary to check the spelling or definitions of any words you're not sure about.
2. Use spell-check, but use it carefully. Spell-check won't catch words that are spelled correctly but used incorrectly, such as *their* for *there* or *hear* for *here*. (See page 325 for a list of commonly confused words.)

Proofreading Symbols

Symbol	Meaning
℘	Delete.
∧	Add.
⊙	Add a period.
∧ with comma	Add a comma.
/	Make lowercase.
∩∪	Switch order.
≡	Capitalize.
¶	Start a new paragraph.

➡ As you edit and proofread, use **proofreading symbols** to mark any errors that you find. In the margin, you'll see a list of commonly used proofreading symbols.

Notice how one writer used proofreading symbols to edit and proofread this paragraph.

Writing Model

Galileo correctly beleived that our solar system is is sun-centered. He based his belief on the things he observed with his powerful telescope. However, the Authorities of his day, especially church leaders, believed that the other planets and the sun revolved around Earth. Unlike galileo, they did not base their theories on observation. Instead, their theories had been passed down through the generations. Because he threatened their ~~there~~ ideas, Galileo was made to defend his new positions.

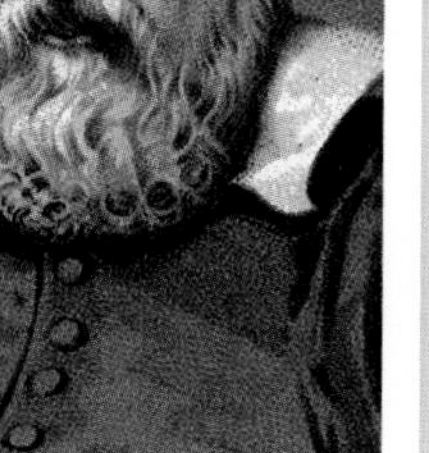

Galileo

Copyright © 2014 by William H. Sadlier, Inc. All rights reserved.

Exercise 1 Proofreading a Draft

Use the proofreading tips and checklist on page 17 to help you edit and proofread the draft below. Use the proofreading symbols on the previous page to correct any mistakes you find.

> [1]The Bald Eagle is one of America's most majestic sights. [2]It's enormous wingspan and instantly recognizable colors make it hard to miss. [3]When I was ten, my family and I traveled to Yellowstone national park in Wyoming. [4]On our very first day we saw several Eagles floating around the sky, Hunting for food and surveying the mountans. [5]It was amazing I could barely beleive my eyes. [6]I thought to myself, "This is the most fascinating animal I have ever seen."

Exercise 2 Editing and Proofreading Your Writing

Now edit and proofread the paper that you revised in Exercise 2 on page 16.

1. Begin by reading and rereading your paper. Use the checklist on the first page of this lesson as a guide.
2. Use proofreading symbols to make your corrections neatly.
3. After you make the changes, create a clean copy of your paper.
4. Then, have a classmate review your work, looking for any errors that you have missed.
5. Make any final corrections.

LESSON
1.5

Publishing and Presenting

The last stage in the writing process is **publishing and presenting,** when you create a final copy of your work and share it with others.

Remember

Follow these guidelines to give more effective presentations:

- Speak loudly and clearly.
- Pace yourself. Don't rush.
- Make eye contact with your audience.
- Use gestures and facial expressions to emphasize key ideas.
- Practice several times.

➡ Proofread your paper one last time, checking that it is free of any distracting errors and that you have met all of the format requirements for the assignment.

➡ You can publish your work in many different ways:

- Submit your work to a school or local newspaper.
- E-mail your work to friends and family.
- Post your paper on a Web site for young writers.
- Share your paper with your classmates on a class blog.

➡ You can also present your work aloud in a variety of ways:

- Turn your paper into a speech.
- Have a discussion with your class or family.
- Give a presentation that includes photographs, drawings, other visual aids, or music.

If you give a presentation, make sure to choose a format that is appropriate for the type of writing you did. How else could you share each type of writing listed below?

Type of Paper	Type of Presentation
How-to Essay	give a demonstration or show photos
Persuasive Essay	make a speech or hold a panel discussion
Research Report	create a video or give a slide show
Short Story or Poem	give a dramatic reading or present a skit

➡ Throughout the school year, maintain a **writing portfolio,** a collection of your best writing. Collect copies of your best work, and keep track of your growth as a writer.

Copyright © 2014 by William H. Sadlier, Inc. All rights reserved.

Exercise 1 Creating a Portfolio

Begin a writing portfolio. Keep your work in a binder or folder.

1. Create a cover sheet for the final paper you edited in Exercise 2 on page 19. List the title of your work, your name, and the date.
2. Write at least one paragraph in response to these questions:
   - What did you learn as a writer from this assignment?
   - How does this paper compare to other papers you have written?
   - What are your strengths and weaknesses as a writer?
3. Attach your paragraph(s) to your paper.

Include answers to questions like these in the paragraph(s) you attach to your paper:

- What did you find easy about writing this piece?
- What did you find difficult?
- How effective do you think your writing is? Why?
- What kind of writing would you like to try next? Why?

Exercise 2 Making a Presentation

Make a presentation of your paper. Be sure the format is appropriate for the kind of paper you wrote.

1. Determine the kinds of materials (visual aids, graphics, audio or visual technology, or costumes) that you will need for your presentation.
2. Present your work to the class, following the guidelines on the previous page.

Exercise 3 Publishing Your Work

Exchange your paper with a partner. Discuss which kind of publication would best suit your work.

1. Research places where you could publish your work, including blogs, local and school newspapers, and magazines.
2. Create a list of at least five different places where you could publish your work. Choose one place, and submit your work.

ONLINE MODEL
www.grammarforwriting.com

Personal Narrative

A **personal narrative** is a type of autobiographical writing. It tells a true story about something that happened to you. In this workshop, you will have the opportunity to write a personal narrative about an interesting experience in your life. The Web below lists a special experience from one writer's life.

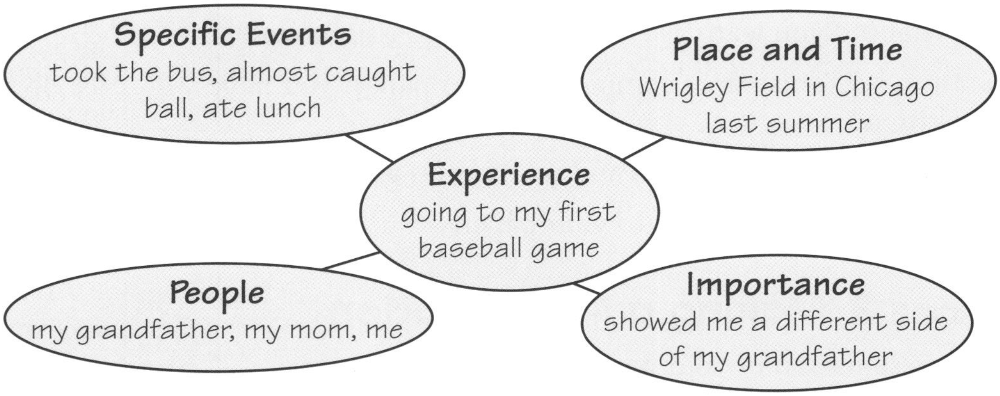

Specific Events
took the bus, almost caught ball, ate lunch

Place and Time
Wrigley Field in Chicago last summer

Experience
going to my first baseball game

People
my grandfather, my mom, me

Importance
showed me a different side of my grandfather

Your personal narrative should have the following features.

Key Features

- logically organized event sequence
- narrative techniques, such as dialogue and description, to develop experiences and events
- transitions to signal shifts in time and setting
- sensory details and precise language
- ending that concludes and reflects on the events

ASSIGNMENT

TASK: Write a three- to four-page **personal narrative** about an experience you had doing something for the first time.

AUDIENCE: your teacher, classmates, family, and friends

PURPOSE: to tell about and reflect on a meaningful experience

Copyright © 2014 by William H. Sadlier, Inc. All rights reserved.

Prewriting

Pick a Good Topic To write a good narrative, you need a topic that is specific, interesting, and important to you.

1. First, brainstorm topics you might write about. Think about these possible "first times":

   - trying a sport or hobby
   - going to an unusual place
   - learning how to do something

2. Pick an experience that took place in a short time. Avoid broad topics. For example, instead of writing the story of what you did last summer, focus on one specific experience.

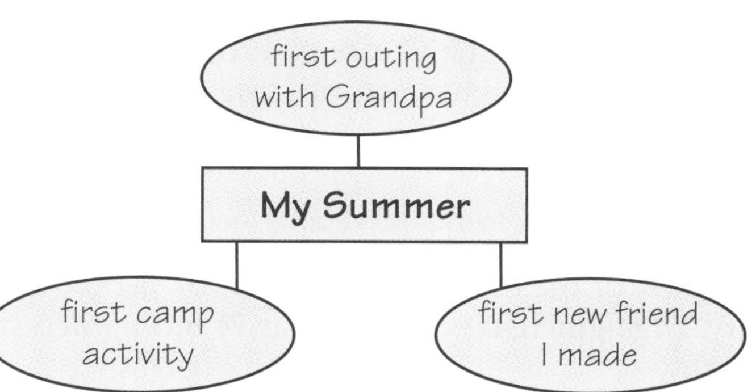

Gather Details Details are the heart of your story. To gather details about the experience, do the following:

- **Ask yourself questions.** Jog your memory by asking *Who? What? When? Where? Why?* and *How?*
- **Brainstorm.** List all specific details that come to mind.
- **Use a graphic organizer.** Use a Web or chart to collect and organize details you might want to include.

WRITING HINT

During prewriting, think about your audience. Pick a topic that your readers may find interesting. As you gather details, jot down those your audience will need to understand your narrative.

Real-World Writing

Note this author's advice about prewriting.

"Jot down your thoughts as they come without worrying if an idea is 'good' or 'bad.'"

—Marion Dane Bauer

Drafting

Write a Beginning, Middle, and End To make drafting easier, organize your narrative into three parts.

Beginning	Middle	End
• Grab the readers' attention. • Set the scene, and tell who was involved.	• Present the events in chronological order, or the order in which they happened. • Use transitional words and phrases, such as *first* and *next*, to signal what happened when.	• Share your feelings about the experience. • Tell why it was important.

WRITING HINT

In a personal narrative, *you* are telling the story. Remember to tell the story from your **point of view,** or perspective. Use pronouns such as *I*, *me*, and *we* to describe what happened.

Keep It Interesting Create pictures in the readers' minds with **sensory details** (sights, sounds, smells, tastes, and textures).

ORIGINAL I was upset.

REVISED I rolled my eyes and let out a long, loud sigh.

Add **dialogue,** or the exact words spoken by people in your story. Dialogue makes your narrative more interesting and realistic.

Writing Model

First-person pronouns

Dialogue

Sensory details

[1]Mom gave me a hard stare as she whispered, "No, you can't back out now. [2]Grandpa has been excited about taking you to this game for weeks." [3]With a sigh, I glanced in the kitchen where my seventy-year-old grandfather was cramming yet another bottle of cold water into an already bulging black backpack.

Copyright © 2014 by William H. Sadlier, Inc. All rights reserved.

Revising

Use the Revising Questions to help you decide how to improve your draft. The model below shows the revisions one writer made to the middle of a draft.

As you revise, keep in mind the traits of good writing. See **Lesson 1.3.**

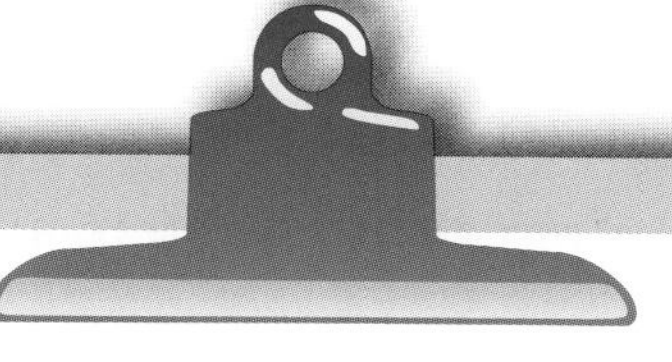

Revising Questions

- ❏ How effectively have I used first-person point of view?
- ❏ How clearly have I presented the order of events?
- ❏ How well does the opening capture the readers' attention?
- ❏ Where should I add sensory details or dialogue?
- ❏ How well have I shown why the experience is meaningful?

Writing Model

dripping with sweat climbed the steep steps
[1]We were ~~hot~~ as we ~~made our way~~ to our seats. Add sensory details.
[2]All kinds of noises overwhelmed us. [3]Grandpa and I could barely hear ourselves talk because of the
clapping and yelling
fans and the music blaring. [4]After a lunch of hot
excitedly
dogs and popcorn, we turned our attention to the players on the field. Express feelings.

Revising

Make Your Sentences Smooth Sentences that all sound the same are boring to read. Make your personal narrative more interesting by following the suggestions below.

For more help with sentence variety, see **Lessons 3.1** and **3.2.**

- **Mix up the sentence lengths.** Create a lively style by using long and short sentences. Use a short sentence to surprise the reader or call attention to an idea or detail.
- **Start in different ways.** Not every sentence should start with the same subject. Try a subordinate clause or phrase at the beginning to add variety. (See Lessons 3.3 and 3.5 for more about clauses and phrases.)

SUBORDINATE CLAUSE	**Whenever our team scored,** we clapped.
PHRASE	**Cheering wildly,** the fans stood up.

- **Combine choppy sentences.** Avoid using too many short sentences in a row. Look for ways to connect ideas smoothly.

Writing Model

Combine sentences.

Begin with a subordinate clause.

End with a short sentence.

[1]I was surprised that Grandpa paid so much attention to the game, and [2]I was surprised that he knew so much about baseball. Although [3]I liked hearing about the players and the teams, [4]My favorite part of the afternoon was the memories he shared [5]~~The stories were~~ about going to baseball games with his dad~~, and~~. Grandpa is a great storyteller.

Copyright © 2014 by William H. Sadlier, Inc. All rights reserved.

Editing and Proofreading

Proofread Your Draft Using the Editing and Proofreading Checklist, read your narrative for errors in grammar, usage, mechanics, punctuation, and spelling. Go slowly, concentrating on one sentence at a time.

Editing and Proofreading Checklist

- ❑ Did I indent each paragraph?
- ❑ Have I checked that all words are spelled correctly?
- ❑ Have I capitalized the first word of each sentence?
- ❑ Did I leave out or run together any words?

Fix Run-on Sentences Sometimes you might connect sentences with only a comma or without any punctuation at all. When you run together two complete sentences as if they were one sentence, you create a **run-on sentence.**

RUN-ON It began to rain hard, we stayed until the end of the game.

See **Lesson 2.2** for more about correcting run-on sentences.

Run-ons can confuse readers. They make it hard to tell where one idea ends and another one begins. Use one of these ways to fix a run-on.

1. Divide the run-on into two sentences.

It began to rain hard**. W**e stayed until the end of the game.

2. Connect the sentences with a comma and a coordinating conjunction (such as *and, but,* or *or*).

It began to rain hard**, but** we stayed until the end of the game.

Editing and Proofreading

Proofreading Symbols

Symbol	Meaning
^	Add.
#	Add a space.
℘	Delete.
¶	Start a new paragraph.
⊙	Add a period.

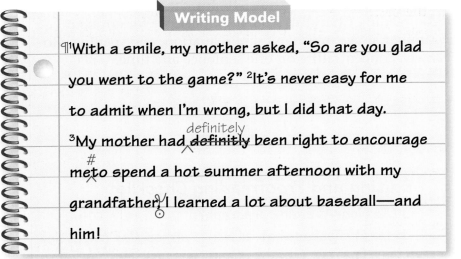

Writing Model

¶[1]With a smile, my mother asked, "So are you glad you went to the game?" [2]It's never easy for me to admit when I'm wrong, but I did that day. [3]My mother had ~~definitly~~ definitely been right to encourage me to spend a hot summer afternoon with my grandfather, I learned a lot about baseball—and him!

Publishing and Presenting

Choose one of these ways to share your personal narrative.

- **Include it in a letter or an e-mail.** Send it to a friend or family member, and ask for his or her reaction to it.
- **Read your story to classmates.** Be ready to answer their questions about the experience.
- **Post your work on a class bulletin board.** Include photos of the people, places, or things your narrative describes.

Reflect On Your Writing

- What detail in your narrative is the clearest or the most important? Why do you think so?
- What do you like best about your narrative?
- What was the hardest part to write?

Copyright © 2014 by William H. Sadlier, Inc. All rights reserved.

Chapter Review

A. Practice Test

In the passage below, there is a question *for each numbered item.* Read the passage carefully, and circle the best answer to each question.

My First Garden

Have you ever wanted to grow a garden? It can be hard work, involving many hours in the mud and hot sun. However, growing a garden can be satisfying. Especially if your[1] garden produces delicious food.

I grew my first garden when I was ten years old. It was summer vacation. I was really bored[2]. For years, my mom had been talking about planting a vegetable and herb garden in our backyard. She suggested that the two of us work together to plant and grow her dream garden. I was unsure at first, but I soon got interested.

We began by choosing the vegetables and herbs that we wanted to plant. I wanted eggplants and tomatoes because they are good[3]. She picked sweet potatoes, pumpkins, basil, and chives.

1. What is the best replacement for the underlined section?
A. NO CHANGE
B. be satisfying, especially if your
C. satisfy, especially if you're
D. be satisfying. If your

2. How could this underlined section be improved?
A. NO CHANGE
B. Move it to the next paragraph.
C. Change the period after *vacation* to a comma.
D. Combine the sentences using a coordinating conjunction.

3. What is the best replacement for the underlined section?
A. NO CHANGE
B. because their really good.
C. because they are tender and delicious.
D. because eggplants and tomatoes are pretty good.

First, we turned the soil and checked that it was healthy. Then, we created little rows for our seeds. Next, we planted them. We marked our rows with signs[4] that showed where the different vegetables and herbs were planted.

By the beginning of fall, we were making pumpkin and sweet potato pies. While not everyone[5] will like the work that it takes to grow a garden, the delicious foods produced definitely make the experience worthwhile.

4. What is the best replacement for the underlined section?
- **A.** However, we marked our rows with signs
- **B.** Therefore, we marked our rows with signs
- **C.** First, we marked our rows with signs.
- **D.** Finally, we marked our rows with signs

5. Which of the following best describes this sentence?
- **A.** It is a restatement of the thesis statement.
- **B.** It is an example of freewriting.
- **C.** It is part of the body.
- **D.** It is a restatement of the topic.

B. Matching Stages to Tasks

Match the writing stage in the first column with the task listed in the second column. Write the letter of your choice in the space provided.

___ **1.** prewriting

___ **2.** drafting

___ **3.** revising

___ **4.** editing and proofreading

___ **5.** publishing and presenting

a. correcting spelling errors

b. writing body paragraphs

c. identifying and replacing vague words

d. e-mailing your essay to a friend

e. brainstorming and gathering details

Chapter Review

Copyright © 2014 by William H. Sadlier, Inc. All rights reserved.

C. Evaluating Writing Tips

Read each tip about the stages of the writing process. Is it a good tip to follow? Write *Y* for yes or *N* for no.

___ **1.** Include the thesis statement in each body paragraph.

___ **2.** Ask a classmate to review your paper as you revise.

___ **3.** Use the *5-W and How?* questions when you proofread.

___ **4.** As you edit, focus most on narrowing your topic.

___ **5.** Before you draft, analyze your audience.

D. Proofreading a Personal Narrative

Use proofreading symbols to correct any errors in the draft below.

Proofreading Symbols		
Delete.	Add.	Switch order.
Capitalize.	Add a comma.	Start a new paragraph.

[1]Ever since I was in fith grade, I have ridden my bike to school almost every day. [2]I enjoy the interesting sights, the queit time to myself, and the fresh air. [3]Its hard for me to imagine being stuffed inside a school bus with all that noise. [4]Who would want to start the day like that. [5]The most interesting part of my ride to school is going over the bridge above the Root river. [6]I usually see poeple fishing off the rocks. [7]I have also seen many different kinds wildlife, including raccoons possums and herons.

CHAPTER 2 Effective Sentences and Word Choice

Copyright ©2014 by William H. Sadlier, Inc. All rights reserved.

Sentence Fragments

LESSON 2.1

A **sentence fragment** is a group of words that is incorrectly punctuated as a complete sentence. A sentence fragment may be missing a subject, a verb, or both. Sentence fragments express incomplete thoughts.

Try these three strategies to correct sentence fragments.

1. Add the missing subject, verb, or other words necessary to make the group of words into a grammatically complete sentence.

   FRAGMENT At the end of the race, a checkered flag. [The verb is missing.]

   SENTENCE At the end of the race, a checkered flag was flying.

2. Attach the fragment to a complete sentence before or after it.

   FRAGMENT Race officials wave a red and yellow striped flag. In cases of danger, such as spilled oil. [The second word group has no subject or verb.]

   SENTENCE Race officials wave a red and yellow striped flag in cases of danger, such as spilled oil.

3. Eliminate the word that makes the fragment sound incomplete.

   FRAGMENT When officials wave a black flag to signal drivers to stop. [The word *When* is a subordinating conjunction that makes the word group a subordinate clause.]

   SENTENCE Officials wave a black flag to signal drivers to stop.

Exercise 1 Analyzing a Literary Model

Read the literary model on the next page. Identify the sentence fragments, and explain what makes them fragments. Rewrite each fragment as a complete sentence on a separate sheet of paper.

Real-World Writing

Sometimes writers intentionally use sentence fragments in ads or stories to grab readers' attention, create an informal style, or make dialogue realistic.

Silky Shampoo. Because it's the best.

However, you should avoid fragments in your own academic writing.

Common Subordinating Conjunctions

after	since
although	unless
because	until
before	when
if	while

See **Lesson 3.3** for more about subordinate clauses and fragments.

Literary Model

[1]It is so hot now that Abuelo has decided we should do our exercise walks after dinner, when it's almost nightfall. [2]Every day this week, though, it has rained on our plans. [3]"That's summer in the tropics," Abuelo says. [4]"Rain, rain, and more rain." [5]We were finally able to walk today, and along the way we saw many beautiful plants and flowers as well as dragonflies and butterflies, grasshoppers, snails, slugs, and tiny aphids. [6]Plenty of mosquitoes, too, unfortunately. [7]We kept having to flap away the bugs.

—Excerpt from *Flight to Freedom* by Ana Veciana-Suarez

Exercise 2 Correcting Sentence Fragments

Label each group of words *S* for sentence or *F* for fragment. On a separate sheet of paper, correct each fragment using the strategies in this lesson.

EXAMPLE Bollywood is an India-based film industry. S

___ **1.** Bollywood more than 1,000 films a year!

___ **2.** Because, unlike Hollywood, Bollywood isn't a physical place.

___ **3.** Many Bollywood films musicals with dance numbers.

___ **4.** New Delhi is the capital of India.

___ **5.** Since it is located on the west side of the country.

___ **6.** It is usually either dry or humid.

___ **7.** Sixteen million people in Mumbai alone.

___ **8.** The Suez Canal made Mumbai one of the largest seaports in the Arabian Sea.

___ **9.** Since I've always wanted to go to India.

Copyright © 2014 by William H. Sadlier, Inc. All rights reserved.

___ **10.** The plane ride takes many hours from my home.

___ **11.** They serve Indian food on the plane.

___ **12.** While we travel this summer to visit family.

___ **13.** To learn about different customs.

___ **14.** India, even hot in the winter.

___ **15.** My piano teacher moved to New Delhi.

Exercise 3 Writing from Notes

Use the notes below to write five sentences about India. Use a separate sheet of paper, and make sure you have no sentence fragments.

- main religions—Hinduism and Islam
- colonized by Britain, independence in 1947
- population—more than a billion people
- world's largest democratic nation
- official language—Hindi

Exercise 4 Editing an Invitation

Read the book-signing invitation below. Correct any fragments, and rewrite the invitation on a separate piece of paper.

[1]The hottest teen author this year holding a book signing at the City Bookstore on Rand Road. [2]Anjali Banerjee will read selections from her new novel, Maya Running. [3]Approximately 7 P.M. [4]Will give autographs for one hour following the reading. [5]Plenty of time to meet her and browse the entire collection. [6]Be there!

LESSON 2.2

Run-on Sentences

A **run-on sentence** occurs when two or more sentences are incorrectly written as a single sentence.

RUN-ON Glaciers are large masses of moving snow and ice they created many of the lakes in the United States.
[There is no punctuation between the two sentences.]

RUN-ON Glaciers are large masses of moving snow and ice, they created many of the lakes in the United States.
[Only a comma joins the two sentences.]

CORRECT Glaciers are large masses of moving snow and ice**. T**hey created many of the lakes in the United States.

Use one of these four strategies to correct run-on sentences.

1. Create two separate sentences by adding end punctuation and a capital letter.

RUN-ON Many high mountains contain glaciers, did you know that Mount Rainier in Washington has several small glaciers?

CORRECT Many high mountains contain glaciers**. D**id you know that Mount Rainier in Washington has several small glaciers?

2. Use a **coordinating conjunction** preceded by a comma to join the sentences.

RUN-ON Some glaciers form in the polar regions these ice caps may cover millions of square miles.

CORRECT Some glaciers form in the polar regions**, and** these ice caps may cover millions of square miles.

3. Use a **semicolon** by itself or before a **conjunctive adverb** to join two closely related sentences. Place a comma after the conjunctive adverb. (See Lesson 11.5.)

RUN-ON The largest glacier in the world is Humboldt Glacier it is in Greenland.

CORRECT The largest glacier in the world is Humboldt Glacier**;** it is in Greenland.

RUN-ON Icebergs break off glaciers and drift into the sea only a small part of an iceberg is visible above the water.

Coordinating Conjunctions

and	or
but	so
for	yet
nor	

Common Conjunctive Adverbs

also	meanwhile
besides	still
however	then
instead	therefore

Copyright © 2014 by William H. Sadlier, Inc. All rights reserved.

CORRECT Icebergs break off glaciers and drift into the sea**; however,** only a small part of an iceberg is visible above the water.

4. Change one sentence into a **subordinate clause** or a **phrase,** adding or changing words and punctuation as needed. (See Lessons 3.3 and 3.5.)

RUN-ON Crevasses are cracks in a glacier they can make mountain climbing dangerous.

CORRECT Crevasses**, which are cracks in a glacier,** can make mountain climbing dangerous. [subordinate clause]

CORRECT Crevasses**, or cracks in a glacier,** can make mountain climbing dangerous. [appositive phrase]

Exercise 1 Recognizing Run-on Sentences

Label each sentence *C* if it is correct and *R* if it is a run-on sentence. Correct the run-on sentences on a separate sheet of paper. Use a variety of strategies.

___ **1.** The notion of brewing coffee emerged in Arabia around the year 1000 it quickly became a craze.

___ **2.** The popularity of coffee spread to North African and Mediterranean countries.

___ **3.** Coffee beans appeared in Europe in 1615, the Dutch were the first to bring an actual coffee plant to the continent.

___ **4.** In 1714, the Dutch gave Louis XIV a gift of a coffee plant it was stolen from the Royal Garden.

___ **5.** Between 1727 and 1800, Brazil became the world's leading coffee exporter it still is today.

___ **6.** The best growing conditions for coffee include sun, rain, and moderate temperatures.

___ **7.** Coffee is the most consumed drink in the world.

R **8.** In Great Britain, people drank coffee with mustard, butter, and oatmeal different ingredients are added today.

R **9.** The Indian Coffee Board controls Indian coffee plants, they produce about 3.8 million bags of coffee beans a year.

__ **10.** Nowadays, coffee is an everyday drink for many people.

Exercise 2 Correcting a Run-on Sentence

Read the run-on sentence and the proposed revisions below. With a partner, choose the correct revision. Discuss your reasoning.

The run-on sentence consists of three sentences that are incorrectly joined. Be sure to choose the revision that joins all three ideas correctly.

If you like oatmeal, you should eat OatTidbits, the treats are bite-sized and tasty they melt in your mouth.

1. If you like oatmeal, you should eat OatTidbits. The treats are bite-sized and tasty, and they melt in your mouth.
2. If you like oatmeal, you should eat OatTidbits. The treats are bite-sized and tasty, they melt in your mouth.
3. If you like oatmeal; you should eat tasty OatTidbits. They are bite-sized. They melt in your mouth.

Exercise 3 Editing a Speech

Read the speech below. Correct all of the run-on sentences on a separate sheet of paper. You may add or delete words.

[1]As cooking club president, I hope to have cook-offs once a semester, after all, competition is healthy. [2]I think that members should be given more responsibility for example, we should try to cook more difficult dishes if we feel prepared. [3]If I am cooking club president, I am going to make cooking club time longer students should spend more time in the activities that interest them. [4]Vote for me!

Copyright © 2014 by William H. Sadlier, Inc. All rights reserved.

LESSON 2.3

Parallel Structure

Which of the sentences below do you prefer? Why?

> Anisa slipped off the stool, dropped the bowl, and spilling soup everywhere.
>
> Anisa slipped off the stool, dropped the bowl, and spilled soup everywhere.

The second sentence has **parallel structure,** or **parallelism,** the use of two or more words, phrases, or clauses that have the same grammatical structure. (It contains three past tense verbs.) Using sentences with parallel structure creates balance and a pleasing rhythm in your writing.

NOT PARALLEL	**Surprised, embarrassed,** and **with anger,** Anisa looked down. [two adjectives and a prepositional phrase]
PARALLEL	**Surprised, embarrassed,** and **angry,** Anisa looked down. [three adjectives]
PARALLEL	With **surprise, embarrassment,** and **anger,** Anisa looked down. [three nouns]

When you combine short sentences by using compound parts (such as subjects, verbs, or modifiers), be sure that the grammatical forms are parallel.

ORIGINAL	The hot soup dripped from the table. It spread onto the floor. It made a mess that was sticky.
NOT PARALLEL	**Dripping from the table** and **as it spread onto the floor,** the hot soup made a sticky mess. [one participial phrase and one subordinate clause]
PARALLEL	**Dripping from the table** and **spreading onto the floor,** the hot soup made a sticky mess. [two participial phrases]

Parallel elements may appear anywhere in a sentence or even throughout an entire paragraph. Not only the same grammatical forms but also the same exact words may be repeated.

WRITING HINT

Use parallel structure in headings, labels, and lists in charts, graphs, and outlines. For example, use nouns for all three subtopics.

I. Background
   A. Childhood
   B. ~~The~~ Education ~~that he had~~
   C. Family

See **Lesson 3.6** for more about combining sentences with compound parts.

Literary Model

The repeated words and sentence structure with semicolons give the paragraph unity.

[1]Matthew Alexander Henson was born in 1866 into a United States of two worlds, a white world and a black world. [2]Matt Henson was black. [3]Robert E. Peary, the man he assisted for 22 years, was white. [4]In the Arctic they ate from the same chunk of frozen walrus; in the United States they did not sit at the same table or even in the same room. [5]In the Arctic they slept in the same igloo; in the United States Henson couldn't enter the same hotel as Peary. [6]In the Arctic they worked side by side, often close to death; in the United States Henson was only Peary's "faithful colored servant."

—Excerpt from *Arctic Explorer: The Story of Matthew Henson* by Jeri Ferris

Exercise 1 Making Sentences Parallel

Read the sentences below. On a separate sheet of paper, revise the sentences to fix faulty parallelism or add parallel elements. Underline the parallel parts.

1. The librarian always suggests paper topics and is answering our questions.
2. Choosing a topic takes time. It also involves patience. Research is also required.
3. Carla's topic may come from our textbook or coming from a recent news article.
4. Does Carla like going to the library or to work at home?
5. She needs note cards, her book, and to have time to finish her draft.
6. Nervous but feeling excitement, Carla began writing her report.
7. Yesterday she did research, brainstorming ideas, and was narrowing her topic.

HiNT

Read your sentences aloud when you revise for parallel structure. Sentences with errors in parallelism will sound awkward.

Copyright © 2014 by William H. Sadlier, Inc. All rights reserved.

8. Her teacher answered her questions with quickness, patiently, and with care.
9. Finding good sources and to make an outline with details took Carla several hours.
10. Does she like to draft and editing on a computer?
11. She will use books and interviewing an expert.
12. Tomorrow Carla will start writing and to work on revising.
13. Her computer has a spell-check program, and a dictionary is also on it.
14. Carla will read her paper and be giving a presentation to our class on Friday.
15. As long as she remembers to look the audience in the eye and reading slowly, she will be fine.

Exercise 2 Using Parallel Structure

Write one or two paragraphs that describe your habits, likes, or dislikes as a writer. You may focus on one particular piece of writing or discuss your writing more generally.

1. At least three sentences should have parallel structure.
2. Exchange paragraphs with a partner. Read each other's paragraphs, looking for errors in parallelism.
3. Discuss possible revisions with your partner.

Exercise 3 Improving Your Writing

Find an essay you wrote for this or another class. Read it aloud, looking for sentences that lack parallel structure. Then rewrite those sentences to fix errors in parallelism.

LESSON 2.4

Stringy Sentences

Stringy sentences are long and hard to follow. They contain too many ideas strung loosely together by the conjunction *and*.

Stringy	One of the first European novels was *Don Quixote*, and it was written in 1605, and the author was Miguel de Cervantes, and he was a Spanish writer.
Revised	*Don Quixote*, one of the first European novels, was written in 1605 by Spanish writer Miguel de Cervantes.

The rambling structure of stringy sentences makes it difficult for readers to understand how the ideas in them are related.

Use one or more of these strategies to rewrite a stringy sentence.

1. Break it into two or more separate sentences, each presenting only one or two ideas.

Stringy	Folktales are traditional stories, and they have been passed down orally, and some specific types of traditional stories include fairy tales and trickster stories and legends.
Revised	Folktales are traditional stories that have been passed down orally**. S**ome specific types of traditional stories include fairy tales, trickster stories, and legends.

2. Delete less important details, or turn them into phrases or subordinate clauses.

Stringy	*Beowulf* tells the story of a hero, and he fights a monster, and its name is Grendel, and *Beowulf* is one of the oldest poems in English.
Revised	*Beowulf*, **one of the oldest poems in English,** tells the story of a hero **who fights a monster named Grendel.**

To correct stringy sentences, you may use **appositive phrases.** They follow and explain a noun or pronoun. Use commas to set off an appositive phrase that is not essential to understanding the sentence.

Jane Austen wrote *Pride and Prejudice*, **her most famous novel,** in 1813.

See **Lesson 11.4** for more about this comma rule.

Copyright © 2014 by William H. Sadlier, Inc. All rights reserved.

3. Include **transitions** (such as *although, because,* and *then*) to clarify the connections among ideas. (See Lesson 4.5.)

Stringy	Most myths are ancient, and people still enjoy them, and they explore common themes, and they are love, evil, and courage.
Revised	**Although** most myths are ancient, people still enjoy them **because** they explore common themes, **such as** love, evil, and courage.

Exercise 1 Revising Stringy Sentences

Revise the stringy sentences below on a separate sheet of paper.

EXAMPLE *Robinson Crusoe* was written by Daniel Defoe in 1719 and is often considered the first novel written in English, and the plot tells about a man who is stranded on an island.

Robinson Crusoe, written by Daniel Defoe in 1719, is often considered the first novel written in English. The plot tells about a man who is stranded on an island.

1. The book is fictional and is based upon the life of Alexander Selkirk, and he was trapped on an island, and it was known as Más a Tierra in the Pacific Ocean.
2. That island is now called Robinson Crusoe's Island, and Defoe's description was probably based on the island of Tobago, and it is near Trinidad and in the Caribbean Sea.
3. The book was first published in England and was followed by a sequel, and its title was *The Further Adventures of Robinson Crusoe.*
4. *Robinson Crusoe* became popular, and it happened almost immediately, and the book was soon translated into many languages.
5. Defoe was born around 1660 and in London and was the son of a butcher and candlestick maker and was interested in politics throughout his life.

LESSON **2.5**

Wordy Sentences

Make your writing concise. **Wordy sentences** can confuse and bore readers. Use as few words as possible to express your meaning clearly.

Wordy	Because of the fact that there were problems with electricity, which happened in the gym, the basketball games to be played tonight were cancelled by Mr. Rodriguez, who is the principal. [31 words]
Concise	Because of electrical problems in the gym, the principal, Mr. Rodriguez, cancelled tonight's basketball games. [15 words]

Follow these strategies to eliminate extra words.

Strategies	Example
1. Eliminate redundancies. Look for places where you have unnecessarily repeated words or ideas.	The four teams had little difficulty ~~or trouble~~ cooperating ~~together~~ to schedule make-up games for 5:00 ~~P.M~~ tomorrow afternoon.
2. Reduce a clause to a phrase. Consider replacing the phrases *which is/are* and *who is/are.*	The games, ~~which are~~ part of the Holiday Finals, will feature Tonya Wilson, a talented forward.
3. Replace a phrase with a single word. Simplify wordy expressions, such as *due to the fact that (because)* or *at the present time (now).*	Hill Middle School fans will cheer ~~with enthusiasm~~ enthusiastically until ~~such time as~~ our team is eliminated from the weekend competition ~~over the weekend~~.
4. Rewrite sentences to eliminate empty phrases. Look especially for sentence openers that add little or no meaning.	~~In my opinion, it is important that~~ Our school's staff and students should show more school spirit.
5. Use strong verbs in the active voice. Avoid using many forms of the verb *to be (is, are, was, were)* and verbs in the passive voice.	The eighth grade student council ~~is in charge of making~~ makes posters and ~~selling~~ sells tickets, and seventh graders sell popcorn ~~is sold by seventh graders~~ at halftime.

Real-World Writing

Note these authors' ideas about wordiness.

"A sentence should contain no unnecessary words, a paragraph no unnecessary sentences, for the same reason that a drawing should have no unnecessary lines and a machine no unnecessary parts."

—William Strunk and E. B. White

For more on using clauses and phrases, see **Lessons 3.3** and **3.5.**

Copyright © 2014 by William H. Sadlier, Inc. All rights reserved.

Exercise 1 Revising Wordy Sentences

Use the five strategies introduced in this lesson to revise the following wordy sentences. Make sure you use each strategy at least once. Write your revisions on a separate sheet of paper.

EXAMPLE Puerto Rico is an island that is surrounded by water on all sides and is between the Caribbean Sea and the Atlantic Ocean.

Puerto Rico is an island located between the Caribbean Sea and the Atlantic Ocean.

1. The fact of the matter is that after Columbus landed on the island in 1493, the island was claimed by the Spanish Crown for a period of four hundred years.
2. The island is visited by people who are tourists who want to enjoy the scenery that is tropical.
3. In all honesty, it is true that Puerto Rico is about triple the size of the state of Rhode Island.
4. The official languages, which are Spanish and English, are both spoken by many residents.
5. The name *Puerto Rico* has the meaning of "Rich Port" in the language of Spanish.
6. The tropical island boasts a tropical climate that is pleasant.
7. The major exports from Puerto Rico, which are exported, include the products of coffee, pineapple, mangoes, and melons.
8. It has been noted that about 85 percent of the population of the island is Roman Catholic.
9. Sometimes there are droughts that occur, and sometimes there are hurricanes that occur in Puerto Rico.
10. The country of Venezuela lies about five hundred miles in the southern direction of the country of Puerto Rico.

Remember

In sentences with verbs in the active voice, the subject performs the action of the verb.

ACTIVE VOICE We **won** the game.

PASSIVE VOICE The game **was won** by us.

See **Lesson 8.6** for more about verbs in the active voice.

Exercise 2 Revising a Paragraph

Revise the wordy paragraph below on a separate sheet of paper. Share your revision with a partner.

[1]It is true that the period of the Great Depression, which started in the United States in the year 1929 and soon after spread to Europe, was an economic slump that started with the time of the crash of the stock market on Black Friday and continued and lasted for almost ten years. [2]It was the worst depression ever in the entire history of the Western world.

Exercise 3 Writing a Paragraph

Write a paragraph describing the photograph and your reactions to it. On a separate sheet of paper, write at least five sentences. Read your draft aloud to a partner. Work with your partner to revise any wordy sentences.

Copyright © 2014 by William H. Sadlier, Inc. All rights reserved.

LESSON 2.6

Colorful Language

Good writers use **colorful language** to express their meaning precisely and engage their readers with specific details and a lively style. For example, notice the differences in these two descriptions of the same event. Why does the second one give readers a more vivid picture of the scene?

[1]The man looked at the sky as he drove away from the people's house. [2]The weather was unusual. [3]In the darkness, lightning was visible. [4]Hard snow fell on the front part of the car.

Literary Model

[1]Deputy Brewster Bingham eyed the sky as he sped out of the McGuires' driveway. [2]This storm defied the laws of nature. [3]Ragged bolts of lightning forked into a black horizon. [4]Icy pellets pounded the windshield.

—Excerpt from *Rescue Josh McGuire* by Ben Mikaelsen

Remember

A proper noun names a particular place, person, thing, or idea. Begin proper nouns with a capital letter.

a doctor	**D**r. **J**ane **A**bbott
the city	**D**enver

Follow these suggestions to add colorful language that will make your meaning precise and create strong word pictures for your readers.

1. Use specific, rather than general, nouns.

General	More Specific	Most Specific
publication	magazine	*Time*
creature	bird	pelican
people	explorers	Lewis and Clark
object	tool	screwdriver

Original	Two students won prizes for their act in the school event.
Revised	**Sofia** and **Hannah** won a gold **trophy** and **fifty dollars** for their **skit** in **Murphy Middle School's talent show.**

2. **Choose vivid verbs.** Where possible, replace forms of the verb *to be* (*is, are, am, was, were*) with strong verbs that "show," rather than "tell" the reader your meaning. Also, choose one precise verb over a vague verb and an adverb.

Original	As the audience rose to their feet, the girls felt happy and moved quickly offstage.
Revised	As the audience **leaped** to their feet, the girls **grinned** and **dashed** offstage.

3. **Include strong, precise modifiers.** Replace vague, overused adjectives and adverbs that convey little meaning.

Original	After the nice show, the lobby filled with hot, tired performers lining up for cups of water and good cookies.
Revised	After the **fantastic** show, the lobby filled **rapidly** with **sweaty** and **exhausted** performers lining up for cups of **ice** water and **sugar** cookies.

Real-World Writing

As this author notes, with modifiers, less is sometimes more. "Adding a ton of adjectives is like pouring too much syrup on a waffle. It won't make your writing strong."
—Ralph Fletcher

Exercise 1 Adding Colorful Language

Read the sentences below. On a separate sheet of paper, revise the sentences. Make them more interesting by adding the details specified in the parentheses.

EXAMPLE The girl wanted some food. (specific nouns)

My *best friend, Sheila,* wanted *a chicken sandwich.*

Copyright © 2014 by William H. Sadlier, Inc. All rights reserved.

1. The building was not in good shape. (strong modifiers and specific nouns)
2. My dad said that he had once eaten several apples in ten minutes. (vivid verbs)
3. The artwork is made of different materials. (specific nouns)
4. We ate a meal at a restaurant that served good seafood and loaves of bread. (strong modifiers and specific nouns)
5. I quickly took off my shoes and lay down on the bed. (vivid verbs)

Exercise 2 Improving Your Own Writing

Find a story or essay you wrote for this or another class.

1. Read it aloud, looking for sentences that use dull, general, or vague language.
2. Rewrite the sentences, adding specific nouns, vivid verbs, and strong, precise adjectives and adverbs.
3. Share your revisions with a partner. Discuss the effectiveness of the colorful language each of you added.

Write What You Think

On a separate piece of paper, write two paragraphs in response to the question below.

What makes your town, city, or neighborhood interesting or unusual?

1. Explain your answer by describing two examples, reasons, or specific places or people. Support each one with details.
2. After you have finished writing, revise your sentences to make sure that you have included a variety of specific nouns, vivid verbs, and strong modifiers.

LESSON 2.7

Denotation and Connotation

Choosing the right word means paying attention to two types of meaning: denotation and connotation.

A dictionary shows a word's **denotation,** or definition. To add precision and variety to your writing, consult a thesaurus, which lists **synonyms,** or words with similar meanings. Even words with the same denotation may express slightly different shades of meaning.

For example, notice the variety of synonyms one thesaurus lists for the word *nervous*.

The entry shows two related meanings and sixteen synonyms.

nervous *adjective*

1. In a state of anxiety or uneasiness : agitated, anxious, concerned, distressed, solicitous, uneasy, unsettled. *See* FEELINGS. **2.** Feeling or exhibiting nervous tension : edgy, fidgety, jittery, jumpy, restive, restless, skittish, tense, twitchy.

—Excerpt from *Roget's II The New Thesaurus*

The **connotation** of a word is what it suggests beyond its dictionary definition. Connotations are the thoughts and emotions that people associate with a word.

Words with similar denotations may have various connotations, some positive and some negative.

Remember

A word that does not arouse strong favorable or unfavorable emotions has a neutral connotation.

Connotations

Positive	Neutral	Negative
economical	inexpensive	cheap
pride	self-respect	arrogance
aroma	odor	stench
curious	interested	nosy

Copyright © 2014 by William H. Sadlier, Inc. All rights reserved.

Check that the connotations of your words are appropriate for your topic, audience, and purpose. Choose words that match the **tone,** or attitude, you want to express.

Fortunately, the movie was filmed in a beautiful, ~~desolate~~ secluded location in Australia.
[Both words mean "far from people." The connotation of *desolate* is too negative.]

The critic's negative review singled out the ~~extraordinary~~ outlandish costumes in the final scene.
[Both words mean "unusual." The connotation of *extraordinary* is too positive.]

The movie star ~~smirked~~ smiled at the crowd outside the theater.
[Both words refer to a facial expression. The connotation of *smirked* is too negative.]

Exercise 1 Identifying and Using Synonyms

Working Together

Work with a partner to choose ten of the words listed below.

1. Look up their meaning(s) in an online dictionary or thesaurus.
2. Find five synonyms for each of the ten words. List them on a separate piece of paper, and discuss their different shades of meaning and connotations.
3. Then, pick two synonyms for each of the words you chose. Write a sentence that uses each synonym appropriately.

beautiful	loud	old	shy
confident	move	quick	smart
fragile	nervous	sad	soft
fresh	nice	say	strong
idea	odd	see	wet
lively			

Exercise 2 Revising Sentences

Replace the underlined word in each of the sentences below. Use a word with a connotation that matches the description in the parentheses and fits the meaning of the sentence better.

EXAMPLE When the young child spoke in an annoying voice, his mother told him to please stop. (more negative)

whined

1. Winners walked around the stadium, proudly showing off their trophies. (more positive)
2. A gathering of angry fans stormed the stage and started heckling the performers. (more negative)
3. Unfortunately, Marcus firmly insists that he is right even when he has made a mistake. (more negative)
4. The room was dark, except for the warm glare of a brass lamp on the desk. (more positive)
5. The celebrity's wig was so poorly made that you could easily see it was unreal. (more negative)

Exercise 3 Writing Reviews

On a separate sheet of paper, write two brief reviews of a restaurant, a store, or a product of your choice.

1. One should be favorable, using several words with positive connotations. In the other review, use words that convey a more negative feeling.
2. Share your writing with a partner, and discuss specific word choice and connotations.

EXAMPLE The waitress explained the menu items in abundant detail. (positive)

The waitress droned on and on, describing the menu items in excessive detail. (negative)

Copyright © 2014 by William H. Sadlier, Inc. All rights reserved.

LESSON 2.8

Figurative Language

Because **figurative language** goes beyond the literal meanings of words, it appeals to the imagination.

Writers use **figures of speech,** such as similes, metaphors, and personification, to create vivid pictures in their readers' minds. Figurative language helps readers see people, places, and things in new ways.

1. A **simile** compares two unlike things using the word *like* or *as*.

"A person without a sense of humor is like a wagon without springs, jolted by every pebble in the road."

—Henry Ward Beecher

"Writing a novel is like driving a car at night. You can only see as far as your headlights, but you can make the whole trip that way."

—E. L. Doctorow

2. A **metaphor** compares two unlike things by saying that one thing is another. A metaphor does not use the words *like* or *as*.

"The wastebasket is a writer's best friend."

—Isaac Bashevis Singer

"The unread story is not a story; it is little black marks on wood pulp."

—Ursula K. LeGuin

3. You use **personification** when you give human qualities to animals, objects, places, or ideas.

"It seems to me that those songs that have been any good, I have nothing much to do with the writing of them. The words have just crawled down my sleeve and come out on the page."

—Joan Baez

"Books want to be born: I never make them. They come to me and insist on being written, and on being such and such."

—Samuel Butler

Exercise 1 Identifying Figurative Language

As you read the passage below, note the writer's use of figures of speech to build a vivid description.

The passage describes a wintry scene.

Literary Model

[1]The entire street was smothered in snow, right up to the doorways of each house. [2]Gone were streets and sidewalks. [3]Driveways were invisible. [4]Telephone wires hung heavy, looking every bit like clotheslines draped with wet, white laundry. [5]Mailboxes and telephone poles were skinny islands in a sea of powder. [6]The house across the street looked like a gingerbread house with powdered sugar on the rooftop.

—Excerpt from *The Road to Paris* by Nikki Grimes

Reading as a Writer

1. What two similes does the writer use to describe ordinary objects? How effective are they?
2. Where does the writer use a metaphor? Explain what is being compared.
3. Continue the description using personification. Write a sentence that gives human qualities to an object, such as a car, traffic sign, snowman, or streetlight.

Think creatively. Avoid using similes that you have heard many times before. These **clichés** convey little meaning.

flat as a pancake

cold as ice

quiet as a mouse

Exercise 2 Using Figures of Speech

Rewrite each sentence, using the figure of speech indicated in the parentheses. Refer to the examples on page 53 as models.

EXAMPLE The pancakes were not good. (simile)

The pancakes were as soggy as socks straight out of a washing machine.

Copyright © 2014 by William H. Sadlier, Inc. All rights reserved.

1. Ray seemed emotional. (metaphor)
2. The loud noise annoyed me. (personification)
3. The hat was red. (simile)
4. Firefighters are strong. (simile)
5. The girl ran quickly. (metaphor)
6. The football flew through the air. (simile)
7. The athlete looked tired. (metaphor)
8. The fire truck was bright. (personification)
9. After playing in the rain, my dog smelled bad. (simile)
10. Kids played in the sandbox. (simile)

Exercise 3 Writing a Poem

Working Together

On a separate sheet of paper, write a poem about a person or place that is important to you.

1. Give your poem a title. (See page 217 for information about writing a poem.)
2. Include vivid details, and use at least one simile, one metaphor, and one example of personification.
3. Read your poem aloud to a partner. Ask him or her to identify the figures of speech that you used. Discuss which ones are the most effective.

CALVIN AND HOBBES © (1992) Watterson. Dist. By UNIVERSAL PRESS SYNDICATE. Reprinted with permission. All rights reserved.

WRITING APPLICATION

Character Sketch

Think about a movie you saw recently. How would you describe the villain? Would you give details about his or her appearance, personality, or behavior? Would you describe how those traits affected other characters? A good description would include all of these details.

When you write a description of a real person or a fictional character, you are writing a **character sketch.** A character sketch describes the following:

- the character's actions and appearance
- the character's thoughts and behavior
- the reactions others have to the character

Remember to include the following features in your character sketch.

Key Features

- specific details about the character's personality, actions, thoughts, and physical traits
- main impression of the character
- specific incidents and dialogue that reveal what the character is like
- imagery and colorful language

ASSIGNMENT

TASK: Write a two-page **character sketch** in which you create a new character based on people you know, have seen, or have read about.

PURPOSE: to describe a character and entertain readers

AUDIENCE: your classmates

KEY INSTRUCTIONS: Make your character realistic, and develop one personality trait in great detail.

Copyright © 2014 by William H. Sadlier, Inc. All rights reserved.

Brainstorm a Character First, make a list of people you know who possess personality traits or physical characteristics that make them stand apart from others.

- Sherry—tall, very competitive
- Frankie—long hair covers his eyes, won talent show for song he wrote and performed
- Jocelyn—bold, funny, athletic

Now choose at least two traits, and use a Character Map to create your own character. In the center box, name your character.

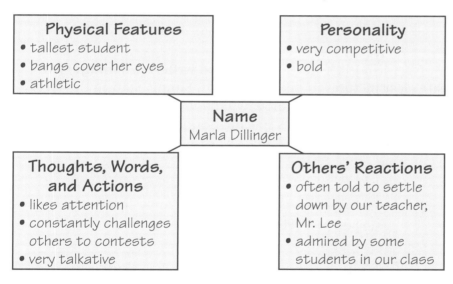

Physical Features
- tallest student
- bangs cover her eyes
- athletic

Personality
- very competitive
- bold

Name
Marla Dillinger

Thoughts, Words, and Actions
- likes attention
- constantly challenges others to contests
- very talkative

Others' Reactions
- often told to settle down by our teacher, Mr. Lee
- admired by some students in our class

WRITING HINT

Use the Character Map to organize your draft. Each outside box can serve as a body paragraph. The outline below shows one way to organize your sketch.

I. Physical features
II. Personality
III. Thoughts, words, and actions
IV. Others' reactions

Determine a Main Impression Next, determine the **main impression** that you want to create about your character. What feeling do you hope your audience will have about the character after reading your sketch? To help you decide, complete a sentence such as this one:

> The main impression, or overall idea, I want to create about my character is...**Marla is exceptionally competitive.**

Make Your Character Come Alive Although your character is fictional, you want your audience to believe that he or she could exist in real life. Support the traits you give your character with specific **incidents** from his or her life, as well as with **dialogue**, or conversations with other characters.

Traits	Incidents	Dialogue
bangs cover eyes	classmate lifts bangs to see if sleeping	"You could hide a horse under those."
very competitive	challenges older boy to race	"I'll even run barefoot to make it easier on you."
loud	constantly tells others she can beat them at anything	"I bet I can win," Marla insisted.

Use Colorful Language Good writers use **imagery** to create clear pictures in people's minds. Simply stating the facts won't create imagery. To show what you mean, use **colorful language,** which includes specific nouns, vivid verbs, and precise modifiers.

For more help with colorful language, see **Lesson 2.6.**

VAGUE Marla liked to win things.

PRECISE Marla liked to win **board games, races,** and **other contests.** [specific nouns]

VAGUE Marla was competitive.

PRECISE Marla **oozed** competition. [vivid verb]

VAGUE Marla defeated her classmates in sports.

PRECISE Marla **effortlessly** defeated her classmates in sports. [precise modifier]

Copyright © 2014 by William H. Sadlier, Inc. All rights reserved.

Check Your Character Sketch Use the checklist below to review your draft. The model that follows shows the beginning of one writer's character sketch.

WRITING CHECKLIST

Did you...

- ✔ provide specific details about the character's personality, actions, and physical traits?
- ✔ create a main impression of your character and include specific incidents and dialogue?
- ✔ use imagery and colorful language?
- ✔ write two pages and develop one trait in great detail?

Writing Model

1"I'll even run barefoot to make it easier on you, Lee." 2Lee stared in frustration at Marla, who swept a blunt chunk of hair from her eyes and continued her offer. 3"C'mon, give it a try," Marla insisted in a loud voice. 4Her offer was a race around the school, and it wasn't the first one of the week.

5Marla Dillinger was a competitor, above all else, and losing wasn't an option. 6She started every match by raising one eyebrow like an arrow and curling the other like a cheetah ready to pounce. 7With a swift flick of the wrist, she grabbed a chunk of her long hair with her left hand and twirled it around like a baton while she sized up her opponent.

Specific incident and dialogue reveal Marla's competitiveness.

Emphasis on Marla's competitiveness creates the main impression.

Colorful language paints a clear image of Marla.

CONNECTING Writing & Grammar

A run-on sentence contains two or more sentences that are incorrectly written as one. **See Lesson 2.2.**

The teacher stopped talking he told Marla to stop speaking out of turn.

One way to fix a run-on sentence is to separate it into two sentences.

The teacher stopped talking**. H**e told Marla to stop speaking out of turn.

CHAPTER 2

Chapter Review

A. Practice Test

Read each sentence below carefully. If you find an error, choose the underlined part that must be changed to make the sentence correct. Fill in the circle for the corresponding letter. If there is no error, fill in circle *E*.

EXAMPLE

Ⓐ Ⓑ Ⓒ Ⓓ Ⓔ Social dancing has always (A) been a part (B) of American (C) culture. Changes over the years. (D) No error (E)

● Ⓑ Ⓒ Ⓓ Ⓔ **1.** Many early dances were done in rows. With (A) men on one side and (B) ladies (C) on the other. (D) No error (E)

Ⓐ Ⓑ ● Ⓓ Ⓔ **2.** The waltz (A) required a close embrace (B) between men and women, it was (C) controversial for its time. (D) No error (E)

Ⓐ Ⓑ ● Ⓓ ● **3.** Group dances were also (A) popular throughout (B) the 1900s. For example, (C) the quadrille. (D) No error (E)

Make sure to familiarize yourself with scoring rules before taking any test. Some tests do not penalize for wrong answers, while others do. Therefore, if you don't know an answer for sure, it may be smarter to make a guess on some tests and better to leave the answer blank on others.

Copyright © 2014 by William H. Sadlier, Inc. All rights reserved.

Ⓐ Ⓑ Ⓒ Ⓓ Ⓔ **4.** The 1920s introduced (A) the Charleston a dance (B) craze that (C) swept the nation (D). No error (E)

Ⓐ Ⓑ Ⓒ Ⓓ Ⓔ **5.** The jitterbug, with (A) its jazzy rhythms (B), bouncy movements (C), and it also has a lot of twirling (D), first became popular in the 1930s. No error (E)

Ⓐ Ⓑ Ⓒ Ⓓ Ⓔ **6.** In the 1950s, Latin rhythms became more popular (A). They led (B) to new dance trends, such as (C) the cha-cha and the mambo (D). No error (E)

Ⓐ Ⓑ Ⓒ Ⓓ Ⓔ **7.** Dances included the hitchhiker (A), the frug, and the jerk, social (B) dancing became more individualized (C) in the 1960s (D). No error (E)

Ⓐ Ⓑ Ⓒ Ⓓ Ⓔ **8.** The hustle was a hot new trend (A) in the 1970s, however (B), it was actually based (C) on the graceful moves of the mambo (D). No error (E)

Ⓐ Ⓑ Ⓒ Ⓓ Ⓔ **9.** The 1990s were marked (A) by the comeback of swing; (B) couples again (C) ruled the dance floors (D). No error (E)

Ⓐ Ⓑ Ⓒ Ⓓ Ⓔ **10.** Social dances can come into fashion (A), go out (B), and then (C) come back in again. Just (D) like clothing styles. No error (E)

Chapter Review

B. Revising Sentences

On a separate sheet of paper, revise each sentence to include colorful or figurative language. Add the elements indicated in the parentheses.

1. My trip to the city was good. (specific nouns, precise modifiers)
2. There was a lot of traffic. (personification)
3. Swarms of people came up from the subway. (simile)
4. Nighttime in the city is exciting. (metaphor)
5. As I walked along the city streets, something happened in front of me. (vivid verbs, precise modifiers, specific nouns)

C. Identifying Connotations

The table below shows words with positive, neutral, and negative connotations. In the blank in each row, write a word with an appropriate connotation.

Positive	Neutral	Negative
slender	thin	Skinny
gazed	looked	glared
chat	talk	babble
stroke	touch	punch
Mansion	house	shack
stroll	Walk	trudge
Brave	fearless	reckless
unique	uncommon	weird
reflect	think	brood
youthful	young	immature

Copyright © 2014 by William H. Sadlier, Inc. All rights reserved.

D. Revising a Character Sketch

On a separate sheet of paper, revise the draft of the character sketch below. Shorten and clarify any wordy or stringy sentences. Revise sentences for parallel structure. Add colorful and figurative language to create a vivid picture of the person.

[1]My little brother Eric appears silly and easily distracted to some people, and he forgets things easily, and they think he is ignorant, and actually it's due to the fact that he's super smart. [2]The fact of the matter is, if you want to know the truth, my brother is just too brilliant to think about the things the rest of us think about.

[3]For instance, Eric often gets lost on the way home from school, and he's been using the same route for a long time. [4]Instead of thinking about left and right turns, he's busy looking up at the sky, seeing things in the sky, and he makes weather predictions.

[5]In addition, to give you an additional example, Eric often loses track of conversations. [6]His most common response to a question is, "Huh?" [7]This makes him look odd, and it's usually because his mind is hard at work, and in his head, he has already skipped to the next thing.

[8]Anyone who knows my brother really well can tell you he's smarter than he seems. [9]He is in point of fact one of the smartest people that will ever be met by you.

Chapter Review

CHAPTER 3

Sentence Variety and Structure

Copyright © 2014 by William H. Sadlier, Inc. All rights reserved.

LESSON 3.1

Varying Sentence Length

Pay attention to the length of your sentences as you write. A string of sentences of the same length—short or long—sounds monotonous. For example, read the draft below aloud.

DRAFT

[1]Have you heard the phrase "Big Brother is watching"? [2]Well, many people feel that way. [3]They feel as if they are almost always being watched. [4]Schools across the country use video cameras. [5]The video cameras are used to monitor student behavior. [6]They record students in hallways. [7]They record students in the cafeteria and at dances. [8]We live in a world of hidden cameras and constant surveillance. [9]Perhaps such advances in technology have violated our right to privacy.

These same-length sentences create a boring style.

Add or delete words, and combine sentences to create an interesting mixture of long and short sentences and a smooth flow from one to another. As you read the revision below, notice the wide range of sentence lengths.

Writing Model

[1]Did you ever hear the phrase "Big Brother is watching"? [2]Well, it may be true. [3]For example, schools across the country use video cameras to monitor student behavior—in hallways and cafeterias and at dances and sporting events. [4]We live in a world of high-resolution surveillance cameras, digital recorders, satellite photos, and video-sharing Web sites. [5]Have such advances in technology violated our right to privacy?

Using a variety of lengths helps sentences flow smoothly.

Use an occasional short sentence to emphasize a key detail or add a sense of drama or humor. As you read the following part of a story, think about the effect of the two short sentences.

Literary Model

A three-word sentence

A two-word sentence

[1]When Jimmy opened his eyes he didn't know where he was. [2]The car was stopped at the side of the road. [3]It was night. [4]Up the road there were tall poles that stretched over the road like alien giraffes, their great shiny eyes lighting up the night. [5]Jimmy could see small insects flying through the green halos around the lights on the poles. [6]Jimmy looked over to see if Crab was in the backseat. [7]He wasn't.

—Excerpt from *Somewhere in the Darkness* by Walter Dean Myers

Reading as a Writer

1. Why might Myers have made sentences 3 and 7 so short?
2. Overall, how well has the author varied the lengths of his sentences?

Exercise 1 Varying Sentence Lengths

Read the paragraphs below. Revise them so that the sentences within the paragraphs vary in length. Use a short sentence in each paragraph to grab a reader's attention.

See **Lessons 3.6, 3.7,** and **3.8** for more about combining sentences.

[1]Recently, a leopard that had befriended a cow was discovered. [2]The leopard visited the cow outside of Antoli, in India. [3]The two animals met at night in a sugarcane field. [4]According to zoologists, their friendship is an example of a predator-prey friendship. [5]These kinds of friendships occur very rarely in nature.

[6]The forestry department stopped trying to capture the leopard after learning of the friendship. [7]According to wildlife warden Rohit Vyas, the leopard was keeping other animals away. [8]As a result, the leopard unintentionally improved crop yields by 30 percent.

Copyright © 2014 by William H. Sadlier, Inc. All rights reserved.

Exercise 2 Writing a Public Service Announcement

On a separate sheet of paper, write a public service announcement to advise Antoli villagers not to harm the leopard. Use a variety of sentence lengths.

1. Include facts from the paragraphs to explain why the leopard should be left alone. You may add other details.
2. When you are done, share your work with a partner. Exchange suggestions about sentence variety.

Exercise 3 Emphasizing Details

Find a brief newspaper or magazine article that interests you. Read it aloud, listening for a passage that sounds monotonous because sentences are almost all the same length. Rewrite the passage to vary sentence lengths. Use at least one short sentence to emphasize details that are not emphasized in the original.

Exercise 4 Revising a Passage

Read the passage below about the African country of Tanzania. Notice that all of the sentences are short.

1. On a separate sheet of paper, revise the passage.
2. Keep the same information, but vary the length of sentences.
3. You may change word order, add or delete words, and combine sentences.

[1]Tanzania borders the Indian Ocean. [2]Its official name is the United Republic of Tanzania. [3]Its capital city is Dodoma. [4]Tanzania features a variety of stunning scenery. [5]Among the features is Mount Kilimanjaro. [6]It is the highest peak in Africa. [7]Another feature is the Serengeti National Park.

LESSON 3.2

Varying Sentence Beginnings

Reading too many sentences that sound the same can be boring. Make your writing more lively and interesting by paying attention to **sentence variety.** One way to do this is by **varying sentence beginnings.**

➡ As you write, start most of your sentences in different ways.

Ways to Begin	Example
Subject	**Tornadoes** tend to occur during spring or early summer.
Adverb or Transition Word	**Typically,** a tornado begins as a funnel cloud of water droplets.
Subordinate Clause	**As the funnel reaches ground,** it begins sucking objects upward.

➡ Try beginning sentences with different types of phrases. (See Lesson 3.5 for more about phrases.)

Type of Phrase	Example
Prepositional Phrase	**In the most powerful tornadoes,** wind speeds may exceed 300 miles per hour.
Verbal Phrase	**To stay safe,** go to a hallway, crouch down, and cover your head with your hands.

➡ You can also add inverted sentences, where the verb **(v)** or part of the verb appears before the subject **(s)**. Note that questions usually use inverted order.

REGULAR The air (s) swirls (v) rapidly.

INVERTED Rapidly swirls (v) the air (s).

INVERTED Does (v) the air (s) swirl (v) rapidly?

Notice how the sentences in the draft on the next page all begin with the subject.

Common Transitions

also	for example
as a result	for instance
finally	in addition
first	similarly
however	therefore

See **Lesson 4.5** for additional transitions.

Common Words That Begin Subordinate Clauses

after	since
although	until
because	when
before	where
if	while

For more about subordinate clauses, see **Lesson 3.3.**

Copyright © 2014 by William H. Sadlier, Inc. All rights reserved.

DRAFT

[1]E-mails are now common in business. [2]E-mails should avoid using all capital letters. [3]The use of all capital letters resembles shouting. [4]This is one fine point of Netiquette, a set of guidelines for sending formal e-mails.

The revision below shows how one writer made changes to improve sentence variety. How effective are the changes? Can you think of other ways to revise?

Writing Model

[1]In business, it's now common to send e-mails. [2]Have you ever received e-mails in all capital letters? [3]Avoid this type of shouting. [4]This is one fine point of Netiquette, a set of guidelines for sending formal e-mails.

Exercise 1 Revising Sentences

Read the sentences below. Keep one sentence in each set the same. Rewrite the others so that each sentence begins in a different way.

1. Claudia boarded the train hesitantly. Claudia was nervous. Today Claudia was starting her volunteer job at the library. Claudia was on summer vacation.
2. Claudia always wanted to volunteer. She enjoyed reading stories aloud. She was very good at it. She had a talent for working with children. She knew how to grab their attention.

EXERCISE 2 Revising an Application Letter

Rewrite the letter below to add sentence variety. You may combine sentences and add or change words. Discuss your revisions with a partner.

1. Use the charts on page 68 to help you write sentences that begin in different ways.
2. As you vary sentence beginnings, include two different types of phrases. Include at least one inverted sentence.

Dear Mrs. Lee:

[1]I am an eighth grader at Central Middle School. [2]I would like to apply for a position as a Junior Counselor at this summer's nature camp. [3]I believe I am very well qualified and would do a great job.

[4]I like working with young children and have lots of experience taking care of my eight-year-old brother. [5]I also enjoy hiking, swimming, and other outdoor activities. [6]Our family has taken frequent camping trips, which I have enjoyed a lot. [7]I spent a week last summer at an overnight nature camp in Pennsylvania. [8]I learned many things about taking care of the environment.

[9]I promise to work hard to make sure all the kids enjoy camp. [10]I look forward to setting up an interview with you.

Sincerely,

Ben Meyer

EXERCISE 3 Improving Your Own Writing

Choose a paragraph you wrote in a story, article, or essay for this or another class. Read it aloud. Make notes of ways to make it sound more interesting and be more effective by varying sentence beginnings. On a separate piece of paper, revise your original paragraph.

Copyright © 2014 by William H. Sadlier, Inc. All rights reserved.

Independent and Subordinate Clauses

LESSON 3.3

Clauses are groups of words that contain a subject **(s)** and a verb **(v)**. To build sentences, writers use two kinds of clauses: independent and subordinate.

Because an **independent** (or **main**) clause expresses a complete thought, it can stand alone as a complete sentence. Every sentence contains one or more independent clauses.

One Independent Clause	One group (s) of indigenous people of the Arctic regions is (v) the Inuit.
Two Independent Clauses	They (s) live (v) in the cold North, and they (s) are (v) hunters rather than farmers.

A **subordinate** (or **dependent**) clause does not express a complete thought and cannot stand alone as a sentence.

Subordinate Clauses	because they (s) live (v) in Greenland, Canada, and Alaska
	after they (s) arrived (v) in North America

A subordinate clause that is capitalized and punctuated like a sentence is a **sentence fragment.** To make a complete sentence, join a subordinate clause to an independent clause, or delete the word that makes it a subordinate clause. (See Lesson 2.1 for more about fragments.)

Sentence Fragment	Whether a kayak (s) is (v) like a canoe.
Add an Independent Clause	I (s) wonder (v) whether a kayak is like a canoe.
Drop a Word	A kayak (s) is (v) like a canoe.

Remember

When you join two or more independent clauses with a conjunction, use a comma before the conjunction. See **Lesson 11.2** for more practice and examples.

Common Relative Pronouns

that	whom
which	whose
who	

Common Subordinating Conjunctions

after	since
although	than
as	unless
because	until
before	where
if	while

Some Words That Introduce Noun Clauses

how	whether
that	who
what	whom
whatever	whose
when	why

To add variety and detail to sentences, writers use three kinds of subordinate clauses. They may appear in the beginning, the middle, or the end of a sentence.

1. **Adjective clauses** function as adjectives. They modify a noun or pronoun and are often introduced by a **relative pronoun,** such as *that, which,* and *who.*

   Inuit artists carve figures **that are made of ivory.**
   [describes the noun *figures,* telling what they are like]

   That one, **which is the oldest,** is my favorite.
   [describes the pronoun *one,* telling which one]

2. **Adverb clauses** function as adverbs. They modify a verb, an adjective, or an adverb. They are often introduced by a **subordinating conjunction,** such as *after* or *because.*

   While the weather is warm, many hunters live in sealskin tents.
   [describes the verb *live,* telling when the hunters stay in tents]

   Do kayaks go slower **than canoes do**?
   [describes the adverb *slower,* asking to what extent kayaks go slower]

3. **Noun clauses** function as nouns. They are used as subjects, objects, or subject complements. Noun clauses are often introduced by words, such as *what, whoever,* and *whether.*

   What the natural world provides is important to the Inuit.
   [functions as the subject of the verb *is*]

   The Inuit knew **that the igloos were sturdy.**
   [functions as the direct object of the verb *knew*]

Exercise 1 Recognizing Clauses

For each numbered item below, write *I* for independent clause or *S* for subordinate clause. On a separate sheet of paper, revise each subordinate clause to make it a complete sentence.

1. American history is my last class of the day.
2. When Mrs. Alexander assigned a research report.
3. That we cannot use our textbook as a source.

Copyright © 2014 by William H. Sadlier, Inc. All rights reserved.

4. While we are in the library next weekend.
5. Which everyone enjoyed.

Exercise 2 Identifying Subordinate Clauses

Each of the sentences below contains one subordinate clause. Underline it once. Label it as an *adjective, adverb,* or *noun.*

EXAMPLE As Paul Revere rode, he shouted to warn the colonists.

adverb

1. Paul Revere was a silversmith who worked in Boston.
2. Whoever studies American history has heard his name.
3. Revere was a silversmith, whose work is now displayed in many museums.
4. Revere fought in the Seven Years War, which started in 1756.
5. Because British troops were gathering, Revere made his famous midnight ride in 1775.
6. The British did not know what the colonists had planned.
7. After the start of the Revolutionary War, Revere served in the Massachusetts militia.
8. Revere, who died in 1818, was an American patriot.
9. Revere's ride was celebrated in a poem that Henry Wadsworth Longfellow wrote.
10. You should read the poem when you have time.

Use a comma after an adverb clause that begins a sentence.

Unless I leave now, I will be late.

Do not use a comma before an adverb clause at the end of a sentence.

I will be late **unless I leave now.**

Exercise 3 Writing Sentences

Write five sentences about yourself or your family. Include the elements below.

1. two independent clauses
2. two subordinate clauses
3. one adjective clause
4. one adverb clause
5. one noun clause

LESSON 3.4

Types of Sentence Structure

Writers try to vary the lengths and beginnings of their sentences to make their writing interesting. They also vary the structure of their sentences.

The **structure** of a sentence depends on the number and kinds of clauses it includes. There are four types of sentence structures.

Type	Clauses
Simple Sentence	one independent clause and no subordinate clauses
	The world's longest mountain chain (S), the Andes, stretches (V) along the western edge of South America.
Compound Sentence	two or more independent clauses
	The Amazon River (S) is (V) the longest river in South America, but the Nile (S) is (V) the world's longest river. [two independent clauses]
Complex Sentence	one independent clause and at least one subordinate clause
	Glaciers (S) and rocky valleys (S) dot (V) the southern tip of South America, which (S) is (V) very near Antarctica. [subordinate clause after an independent clause]
Compound-Complex Sentence	two or more independent clauses and at least one subordinate clause
	The Atacama Desert (S), which (S) is (V) in Chile, is (V) one of the driest areas on the earth, but dangerous flash floods (S) do occur (V) there. [subordinate clause within first of two independent clauses]

Remember

Every **clause** has a subject **(S)** and a verb **(V).** An independent clause makes sense by itself. A subordinate clause does not.

To review the types of clauses, see **Lesson 3.3.**

Using a variety of sentence structures helps you to express the relationships among ideas and to create an interesting and appealing writing style.

Copyright © 2014 by William H. Sadlier, Inc. All rights reserved.

- The independent clause in a simple sentence focuses the reader on one idea or detail.
- Joining two or more independent clauses links two equally important ideas or details.
- Adding one or more subordinate clauses allows you to express more complex ideas. State the important idea(s) in the independent clause.

  Although the desert is dry, **some plants manage to grow.**
  [The purpose here is to stress that plants grow.]

  Although some plants manage to grow there, **the desert is dry.**
  [The purpose is to stress the dryness of the desert.]

Exercise 1 Identifying Sentence Structure

Identify the structure of each sentence below. Write *simple, compound, complex,* or *compound-complex.*

1. Paula is a wonderful pianist.
2. Paula can play classical piano, and she can play jazz.
3. When she sits down at her piano, her fingers race along the piano keys, and her audience sits in amazement.
4. Paula can play the piano, but she cannot play the organ.
5. Until I heard her perform last summer, I didn't know that she played any instrument.
6. Her brother Mark is a wonderful violinist, and he often accompanies Paula when she gives a concert.
7. Mark has never taken a music class, but he has been studying violin since he was a small child.
8. Paula and Mark performed together last year at our school's spring concert.
9. Although Paula has been playing the piano for years, she still enjoys taking lessons, and she practices for hours each day.
10. To Paula, music is a career, but to Mark, music is a hobby.

Exercise 2 Revising for Sentence Variety

On a separate sheet of paper, revise the thank-you note below, improving its sentence variety.

1. Revise so that all of the sentence types are included. You may add, delete, or rearrange words.
2. Exchange your revision with a classmate, and discuss your changes.

Dear Mr. Roth,

[1]I am writing to thank you. [2]Your music classes have been very helpful. [3]I knew very little at first. [4]I now know so much about music theory and practice techniques. [5]I had a successful recital. [6]I really impressed my parents. [7]I hope you are my teacher for a long time.

Sincerely,
Margaret Bell

Exercise 3 Writing Sentences

HINT

Remember to place quotation marks at the beginning and end of a speaker's words. See **Lesson 11.7.**

As you look at the cartoon below, imagine what the two parent fish might say next.

"MOM, DAD, YOU GUYS NEVER GO OUT AND LEAVE ME HOME ALONE! DON'T YOU TRUST ME?"

Write five sentences in response to the cartoon. Use each sentence type at least once. Label each type.

EXAMPLE "Son, we know that you are frustrated." complex

Copyright © 2014 by William H. Sadlier, Inc. All rights reserved.

Using Phrases

LESSON 3.5

A **phrase** is a group of words that acts like one part of speech. Unlike a **clause,** a phrase does not have both a subject and a verb. A phrase by itself cannot stand alone as a sentence.

Phrases	Clara Barton, a Civil War nurse	working as a teacher
Clauses	Clara Barton was a Civil War nurse.	She worked as a teacher.

Learn to use these three common kinds of phrases to add variety and detail to your sentences.

1. A **prepositional phrase** starts with a preposition and includes the object of the preposition (a noun or pronoun) and any words that describe the object. (See Lesson 9.6 for more about prepositional phrases.)

   Clara Barton was called **by** the unusual **nickname,** (PREPOSITION: by; OBJECT: nickname)
   "The Angel **of** the **Battlefield.**" (PREPOSITION: of; OBJECT: Battlefield)
   [two prepositional phrases]

2. An **appositive** is a noun or pronoun that explains or identifies another noun or a pronoun. An **appositive phrase** includes the appositive and any words that describe it.

   Barton, a dedicated **humanitarian,** treated thousands of American soldiers. (APPOSITIVE: humanitarian)
   [*Humanitarian* identifies *Barton*.]

3. A **verbal** is a verb form that functions like another part of speech. There are three kinds of **verbal phrases:** gerund, participial, and infinitive.

Place phrases as close as possible to the word(s) they modify. Phrases that are in the wrong place can cause confusion.

UNCLEAR **Wounded on the battlefield,** Barton brought medical supplies to soldiers.
[Was Barton wounded?]

CLEAR Barton brought medical supplies to soldiers **wounded on the battlefield.**

Clara Barton

Gerund Phrase	includes a **gerund,** a verb form that ends in *-ing* and is used as a noun
	Barton was proud of **founding** (GERUND) the American Red Cross. [The gerund phrase is the object of the preposition *of.*]
Participial Phrase	includes a **participle,** a verb form that can be used as an adjective and often ends in *-ing, -ed,* or *-d*
	Barton, **raised** (PARTICIPLE) in New England, established a school in New Jersey. [The participial phrase modifies the subject *Barton.*]
Infinitive Phrase	includes an **infinitive,** a verb form that usually begins with *to* and is used as a noun, an adjective, or an adverb
	During the Spanish-American War, Barton led Red Cross efforts **to help** (INFINITIVE) soldiers. [The infinitive phrase is an adjective. It modifies *efforts.*]

See **Lessons 8.7, 8.8,** and **8.9** for more about verbals and verbal phrases.

Exercise 1 Identifying Phrases

On a separate sheet of paper, list the kinds of phrases that are numbered and underlined below.

Literary Model

In fifth [1]grade our teacher asked us to write ab[2]out the most wonderful thing we'd ever seen. I sat in class tap[3]ping my pencil against my head trying to remem[4]ber the colors of butterflies' wings and how the deep blue-green water of Glen[5]wood Springs made you think of som[6]ething that went on forever. But none of the things that came to[7] my mind was the prettiest. When I started writing, it was about [8]my father, the year he won the police department's Medal for Bravery for rescuing[9] a mother and her baby son from[10] a man who was holding them hostage.

—Excerpt from *Hush* by Jacqueline Woodson

Copyright © 2014 by William H. Sadlier, Inc. All rights reserved.

Exercise 2 Using Phrases in Sentences

Use each of the following phrases in a sentence of your own. The type of phrase is indicated in parentheses. Feel free to add as many details as you wish.

EXAMPLE on the ladder (prepositional)

The man on the ladder is Mr. Fields.

1. to paint the front wall (infinitive)

2. lying on the table (participial)

3. with green paint (prepositional)

4. the biggest dog (appositive)

5. searching for a pencil (gerund)

6. near the bottom (prepositional)

7. to stop quickly (infinitive)

8. surprised by the noise (participial)

9. collecting rare coins (gerund)

10. a fourteen-year-old boy (appositive)

Use commas to set off appositive or participial phrases that aren't essential to the meaning of a sentence.

Devon**,** my oldest brother**,** moved to Florida.

See **Lessons 11.3** and **11.4** for more about using commas to set off phrases.

Exercise 3 Writing a Summary

Suppose a friend asked you about a book you've read or a movie or television show you've seen recently.

1. On a separate sheet of paper, write a summary of an exciting incident or scene.

2. Write six to ten sentences. Include at least three different kinds of phrases in your summary.

3. When you finish, underline the phrases you used.

4. Discuss your summary with a partner.

LESSON 3.6

Combining Sentences: Coordinating Conjunctions

Eliminate repetition and improve your style by using **coordinating conjunctions** (*and, or, but, nor, yet, so,* and *for*) to combine a series of short, choppy sentences.

Sometimes you may want to combine two or more short, related sentences to form a **compound sentence.** Remember to place a comma before the coordinating conjunction.

ORIGINAL	Some holidays connect to a culture's religious beliefs. Others celebrate an important historical event.
COMPOUND SENTENCE	Some holidays connect to a culture's religious beliefs**, but** others celebrate an important historical event.

Sometimes you may want to combine sentences by creating a new sentence with **compound elements.** For example, use a conjunction to link compound subjects, verbs, or other sentence parts such as adjectives.

ORIGINAL	Golden fish play a special role in Chinese New Year festivities. So do dragons.
COMPOUND SUBJECT	Golden **fish** and **dragons** play special roles in Chinese New Year festivities.
ORIGINAL	During the Hindu festival of Diwali, people light candles. They share special meals.
COMPOUND VERB	During the Hindu festival of Diwali, people **light** candles and **share** special meals.
ORIGINAL	People wear elaborate costumes during Mardi Gras. The costumes are colorful.
COMPOUND ADJECTIVES	People wear **elaborate** and **colorful** costumes during Mardi Gras.

CONNECTING Writing & Grammar

Avoid joining sentences with a comma alone. To avoid creating a run-on sentence, add a coordinating conjunction after the comma.

RUN-ON Mardi Gras parades can last for hours, they are fun to watch.

CORRECT Mardi Gras parades can last for hours**, but** they are fun to watch.

See **Lessons 3.4** and **6.4** for more examples of compound sentences and compound subjects and verbs.

Copyright © 2014 by William H. Sadlier, Inc. All rights reserved.

Exercise 1 Combining Sentences

On a separate sheet of paper, combine the sentences in each numbered item below. Use *and, or,* or *but,* and follow the method listed in the parentheses.

To combine sentences, you may need to delete or change words and punctuation marks. Be sure to use a plural verb with a plural subject.

Joe and Leo **have** (not *has*) bicycles.

EXAMPLE Commuter trains are crowded. Subways are also crowded. (compound subject)

Commuter trains and subways are crowded.

1. New York City's rapid transit system is the country's oldest. It is also the busiest. (compound adjective)
2. New York's subway operates every day. It is open twenty-four hours a day. (compound verb)
3. The Paris Metro has beautiful stations. It usually runs on schedule. (compound sentence)
4. My dad takes the train to work. My mom does, too. (compound subject)
5. Last week they were late to work. They did not miss anything important. (compound sentence)
6. My uncle drives a cab. My brother drives a cab. (compound subject)
7. The train was hot. It was stuffy. (compound adjective)
8. Airports can be noisy. Train stations are also noisy. (compound subject)
9. My bus driver is strict. She is friendly. (compound sentence)
10. The engine sputtered. Then it died. (compound verb)

Exercise 2 Improving Your Own Writing

Find a story, essay, or report you wrote for this or another class. Read it aloud, listening for a series of short sentences that you can combine by using *and, or,* or *but*. Rewrite the passage on a separate sheet of paper.

LESSON 3.7

Combining Sentences: Key Words and Phrases

You can combine ideas from short sentences by taking a key word or phrase from one sentence and inserting it in another. You may need to change the form of one or more words or leave words out.

ORIGINAL Sean won our school's yo-yo championship! It was the second one. It was an easy win.

COMBINED Sean **easily** won our school's **second yo-yo** championship!

ORIGINAL Pedro Flores was an immigrant from the Philippines. He was the first to manufacture the yo-yo in America.

COMBINED **Pedro Flores, an immigrant from the Philippines,** was the first to manufacture the yo-yo in America.

Explore different options for combining sentences. There is no one "right" way. Remember that you may need to add one or more commas to your new sentence, depending on the phrase you move and where you put it. (See Lessons 11.2, 11.3, and 11.4 for more about using commas.)

ORIGINAL The yo-yo player holds the yo-yo by a string. The string has a loop. The player flicks his or her wrist downward. That causes the yo-yo to spin.

COMBINED **Holding the yo-yo by a loop of string,** the yo-yo player flicks his or her wrist downward **and causes the yo-yo to spin.**

COMBINED A yo-yo player holds the yo-yo by a **loop of** string and then flicks his or her wrist downward, **causing** the yo-yo to spin.

TEST-TAKING TIP

Test questions often ask you to choose which combination of several short sentences is the best. Ask yourself, "Which sounds the most natural? Which uses correct punctuation?" For a sample question, see item 3 on page 93.

Exercise 1 Combining Sentences

On a separate sheet of paper, combine the sentences in each numbered item by inserting key words and phrases from one sentence into another.

Copyright © 2014 by William H. Sadlier, Inc. All rights reserved.

1. Leo went to the pool. The pool is in Lakewood. Leo is an expert swimmer.
2. He went straight to the waterslide. The slide was bright orange.
3. Leo waited in a line before he got to the ladder. The line was long. The line was slow. Leo was impatient.
4. The lifeguard sat at the top of the ladder. She made sure that everyone was safe. Juanita Johnson was the lifeguard.
5. Leo announced he was ready. He said it in a loud voice.
6. Leo hit the water with a splash. The water was cold. Leo was waving his hands.
7. Leo swam quickly. He moved toward a ladder. The ladder was at the edge of the pool.
8. Leo climbed out of the water. He moved quickly. He began to shiver.
9. Leo dried off with his towel. It was a blue and green beach towel. Leo was proud of himself.
10. Leo marched over to the hot dog stand. It was busy. He moved with confidence and quickness.

You may need to change the form of a key word before you can insert it into another sentence.

Juanita **smiled.** She blew her whistle.

Smiling, Juanita blew her whistle.

Exercise 2 Finding and Revising Examples

In small groups, make up three sets of several short sentences.

1. Think of two ways to revise these sentences into one sentence using the information from this lesson.
2. Write the two revisions on a separate sheet of paper. Check that you have used punctuation correctly.
3. Exchange papers with another group, and check their sentences.

LESSON 3.8

Combining Sentences: Subordinate Clauses

You can use **subordinate clauses** to combine short, choppy sentences into longer, smoother ones. A sentence with one independent clause and at least one subordinate clause is a **complex sentence.**

See **Lessons 3.3** and **3.4** to review subordinate clauses and complex sentences.

TWO SIMPLE SENTENCES	The main character of *The House on Mango Street* is Esperanza. The book is set in Chicago.
COMPLEX SENTENCE	The main character of *The House on Mango Street*, **which is set in Chicago,** is Esperanza. [Put the less important idea in the subordinate clause.]

Make a subordinate clause by adding a **subordinating conjunction** (such as *although*, *because*, *before*, *until*, or *when*) that explains how the two ideas are related. When the subordinate clause begins the sentence, set it off with a comma.

ORIGINAL	Esperanza moves to a new house. She makes friends with Lucy and Rachel.
COMBINED	**When Esperanza moves to a new house,** she makes friends with Lucy and Rachel.

You may also turn a short sentence into a subordinate clause by using a **relative pronoun** (such as *who*, *whose*, *which*, or *that*) to replace the subject. When these clauses are not essential to the meaning of the sentence, set them off with commas.

ORIGINAL	Sandra Cisneros wrote the novel. She has a Mexican-American heritage.
COMBINED	Sandra Cisneros**, whose heritage is Mexican-American,** wrote the novel.

If the information in the subordinate clause is essential to the meaning of the sentence, use the word *that*. Do not use commas when you use *that* to combine sentences. See **Lesson 11.4.**

Esperanza learns details about the neighbors. The details surprise her.

Esperanza learns details about the neighbors **that surprise her.**

Exercise 1 Combining Sentences

On a separate sheet of paper, combine the following pairs of sentences by making the second sentence into a subordinate clause. The word in parentheses tells you what word to use to begin the subordinate clause.

Copyright © 2014 by William H. Sadlier, Inc. All rights reserved.

1. Erica catches butterflies for her collection. She keeps her collection in a dresser drawer. (*which*)
2. Julio watched ants climb the side of the watermelon rind. He was sitting in the tall, green grass. (*who*)
3. The sun sank below the horizon. Fireflies and mosquitoes swarmed around the yard. (*while*)
4. The scientist displayed two caterpillars. These caterpillars were poisonous. (*that*)
5. Gabriella works at the park. She is allergic to bees. (*who*)
6. Some cicadas live beneath the ground for seventeen years. Seventeen years is a long time for an insect to live. (*which*)
7. Jack stood still. A wasp was nearby. (*even though*)
8. Bianca has seen few dragonflies. She visited Lake Champlain. (*since*)
9. The wasps will be gone soon. The weather has gotten so cold. (*because*)
10. Mark caught just four fireflies. He spent two hours outside last night. (*although*)

To combine the sentences effectively, you may need to delete one or more words from the second sentence.

Exercise 2 Using Subordinate Clauses

On a separate sheet of paper, write six to ten short sentences describing the photo on the right and your thoughts about it.

1. Work with a partner to combine some of the sentences with subordinate clauses.
2. Write at least five sentences that include subordinate clauses.

ONLINE MODEL
www.grammarforwriting.com

Compare-Contrast Essay

What is your favorite book? To choose that particular book as your favorite, you must have compared and contrasted it to all of the other books you have ever read.

A **compare-contrast essay** is a type of informative/explanatory writing that gives information about a topic. Compare-contrast essays explore the similarities and differences between two or more objects, people, or ideas.

Compare-contrast essays should include the following key features.

Key Features

- clear thesis, or claim, in the introduction
- well-chosen facts, details, and examples that compare and contrast
- logical organization with transitions that show similarities and differences among ideas
- precise language and vocabulary specific to the topic
- formal style and tone
- conclusion that follows from the information given

ASSIGNMENT

TASK: Write a two- to three-page **compare-contrast essay.** Compare and contrast one of the following: two games, a book and its movie version, cats and dogs, or e-mail pen pals and nearby friends.

AUDIENCE: your classmates

PURPOSE: to explain the similarities and differences between two subjects

Copyright © 2014 by William H. Sadlier, Inc. All rights reserved.

Prewriting

Choose and Narrow Your Topic Before you begin, think about the different topics you could write about. To narrow your list, ask yourself these questions:

1. Which topic am I most interested in?
2. Which topic do I know most about?
3. Which topic can I easily find the most information for?
4. Which topic will my audience be most interested in?

After you have answered these questions, complete the following sentences to help you better understand your comparison:

- This would make a strong comparison because...
- The purpose of my comparison is...
- The main similarity between my two subjects is...
- The main difference between my two subjects is...

Make Your Point Your **thesis** states your essay's central claim. In a compare-contrast essay, it must state what is being compared and the purpose for that comparison. Below are common errors that occur when drafting a thesis. The last example shows a strong thesis.

For more information about writing a thesis, see **Lesson 5.2.**

Too Narrow	E-mail pen pals, or e-pals, are better than friends, because they are easier to talk to.
Too Broad	E-mail pen pals, or e-pals, and friends can be great.
Factual	E-mail pen pals, or e-pals, are different from friends who live nearby.
Topic Without a Point	This essay will compare and contrast e-pals and friends who live nearby.
Strong	Though e-pals may come from various backgrounds, the face-to-face contact we have with nearby friends makes them more valuable than e-pals.

Prewriting

Gather Details Next, gather details about your subject. Use a Venn diagram to organize your details.

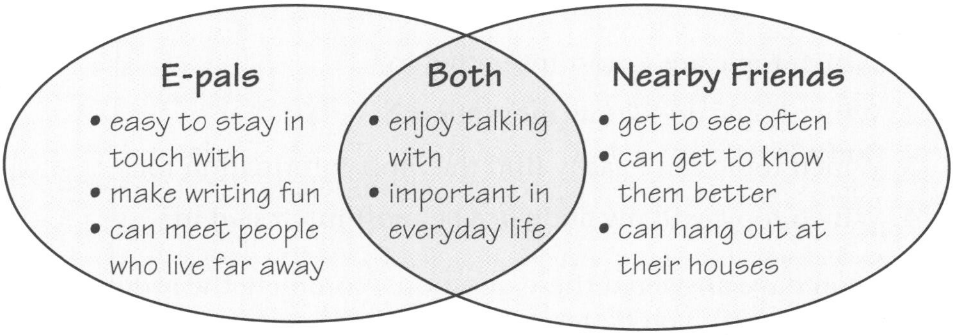

E-pals	Both	Nearby Friends
• easy to stay in touch with • make writing fun • can meet people who live far away	• enjoy talking with • important in everyday life	• get to see often • can get to know them better • can hang out at their houses

Organize Your Ideas Use one of these patterns:

1. **Point-by-Point Method** Focus on one feature at a time. Compare and contrast that feature in both subjects.

Feature 1: Diversity
Subject A: E-pals
Subject B: Friends

Feature 2: Social Life
Subject A: E-pals
Subject B: Friends

Feature 3: Honesty and Closeness
Subject A: E-pals
Subject B: Friends

2. **Block Method** Discuss all the features about one subject first. Then discuss those same features about the next subject.

Subject A: E-pals
Feature 1: Diversity
Feature 2: Social Life
Feature 3: Honesty and Closeness

Subject B: Friends
Feature 1: Diversity
Feature 2: Social Life
Feature 3: Honesty and Closeness

Copyright © 2014 by William H. Sadlier, Inc. All rights reserved.

Drafting

Make It Complete As you draft, be sure to include the three essay parts.

1. **Introduction** Clearly introduce your topic by providing a strong thesis statement, or claim. Preview the features you will discuss and the organizational structure of the body.
2. **Body** The body should include all of the appropriate facts, details, and examples that support your claim. Use either the point-by-point or block method. Establish a formal style and tone, and use precise language and vocabulary specific to your subject matter.
3. **Conclusion** A strong concluding statement should restate your claim and sum up your main points. Be certain that your conclusion follows logically from the information presented in your essay.

The model shows a body paragraph from one writer's essay.

WRITING HINT

Use transitions to signal comparisons and contrasts and to connect sentences and paragraphs.

also	in contrast
conversely	likewise
however	similarly

Writing Model

[1]E-pals are often more diverse than your friends at home. [2]For example, you can be pen pals with a person in Bangladesh, Brazil, Boston, or Botswana. [3]E-pals reveal what it is like to go to a different school, have different customs or traditions, or live in a different country. [4]In contrast, friends who live near each other may not be as diverse. [5]My three closest friends this year, for instance, come from very similar backgrounds to my own. [6]In fact, we all live on the same street, and we have known one another since we were in first grade.

Point-by-point method

Diversity of e-pals

Transitions

Diversity of friends

Revising

Use the Revising Questions to improve your draft. The model below shows one writer's revisions to a body paragraph.

As you revise, keep in mind the traits of good writing. See **Lesson 1.3.**

Revising Questions

- ❑ How clear is my thesis statement, or claim, and where should I add specific details to support it?
- ❑ Where can I clarify the organization or add transitions?
- ❑ How strong are my introduction, body, and conclusion?

Add specific details.

Add a transition to show contrast.

Focus on only one feature in a paragraph when you use the point-by-point method.

[1]It can be difficult to know who your e-pals really are ^(and to feel very close to them.) [2]Through e-mail, e-pals can pretend to be anyone they want to be. [3]Since they are often hundreds—or thousands—of miles away, it is unlikely that you'll ever see how they look and act in real life. [4]~~I~~ ^(In contrast,) in the real world ^(with face-to-face friends,) it is much harder to pretend to be something you are not. [5]~~By keeping a e-pal, you can meet people from all over the world.~~ [6]Because you have firsthand experiences with your friends, you know their personalities well.

Copyright © 2014 by William H. Sadlier, Inc. All rights reserved.

Revising

Smooth It Out By combining two or more short sentences into one longer sentence, you can vary your writing and create more complex ideas. Here are two ways to combine sentences.

1. **Create compound sentences.** In the first sentence, change the end punctuation to a comma. Add a coordinating conjunction, such as *and, or, nor,* or *but* after the comma.

   ORIGINAL E-pals are fun. Friends who live nearby are even more fun.

   COMBINED E-pals are fun**, but** friends who live nearby are even more fun.

2. **Use subordinate clauses.** Turn one sentence into a subordinate clause. In most cases, add a subordinating conjunction at the beginning, followed by a comma.

   COMBINED **While** e-pals are fun**,** friends who live nearby are even more fun.

As you read the model below, notice the sentence variety.

Some Subordinating Conjunctions

after	if
although	when
as	which
because	while

For more help with combining sentences, see **Lessons 3.6, 3.7,** and **3.8.**

Literary Model

[1]Trace Middle School didn't have the world's strictest dress code, but Roy was pretty sure that some sort of footwear was required. [2]The boy might have been carrying sneakers in his backpack, if only he'd been wearing a backpack.

—Excerpt from *Hoot* by Carl Hiaasen

Reading as a Writer

1. Where does Hiaasen use a subordinating conjunction?
2. How well did the author vary his sentences?

CONNECTING Writing & Grammar

When you combine sentences, always add a comma after a subordinate clause that begins a sentence. See **Lesson 11.3.**

While I have e-pals**,** my best friend lives next door.

Editing and Proofreading

Next, use the checklist below to edit and proofread your paper.

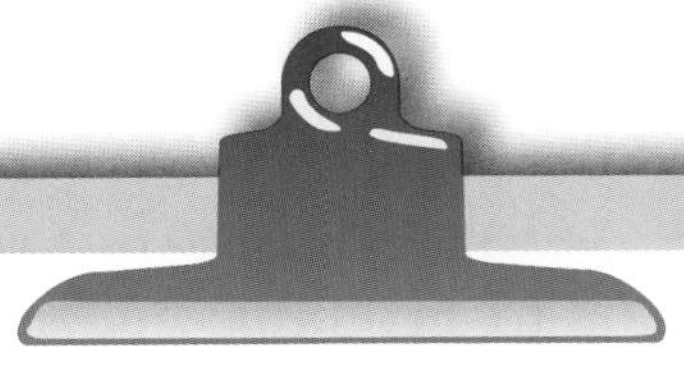

Editing and Proofreading Checklist

- ❑ Have I checked that all words are spelled correctly?
- ❑ Have I correctly used commas when combining sentences?
- ❑ Are any words missing or run together?

Proofreading Symbols

- ^ Add.
- ^, Add a comma.
- Delete.

[1]Although I like my e-pals a lot, the face-to-face contact I have with my nearby friends is extremely important. [2]There are only so many things that can be learned about a person through e-mail. [3]Conversely, I know a whole lot about the ~~the~~ people I see every day.

Reflect On Your Writing

- What is the strongest part of your essay? Why?
- If you had to write the essay again, what would you do differently?

Publishing and Presenting

Use one of these ways to share your essay with others.

1. **E-mail it.** Send it to a friend or family member, and start a correspondence about your topic.
2. **Display it.** Create a poster about your essay.

Copyright © 2014 by William H. Sadlier, Inc. All rights reserved.

Chapter Review

A. Practice Test

Read each sentence below carefully. Decide which answer choice best replaces the underlined part, and fill in the circle of the corresponding letter. If you think the underlined part is correct as is, fill in the circle for choice *A*.

EXAMPLE

Ⓐ Ⓑ Ⓒ Ⓓ Ⓔ Some people feel shy with <u>strangers. They feel shy</u> in crowds.
(A) strangers. They feel shy
(B) strangers, and they feel shy
(C) strangers. Some people feel shy
(D) strangers. Feeling shy
(E) strangers, that feel shy

Ⓐ Ⓑ Ⓒ Ⓓ Ⓔ **1.** Shyness can sometimes cause physical symptoms, such as <u>blushing. It may cause shakiness or shortness of breath</u>.
(A) blushing. It may cause shakiness or shortness of breath.
(B) blushing or shaky. It may cause shortness of breath.
(C) blushing, it may cause shakiness or shortness of breath.
(D) blushing it may cause shakiness or shortness of breath.
(E) blushing, shakiness, or shortness of breath.

Ⓐ Ⓑ Ⓒ Ⓓ Ⓔ **2.** There are some gifts that come with being <u>shy. One of these gifts is being a good listener</u>.
(A) shy. One of these gifts is being a good listener.
(B) shy. Such as being a good listener.
(C) shy, such as being a good listener.
(D) shy. If one of these gifts is being a good listener.
(E) shy one of these gifts is being a good listener.

Ⓐ Ⓑ Ⓒ Ⓓ Ⓔ **3.** Some people would rather not be <u>shy. They'd rather be social. Overcoming</u> shyness takes practice.
(A) shy. They'd rather be social. Overcoming
(B) shy, they'd rather be social. Overcoming
(C) shy, they'd rather be social. To overcome
(D) shy and would rather be social, but overcoming
(E) shy, but they'd rather be social, overcoming

Ⓐ Ⓑ Ⓒ Ⓓ Ⓔ **4.** You may feel shy among new people. Try simple conversation starters. Mention something you have in common with the other person.

(A) You may feel shy among new people. Try simple conversation-starters. Mention something
(B) If you feel shy among new people, try simple conversation starters that mention something
(C) If you feel shy among new people try simple conversation starters, that mention something
(D) If you feel shy among new people. Try simple conversation starters, that mention something
(E) You may feel shy among new people try simple conversation starters, if you mention something

Ⓐ Ⓑ Ⓒ Ⓓ Ⓔ **5.** The more you practice, the more self-confident you will feel you will also feel more relaxed.

(A) you will feel you will also feel more relaxed.
(B) you will feel relaxed.
(C) you will feel, that is being relaxed.
(D) you will feel, you will also feel more relaxed.
(E) and relaxed you will feel.

B. Identifying Clauses

For each sentence below, label the underlined clause *IND* for independent, *ADJ* for adjective, *ADV* for adverb, or *N* for noun.

___ **1.** Origami is a hobby that many people enjoy.

___ **2.** What origami involves is folding paper to form shapes.

___ **3.** When paper was very expensive, only the very rich could afford to practice the art.

___ **4.** For centuries, the directions that explained origami techniques were passed down orally.

___ **5.** In 1797, the first written set of instructions was published.

Chapter Review

Copyright © 2014 by William H. Sadlier, Inc. All rights reserved.

C. Using Phrases and Clauses

On a separate sheet of paper, write a complete sentence using each phrase or clause below. Use it as indicated in the parentheses.

1. shouting with glee (as a participial phrase)
2. finishing the test (as a gerund in a simple sentence)
3. our family's dog (as an appositive in a compound-complex sentence)
4. whose birthday is tomorrow (as an adjective clause)
5. to go skydiving (as an infinitive in a compound sentence)

D. Revising a Compare-Contrast Essay

Rewrite this part of a compare-contrast essay draft. Combine sentences. Include at least one sentence that begins with the subject, one that begins with a subordinate clause, and one that begins with a transition. Fix any problems with organization, and add or delete details as needed.

[1]My two closest friends are Jeremy and Maggie. [2]They each bring out different parts of my personality. [3]I'm serious with Jeremy and silly with Maggie.

[4]Jeremy is quiet. [5]He is thoughtful. [6]He studies very hard. [7]We talk about books. [8]We talk about the news. [9]Maggie's sense of humor is completely wacky. [10]Jeremy brings out my intellectual side.

[11]Maggie is spontaneous. [12]She makes me laugh. [13]She is full of energy. [14]She is always on the go.

[15]Maggie and Jeremy do not have much in common besides my friendship. [16]I value each one of them. [17]They make me happy to be who I am.

Chapter Review

CHAPTER 4

Effective Paragraphs

Copyright © 2014 by William H. Sadlier, Inc. All rights reserved.

LESSON 4.1

Main Ideas and Topic Sentences

Most effective paragraphs focus on a **main idea** or point. Sometimes you may state your main idea directly in a **topic sentence.**

Writers often include a topic sentence as their first or second sentence. A good topic sentence captures the readers' attention and helps them understand what is to come in the rest of the paragraph.

Writing Model

[1]Born in 1877 to the son of a former slave, Garrett Morgan became one of America's most successful African American inventors. [2]In 1914, he developed a gas mask smoke protector that the U.S. Army used during World War I. [3]Several years later, after witnessing a collision between a horse-drawn carriage and an automobile, Morgan patented an inexpensive traffic signal.

Topic sentence at beginning

Examples of Morgan's inventions

Sometimes writers build up to their point rather than begin with it. In these cases, they place topic sentences in the middle or at the end of a paragraph.

Writing Model

[1]In the 1880s, Sarah Goode invented a space-saving cabinet bed that folded into a desk. [2]Mary Anderson invented the windshield wiper to help streetcars operate safely in 1903. [3]In 1950, Marion Donovan invented the disposable diaper. [4]Two years later, Grace Hopper invented the computer compiler, which revolutionized computer programming, and in 1966, Stephanie Kwolek invented kevlar, the fiber used in bullet-proof vests. [5]Although their names may not be widely known, American women have been responsible for an amazing variety of inventions.

Inventions of five women

Topic sentence at end

In some paragraphs, no single sentence expresses the main idea. Instead, writers use details to suggest, or **imply,** a main idea. (See Lessons 4.6 and 4.7 for more about types of paragraphs.)

These sentences support the **implied main idea**—that many of Franklin's inventions were designed to make people's lives safer and easier.

Writing Model

[1]Benjamin Franklin invented the furnace stove so that people in colonial America could heat their homes more safely. [2]Another practical invention of his was bifocals, which allowed people to see up close and far away with one pair of glasses. [3]Interested in protecting buildings from lightning damage, Franklin experimented with electricity. [4]His efforts led to the development of the lightning rod. [5]Another useful invention included swim fins to help swimmers increase their speed.

Exercise 1 Analyzing Paragraphs

Underline the topic sentence in each paragraph. If there is no topic sentence, write the main idea in your own words.

HINT

To find the main idea, first identify the topic. Then ask yourself, "What point is the writer making *about* the topic?"

[1]On May 20, 1883, clouds of ash streamed six miles up into the atmosphere from the mouth of Indonesia's Krakatoa Volcano. [2]Three months later, Krakatoa finished erupting and destroyed itself in the process. [3]People heard shock waves as far away as Australia, while tons of pitch-black ash and fragments of rock were tossed high into the atmosphere. [4]Frighteningly, the ash caused total darkness for two days in surrounding areas. [5]The ash also created massive waves, or tsunamis, the largest of which killed thirty-six thousand people in Java and Sumatra.

Copyright © 2014 by William H. Sadlier, Inc. All rights reserved.

[1]Mount Saint Helens was one of the most violent eruptions in modern history. [2]Mount Saint Helens, which is part of the Cascade range in southwestern Washington, began to erupt in March of 1980. [3]First, steam started to pour from the top of the mountain, and cracks and bulges created by molten rock began to form on its sides. [4]Then, in May of that same year, an earthquake caused a massive landslide on the north slope of the mountain. [5]This event sparked the eruption. [6]Ash and debris were thrown into the atmosphere. [7]Two hundred square miles of land were ruined, the mountain itself lost one thousand feet from its peak, and darkness covered parts of the region.

EXERCISE 2 Writing a Paragraph

Look at the photograph on the right. On a separate sheet of paper, write a paragraph explaining it or a related topic.

1. Include a topic sentence in your paragraph.
2. Exchange papers with a classmate. Ask him or her to identify the topic sentence. Discuss your paragraphs, and determine the effectiveness of the topic sentences. Revise your paragraphs based on this discussion.

Write What You Think

Do you agree or disagree with the statement below? Write a paragraph of at least five sentences to explain your answer.

The best things in life are free.

1. Begin the paragraph with a clear topic sentence.
2. Support your topic sentence with at least two examples.

LESSON 4.2

Methods of Elaboration

In writing, when you **elaborate,** you add **supporting details** that help your readers understand ideas.

The kind of **elaboration** you need depends on your purpose, topic, and audience. The chart below shows several methods of elaboration.

Facts	statements that can be proved true
Statistics	data expressed in numbers
Examples	specific cases or instances
Reasons	statements that explain opinions
Sensory Details	details about how something looks, sounds, smells, feels, or tastes
Anecdotes	brief stories or incidents
Quotations	spoken or written words from an expert

WRITING HINT

Sometimes adding a visual (such as a chart, diagram, photo, or graph) can help explain and clarify your ideas.

To elaborate, ask yourself, "How can I clarify my ideas? What else does my reader need to know?" Some details will come from your own observations and experiences. Others, such as statistics or quotations, will require research.

Notice how the writer of the paragraph below added supporting details to elaborate on the opening topic sentence. What other information would give readers a clearer, more complete picture?

Writing Model

New facts and statistics

New sensory details

New examples

[1]The Great Wall of China is an extraordinary architectural accomplishment. [2]It is the longest structure built by hand, extending more than 4,000 miles. [3]The first emperor of China, Qin Shi Huang, began work on it ~~many centuries~~ more than 2,000 years ago. [4]The top, made of light-colored stone slabs, is a roadway about thirteen feet wide that winds through a variety of harsh landscapes, such as mountains and deserts.

Copyright © 2014 by William H. Sadlier, Inc. All rights reserved.

Exercise 1 Analyzing a Model

Write a paragraph about the following passage. Identify the topic sentence, and evaluate the writer's use of supporting details. Notice what the writer does well. Then, offer specific suggestions about what kinds of details could be added. Compare and contrast your suggestions with those of a classmate.

[1]Although Teddy Roosevelt is popularly thought of as an adventurer and big-game hunter, his actions reveal his commitment to the environment. [2]Even as a young person, Roosevelt was very interested in the natural world. [3]He wrote papers, collected animal specimens, and actively studied environmental issues. [4]During his presidency, Roosevelt helped to create the United States Forest Service. [5]He also greatly increased the amount of land protected from commercial use. [6]Furthermore, Roosevelt created other parks and regularly wrote articles and books supporting conservation.

Exercise 2 Writing a Paragraph

Choose one topic sentence from the list below. Write a paragraph that supports it by using a variety of the methods of elaboration listed on the previous page. Assume your audience is younger children.

1. There is no such thing as luck.
2. The best way to become a good writer is to read a lot.
3. Everyone should learn a second language.

Be sure that all supporting details you add relate to your topic. See **Lesson 4.3** for tips about keeping the focus of a paragraph unified and the details relevant.

EXERCISE 3 Writing a Paragraph from Notes

Read the notes below. Choose several supporting details, and use them to write a well-developed paragraph on a separate sheet of paper. Begin your paragraph with a topic sentence. Remember that you do not need to use all of the information below.

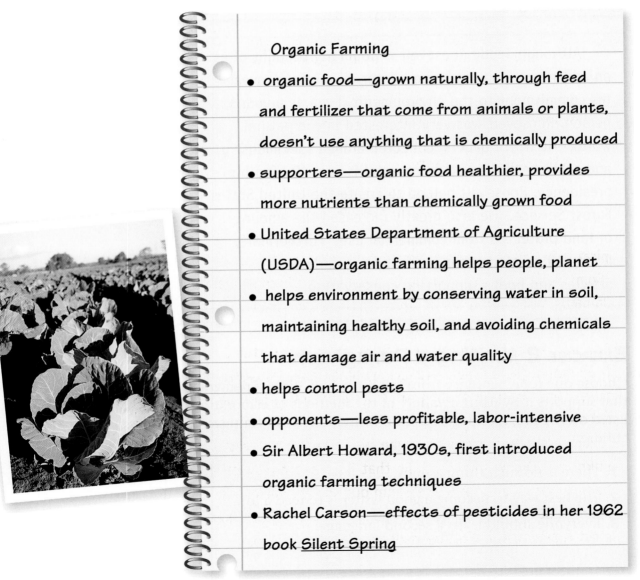

Organic Farming

- organic food—grown naturally, through feed and fertilizer that come from animals or plants, doesn't use anything that is chemically produced
- supporters—organic food healthier, provides more nutrients than chemically grown food
- United States Department of Agriculture (USDA)—organic farming helps people, planet
- helps environment by conserving water in soil, maintaining healthy soil, and avoiding chemicals that damage air and water quality
- helps control pests
- opponents—less profitable, labor-intensive
- Sir Albert Howard, 1930s, first introduced organic farming techniques
- Rachel Carson—effects of pesticides in her 1962 book <u>Silent Spring</u>

Copyright © 2014 by William H. Sadlier, Inc. All rights reserved.

LESSON 4.3

Improving Paragraph Unity

Unity in a paragraph means that all the sentences relate to a single topic. In a unified paragraph, each sentence directly supports one main idea.

Follow these suggestions to write paragraphs with unity.

1. State your main point directly in a strong, clear **topic sentence**. If you write a paragraph without a topic sentence, be clear about the exact idea of your paragraph.
2. Focus on one sentence at a time. Ask yourself, "How does each detail relate to or explain my main idea?"
3. Remove details or sentences that do not develop the paragraph's main idea. If the information is important, you may decide to include it in another paragraph.

For more on topic sentences, see **Lesson 4.1.**

Notice how eliminating three sentences in the paragraph below improves the paragraph's unity.

Writing Model

[1]Although Blackbeard was one of the most feared pirates in history, little is known about his early life. [2]Some sources say he was born in London; others suggest Jamaica or Philadelphia as his birthplace. [3]A number of documents indicate Blackbeard's real name was Edward Teach, but others list his last name as Thatch or Drummond. ~~[4]A tall man with bushy black hair, Blackbeard made sure his appearance terrified his enemies.~~ ~~[5]During battles, he would sometimes coil burning ropes in his hair.~~ [6]Exactly how and when he began his career as a pirate is unknown. [7]A few sources claim that Blackbeard may have been a privateer on a British ship during the War of the Spanish Succession before becoming a pirate. ~~[8]Blackbeard's most famous ship was *Queen Anne's Revenge*.~~

Sentences 4, 5, and 8 tell about Blackbeard's appearance and ship. They do not belong in a paragraph about the mysteries of his early life.

Exercise 1 Revising a Paragraph

On a separate sheet of paper, revise the following paragraph to give it more unity. Underline the topic sentence, and summarize the changes you made.

[1]Jacques Marquette and Louis Jolliet were the first Europeans to explore the Mississippi River and record accurate information about its course. [2]The governor of New France, who wished to learn the direction and the location of the mouth of the river, commissioned Marquette and Jolliet's journey. [3]Jolliet was a former priest who chose a life of adventure. [4]In 1673, these two explorers set out from Green Bay on the Fox River, traveling toward the Wisconsin River. [5]They entered the Mississippi by mid-June. [6]Marquette and Jolliet took the Mississippi from Prairie du Chien, Wisconsin, to the mouth of the Arkansas River, where they stopped, turned around, and headed for home. [7]A university in Wisconsin is named after Marquette. [8]Also, Jolliet has a city south of Chicago named after him.

Exercise 2 Writing from Notes

Study the Timelines on the next page.

1. Read the titles and the information in the Timelines.
2. Choose several related details.
3. Write a unified paragraph of at least five sentences about the life of Louise Boyd.

Copyright © 2014 by William H. Sadlier, Inc. All rights reserved.

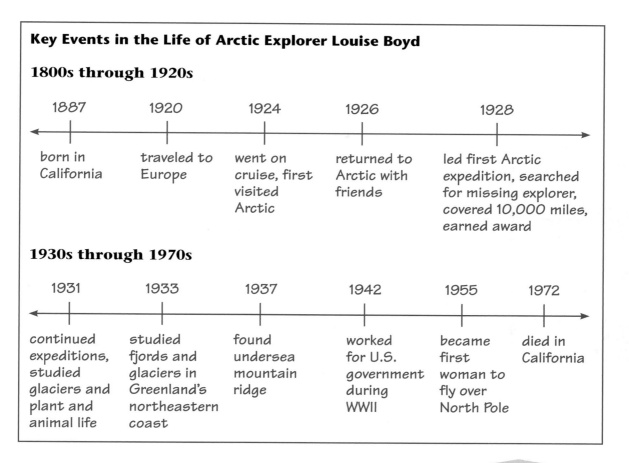

Key Events in the Life of Arctic Explorer Louise Boyd

1800s through 1920s

1887	1920	1924	1926	1928
born in California	traveled to Europe	went on cruise, first visited Arctic	returned to Arctic with friends	led first Arctic expedition, searched for missing explorer, covered 10,000 miles, earned award

1930s through 1970s

1931	1933	1937	1942	1955	1972
continued expeditions, studied glaciers and plant and animal life	studied fjords and glaciers in Greenland's northeastern coast	found undersea mountain ridge	worked for U.S. government during WWII	became first woman to fly over North Pole	died in California

Exercise 3 Writing a Unified Paragraph

Write a one-paragraph description of a recent day at school. Begin your paragraph with a topic sentence that clearly states that the day was or wasn't typical.

1. Use a variety of specific details that explain and support the main idea. Use chronological, or time, order to organize the day's events.
2. When you have finished your draft, ask a partner to read it and check for paragraph unity.

LESSON 4.4

Patterns of Organization

As a writer, you can help your readers understand your ideas better by arranging your sentences and paragraphs in a clear, easy-to-follow order.

Depending on your topic and purpose, choose one of these four common **patterns of organization.** You might use one organizing pattern throughout a paragraph, or you might combine them.

WRITING HINT

Include **transitional words and phrases** (such as *for example, next,* and *however*) to help readers understand how one sentence relates to another. See **Lesson 4.5** for more about transitions.

1. **Chronological Order** This means presenting events or steps in time order: what happened first, what happened next, and so on. Use chronological order to tell a story, explain a process, give instructions, or explain a historical event.
2. **Spatial Order** When you use spatial order, you organize details according to their location in space. You might, for example, start at a specific place and then move from left to right, front to back, top to bottom, or near to far. Use spatial order when writing a description.
3. **Order of Importance** When you organize reasons or details, present them in order of increasing or decreasing importance. Begin with your least important details, and end with your most important ones—or the reverse. Order of importance is especially useful in persuasive paragraphs and essays.
4. **Logical Order** When you organize a paragraph logically, you group together related information and arrange it in an order that makes sense to readers. For example, in a report about the causes of the Revolutionary War, you present key definitions and background information first. If you compare and contrast two historical figures, you might group together all of the similarities and then all of the differences.

The revisions in the model that follows show how one writer moved sentences around to improve the paragraph's organization. Grouping together related ideas makes them much easier to follow. Note the spatial order.

Copyright © 2014 by William H. Sadlier, Inc. All rights reserved.

Writing Model

[1]Scientists divide the ocean into three zones. [2]The sunlit zone is the shallowest. [3] Tiny floating plants, jellyfish, and fish (such as tuna) live there. [4]The deepest, darkest zone is the deep sea zone. [5]It includes the area from 3,300 to 33,000 feet under the surface. [6]The sunlit zone extends about 650 feet below the surface. [7]In the nearly frozen waters of the ocean bottom live species such as gulper eels and anglerfish. [8]Under the sunlit zone lies the twilight zone, the region between 650 and 3,300 feet below the surface. [9]Squid, shrimp, and some whales live in its fading light.

Uses spatial order, moving from top to bottom

Keeps the information about each zone together

EXERCISE 1 Writing a Paragraph from Notes

Working Together

Read the notes on the following page.

1. Use some of the information in the notes to write a well-developed paragraph on a separate sheet of paper.
2. Use one of the four patterns of organization to organize the information.
3. When you are done, exchange your paper with a classmate, and discuss ways to improve your paragraph's organization.

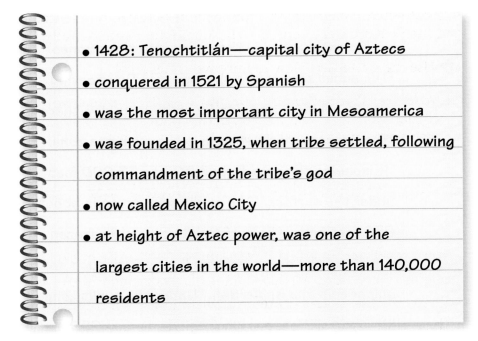

- 1428: Tenochtitlán—capital city of Aztecs
- conquered in 1521 by Spanish
- was the most important city in Mesoamerica
- was founded in 1325, when tribe settled, following commandment of the tribe's god
- now called Mexico City
- at height of Aztec power, was one of the largest cities in the world—more than 140,000 residents

Exercise 2 Revising a Paragraph

Revise the following paragraph. Organize it chronologically by moving and combining sentences and adding or deleting words.

[1]When I was ten, my family drove from Atlanta, Georgia, to Mexico City. [2]The trip was amazing. [3]We started off in Atlanta on a Saturday morning. [4]We drove for seven hours. [5]We finally stopped in Louisiana and spent our first night in a hotel. [6]By the end of the third day, we were pulling into the outskirts of Mexico City. [7]Finally, we had reached our destination! [8]On the second day, we woke up early to get back on the road. [9]When I woke up on the third day, we were in northern Mexico. [10]The last thing I remember before falling asleep in the hotel that second evening was the endless Texas desert.

Copyright © 2014 by William H. Sadlier, Inc. All rights reserved.

LESSON 4.5

Improving Paragraph Coherence

In a **coherent** paragraph, the connections between one sentence and the next are clear. Sentences flow smoothly and logically.

Use the strategies below to improve **coherence**.

See **Lesson 4.4** for information about using common organizational patterns to make your writing coherent.

1. **Add transitional words and phrases.** Transitional words signal the logical relationship between ideas and build links between sentences and paragraphs.

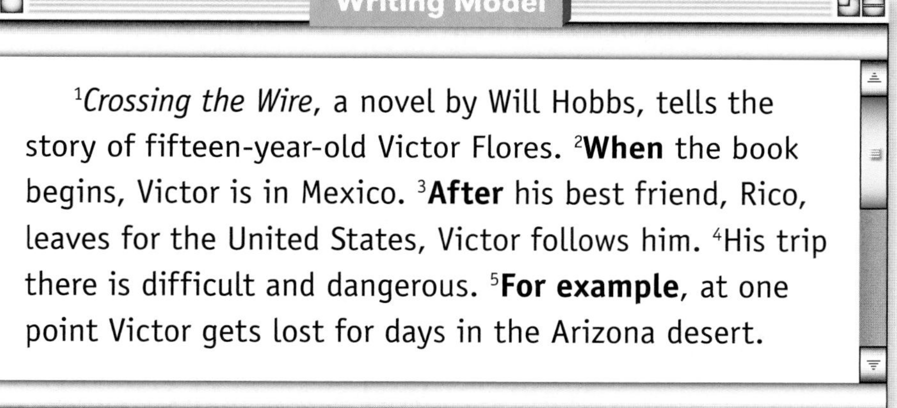

Writing Model

[1]*Crossing the Wire*, a novel by Will Hobbs, tells the story of fifteen-year-old Victor Flores. [2]**When** the book begins, Victor is in Mexico. [3]**After** his best friend, Rico, leaves for the United States, Victor follows him. [4]His trip there is difficult and dangerous. [5]**For example**, at one point Victor gets lost for days in the Arizona desert.

Common Transitional Words and Phrases	
To show **time**	after, as, before, during, immediately, meanwhile, soon, then, when, while
To show **location**	above, behind, below, beyond, in front of, nearby, on top of, opposite, under
To show **order of importance**	above all, first, last, mainly, most important, of least importance, second
To show **examples**	for example, for instance, in addition, such as, to illustrate
To show **cause and effect**	as a result, because, consequently, for this reason, since, so, therefore
To show **similarities and differences**	also, but, however, in contrast, likewise, on the other hand, similarly, yet
To **summarize**	as a result, finally, in conclusion, to sum up, therefore

2. **Repeat key words.** Repeating the same or a related word (*ambition/ambitious*) helps readers link information and ideas.

> [1]The **settings** in *Crossing the Wire* are **described** in vivid **detail.** [2]The Mexican village where the first chapter is *set* is full of dusty dirt paths, overgrown fields, and dilapidated farmhouses. [3]Hobbs contrasts that *setting* with his *description* of Guanajuato, a beautiful big city. [4]He paints a *detailed description* of its stone streets.

3. **Use synonyms and pronouns.** Besides repeating the same word, use a synonym (word with similar meaning) or a pronoun to replace a key word or phrase you used earlier.

> [1]At the end **Victor and Rico** are living in a **city** in Washington. [2]*They* are working hard and sending money back to help *their* **families** in Mexico. [3]Victor decides to stay in the *town*, but *his friend* is **unhappy** and misses *his relatives*.

You do not need to change the order of the sentences.

Exercise 1 Improving a Paragraph

Revise the following paragraph to improve coherence.

> [1]America was plunged into an economic depression after the stock market crash in 1929. [2]Terrible effects happened. [3]Unemployment and widespread poverty occurred. [4]Unemployment and poverty caused a large increase in homelessness. [5]The Depression marked the end of the 1920s. [6]The 1920s were full of optimism. [7]The 1930s had unemployment and economic worries.

Copyright © 2014 by William H. Sadlier, Inc. All rights reserved.

Exercise 2 Analyzing a Model

As you read the following excerpt, look for examples of each of the three strategies described in this lesson.

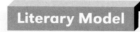

Literary Model

[1]The 1920s were the decade when modern society began. [2]Americans were excited by the technological advances that were becoming a part of their lives—the movies, the automobile, and the airplane. [3]But they were also a little frightened, for technology was changing the world faster than it ever had before. [4]For many Americans, it was a time when they felt torn between the simple, traditional life as lived on the farm, for example, and the new, exciting Jazz Age that beckoned from the city.

[5]Europe, too, was changing and restructuring itself after the First World War. [6]But the spirit of this decade belonged to America and its thirst for the new.

—Excerpt from *The Century for Young People* by Peter Jennings and Todd Brewster

Reading as a Writer

1. What examples of transitional words or phrases did you identify in this passage? Circle them.
2. What key words are repeated? Underline them. Where do the authors use synonyms or pronouns to refer to words used earlier? Enclose them in a box.
3. How coherent is this passage? Explain.

Exercise 3 Writing a News Article

Write a brief news article about an event or person in the news during the last five years. Assume your audience is a person unfamiliar with the subject you chose. When you have finished writing, exchange drafts with a partner, and work together to improve coherence.

LESSON 4.6

Descriptive and Narrative Paragraphs

Depending on your purpose, you may decide to write a descriptive or a narrative paragraph. Sometimes the paragraph will stand by itself. Other times, it will be part of a larger essay.

When you want to give an accurate and detailed picture of a person, a place, an animal, or an object, use these tips to write an effective **descriptive paragraph.**

See **Lessons 2.6** and **2.7** for more about using colorful and precise language to create effective descriptions.

- Use **precise language**, especially specific nouns and adjectives (such as *convertible* and *gold*) rather than general ones (such as *car* and *colorful*).
- Use **sensory details** (sights, sounds, textures, smells, and tastes) to create a strong **main impression.**
- Arrange details in **spatial order,** moving from near to far, left to right, or top to bottom. Use **transitions** (such as *above* and *under*) to signal shifts in setting and to help readers form a clear picture in their minds.

Writing Model

Location of narrator

Sight and sound details

Spatial order: from near (boat and water) to far (the skyscrapers)

[1]Chandra gasped as she stepped onto the deck of the boat. [2]Around her on all sides were the choppy green-blue waters of New York Harbor. [3]The roar of the engines muffled all sounds, except the occasional screech of the gulls that circled several yards in front of the boat. [4]Looming less than a mile ahead through the mist, the Statue of Liberty, with its golden torch, caught Chandra's eye. [5]In the distance, barely visible, stood the skyscrapers of New York City, their tops disappearing into patches of light fog. [6]The spectacular scene took Chandra's breath away.

Copyright © 2014 by William H. Sadlier, Inc. All rights reserved.

When you want to tell a story—fictional or true—or relate the steps in a process, use these tips to write an effective **narrative paragraph.**

- Divide the story or process into a series of separate events or actions.
- Use **chronological order** to tell the events in the order they occurred in time. Include **transitions** (such as *later* and *at the same time*) to help readers follow the sequence.
- Include details that help answer *who, what, when, where, why,* and *how* questions for readers.

Writing Model

[1]In the 1860s, sculptor Frédéric-Auguste Bartholdi began to think about designing a sculpture for France to give to the United States as a symbol of the friendship between the two nations. [2]In 1870, he completed a small-scale model of the standing female figure. [3]Realizing that he needed help constructing the huge copper structure, Bartholdi began working with Gustave Eiffel (designer of the Eiffel Tower). [4]By 1884, the Statue of Liberty was complete. [5]The 214 crates containing pieces of the statue arrived in New York Harbor in June 1885. [6]More than a year later, on October 28, 1886, President Grover Cleveland dedicated the reassembled monument in front of thousands of spectators.

Chronological order of events

Exercise 1 Analyzing a Model

Read the following paragraph from a novel. Then answer the following questions on a separate sheet of paper.

Literary Model

[1]After dinner, Grandma Wu led us to an alcove that was separated from the rest of the living room by special folding screens. [2]Hanging on the wall was a scroll with two large Chinese characters: *Fu Dao*, the Way of Buddha. [3]Below the scroll was an exquisite bonsai tree resting on an antique altar table. [4]Two elaborately carved sandalwood boxes were on either side of the bonsai tree. [5]On the front of each were three Chinese characters: *Gu Yi He*, Memory Vision Box, on the left; and *Wei Lei He*, Future Vision Box, on the right. [6]Otherwise the alcove was bare apart from a small stool.

—Excerpt from *Chinese Cinderella and the Secret Dragon Society* by Adeline Yen Mah

Reading as a Writer

1. Is this mainly a descriptive or a narrative paragraph? Why?
2. How clear is the organization? What, if any, transition words has the author used?
3. What is the writer's purpose?

Exercise 2 Writing a Descriptive Paragraph

Use this sentence to start a descriptive paragraph: *Scott opened the door and was surprised by what he saw.* Use spatial order, and include sensory details in your sentences.

Exercise 3 Writing a Narrative Paragraph

Complete the sentence below, and use it to begin the first paragraph of a story. Mention at least three separate events. Arrange the events in clear chronological order.

It had been a long, tiring day for __________.

Copyright © 2014 by William H. Sadlier, Inc. All rights reserved.

LESSON 4.7

Expository and Persuasive Paragraphs

To inform or persuade your readers, write expository or persuasive paragraphs. Many essays and reports include both of these kinds of paragraphs.

An **expository paragraph** provides information or explains something. Writers use expository paragraphs when they discuss cause and effect, compare and contrast, analyze, explain, or define. Use these tips to write an effective expository paragraph.

- Express your **main idea** clearly. You may state it directly in a topic sentence at the beginning of your paragraph.
- Explain and elaborate on your idea by including **supporting details,** such as facts, examples, and quotations.
- Organize your details logically. Use **transitional words and phrases** (such as *first, for example,* and *in contrast*) to help readers see how one detail or sentence connects to another.

See **Lessons 4.1** and **4.2** for more about using a variety of supporting details to develop your main idea.

Writing Model

[1]Many Americans have never seen or used a $2 bill, and most cash register drawers don't even have slots for them. [2]However, the government still prints $2 bills, and they are, in fact, growing in popularity. [3]The bill, first issued in 1862, features Thomas Jefferson on the front and shows the signing of the Declaration of Independence on the back. [4]Michael Lambert, an assistant director at the Federal Reserve, noticed "the increase in demand beginning in 2001." [5]In 2005, banks, for example, ordered $122 million in $2 bills, more than double the average number ordered from 1991 to 2000. [6]Banking experts are not sure why the bill's use is increasing. [7]Some believe that immigration from Canada and Europe, where currency in twos is common, is one reason.

Main idea

Facts

Quotation

Statistics

The purpose of a **persuasive paragraph** is to convince readers to agree with your opinion or to take a certain course of action. Use these tips to write an effective persuasive paragraph.

- Express your point of view clearly in a **thesis,** or **claim.**
- To support your opinion, give clear **reasons** and **evidence,** such as examples, facts, and statistics.
- Organize your supporting details in **order of importance.** Begin with the least important and end with the most important, or do the reverse, moving from most to least important.
- Explain what you want the reader to do in a clear **call to action,** often at the end of the paragraph.

Writing Model

Clear thesis, or claim

Most important reason at the end

Call to action

[1]Parents should give their children a small allowance if they do certain chores. [2]First, weekly allowances make it easy for parents to help their children recognize coins and practice their counting skills. [3]Second, giving young children an allowance helps them understand the differences between spending and saving. [4]For example, my six-year-old sister decided to save two allowances to buy her friend a special present. [5]Most important, children who have been given an allowance from an early age handle money more responsibly as they grow up. [6]Some experts believe that the earlier children can begin managing their money—and learning from the mistakes they make—the more successful they are in sticking to a budget later on. [7]Parents, if you haven't already done it, give your kids an allowance this week. [8]Start teaching them the value of money.

Copyright © 2014 by William H. Sadlier, Inc. All rights reserved.

Exercise 1 Identifying Paragraphs

Use newspaper or magazine articles, books, or Web sites to find an example of two expository and two persuasive paragraphs. Identify each one as either expository or persuasive.

1. For each paragraph, write a sentence that explains the writer's purpose and main idea or opinion. Explain whether or not you think the paragraph is effective.
2. Show the paragraphs you found to a partner, and discuss any differences in opinion you have about them.

Exercise 2 Writing an Expository Paragraph

Write an expository paragraph on a topic of your choice. Your paragraph should be at least six sentences. Your audience is a friend, and your purpose is to compare and contrast two different things. You may use one of the topics below.

- Compare and contrast two inventions.
- Compare and contrast two historical periods.
- Compare and contrast two people you know.

See pages 86–92 for tips about how to compare and contrast two subjects.

Exercise 3 Writing a Persuasive Paragraph

Write a persuasive paragraph of at least six sentences on a topic of your choice. Your audience is students at your school, and your purpose is to convince readers to agree with your opinion. You may use one of the questions below.

- Which is better—watching a movie at home or watching it in a movie theater? Why?
- Should your school begin at an earlier or later time, or is the starting time just fine as it is now? Why?

See pages 140–146 for tips about how to write persuasively.

WRITING APPLICATION

Summary

When you miss an episode of your favorite television show, what do you do? You probably ask someone to describe what happened. When you do, you are asking for a summary.

A **summary** is a kind of informative/explanatory text, or writing that informs, describes, or explains. Summaries retell the main idea and key details of fiction or nonfiction. They are used in many ways.

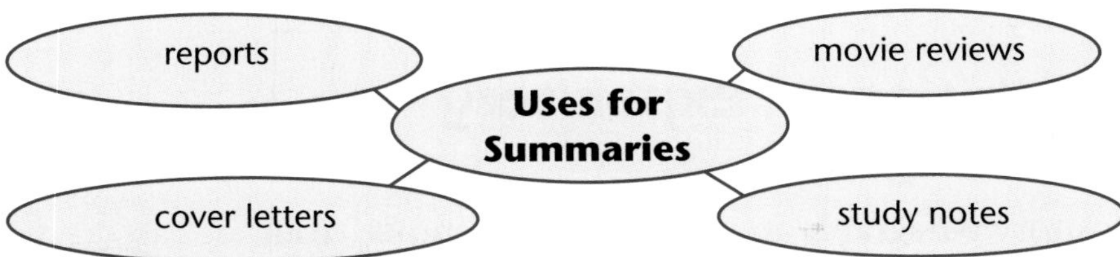

When you write a summary, remember to include the key features below.

Key Features

- clear identification of the text's main idea
- brief retelling of its supporting ideas
- objective tone
- concise language in the student's own words
- paraphrases and short quotations from the original text
- shorter length than the original text

ASSIGNMENT

TASK: Write a **summary** of an article that you have read about a famous person.

PURPOSE: to inform your audience about the main idea and key details of a piece of writing

AUDIENCE: classmates who have not read the article

KEY INSTRUCTIONS: Paraphrase two different sentences from your source. Make sure your summary is no more than one-third of the length of the original text.

Copyright © 2014 by William H. Sadlier, Inc. All rights reserved.

What's the Big Idea? A summary only includes the most important information from the original source.

Leave In	Leave Out
• author's name • title of article • important dates and facts • main idea • key details that support the main idea	• long quotations, descriptions, and explanations • details not related to the main idea • your personal opinion or reactions

To separate the necessary information from the unnecessary information, follow these steps:

For more help with main ideas, see **Lesson 4.1.**

1. Slowly read the material, trying to identify the main idea.
2. Ask, "What overall idea do most of the details support?"
3. Then find the key details that support this main idea.

Start your summary by using your own words to retell the main idea and the key details you found.

Paraphrase Key Ideas In your summary, you may paraphrase important ideas. A **paraphrase** restates an idea in your own words. It can be as long as the original source.

ORIGINAL Michael Jordan was one of the best-known athletes of all time. During his two-decade career, he broke countless records, won six NBA championships, and revived the world of basketball.

PARAPHRASE According to *Slam Dunk!* magazine, few athletes are ever as well known as Michael Jordan, who played basketball for twenty years, leading his team to six NBA championships. He also shattered many records and breathed life back into the sport.

Remember

If you paraphrase, be careful not to **plagiarize,** or present others' ideas or words as your own. Use your own words, and give credit to the source.

See **Lesson 2.5** for more tips on avoiding wordy sentences.

Keep It Brief A summary should be shorter than the original source by at least two-thirds. Follow these guidelines:

1. **Be concise.** Delete empty words and phrases that add little to your summary's meaning.

   WORDY According to the author, Jordan is absolutely the greatest player that has ever been alive.

   CONCISE According to the author, Jordan was the greatest player ever.

   WORDY At this point in time, there are no players who can match what Jordan has accomplished.

   CONCISE Currently, no other players can match what Jordan has accomplished.

2. **Use the active voice.** Avoid passive verbs.

   PASSIVE Jordan's career was made by his slam dunks.

   ACTIVE Jordan's slam dunks made his career.

3. **Combine sentences.** Combine two or more related sentences by moving key words from one sentence to another.

   ORIGINAL Jordan was very fast. He was also very strong.

   COMBINED Jordan was very fast and strong.

For more help with paragraph coherence, see **Lesson 4.5.**

Keep Your Ideas Organized Every paragraph should be coherent. A paragraph has **coherence** when its sentences connect clearly and smoothly from one to the next. Make sure you organize your ideas in a logical, consistent way.

1. Group together related details.
2. Then present the related details in an order that makes sense. For example, give the main idea first. Then present the important details that support the main idea.
3. Use **transitions,** such as *finally, therefore,* and *however.*

Copyright © 2014 by William H. Sadlier, Inc. All rights reserved.

Check for Correctness Use the checklist to review your draft. The model below shows part of one writer's summary.

Check for correct subject-verb agreement. The verb never agrees with a word in a prepositional phrase. See **Lesson 10.1.**

INCORRECT The other **players** on his team **was** aware of his talent.

CORRECT The other **players** on his team **were** aware of his talent.

WRITING CHECKLIST

Did you...

- ✔ clearly restate the main idea and key details?
- ✔ logically organize details and make your summary brief?
- ✔ use concise language and your own words?
- ✔ paraphrase at least two different sentences?

Writing Model

[1]According to Slam Dunk! magazine, few athletes are as well known as Michael Jordan, who played basketball for twenty years, leading the Chicago Bulls to six NBA championships. [2]He also shattered record after record and breathed life back into the sport.

Article's main idea is clearly restated.

[3]During his first year as a professional basketball player, Jordan was named Rookie of the Year. [4]In addition, Jordan led his team to six championships. [5]Also, Jordan was the second player to score 3,000 points in one season. [6]For seven consecutive seasons, he averaged 32 points per game. [7]In his entire career, he was named the Most Valuable Player (MVP) five times.

Key details are listed in logical order.

Transitions connect one sentence to the next.

Chapter Review

A. Practice Test

Read the draft and questions below carefully. The questions ask you to choose the best revision for sentences or parts of the draft. They may ask you to identify parts of the passage. Fill in the corresponding circle for your answer choice.

(1) A recent study has shown that surgeons perform better if they play at least three hours of video games per week. **(2)** The study, performed at Iowa State University in 2003, demonstrated that laparoscopic surgeons who played video games made 37 percent fewer mistakes and finished 27 percent faster than surgeons who played no video games at all. **(3)** Laparoscopic surgery involves inserting a tiny camera and tiny instruments into the body and controlling them with joysticks. **(4)** The camera sends images to a video screen, which doctors watch to perform the surgery. **(5)** Experts believe that the hand-eye coordination used while playing video games is similar to that used in laparoscopic surgery. **(6)** The motor skills used are also very similar. **(7)** However, some video games are very violent. **(8)** Doctors and hospital administrators hope that making video games available will help decrease errors in the operating room.

Copyright © 2014 by William H. Sadlier, Inc. All rights reserved.

Ⓐ Ⓑ Ⓒ Ⓓ Ⓔ **1.** Which sentence best states the paragraph's main idea?
(A) Video games are enjoyable and educational.
(B) Laparoscopic surgery is common.
(C) Doctors must play video games to save lives.
(D) Playing video games may help laparoscopic surgeons perform better.
(E) An important study was performed at Iowa State University.

Ⓐ Ⓑ Ⓒ Ⓓ Ⓔ **2.** Which of the following kinds of elaboration are used in this paragraph?
(A) statistics
(B) quotations
(C) transitions
(D) anecdotes
(E) sensory details

Ⓐ Ⓑ Ⓒ Ⓓ Ⓔ **3.** To improve the coherence of the paragraph, where should sentence 4 be moved?
(A) after sentence 8
(B) after sentence 7
(C) after sentence 1
(D) before sentence 3
(E) No change is needed.

Ⓐ Ⓑ Ⓒ Ⓓ Ⓔ **4.** Which of the following sentences should be removed from the paragraph to improve unity?
(A) sentence 4
(B) sentence 5
(C) sentence 6
(D) sentence 7
(E) sentence 8

Ⓐ Ⓑ Ⓒ Ⓓ Ⓔ **5.** Which of the following best describes this paragraph?
(A) It is persuasive.
(B) It is narrative.
(C) It is expository.
(D) It is descriptive.
(E) It has no main idea.

Chapter Review

B. Understanding Paragraphs

Complete each sentence below.

1. Paragraphs can serve different purposes—to describe, to narrate, to explain, and to ________.

2. The most effective pattern of organization for a descriptive essay about a place is ________.

3. The transitional words and phrases *mainly* and *of least importance* are most likely to occur in an essay organized by ______________.

4. A main idea that is not directly stated in a topic sentence is called an __________. Instead, it is suggested by the details the writer includes.

5. To organize chronologically, you present steps or events ________________.

C. Supporting Topic Sentences

Each statement below could be used as the topic sentence of an expository paragraph.

1. On a separate sheet of paper, write at least two supporting sentences for each topic sentence below. Use the method of elaboration indicated in parentheses.
   - Being in the school play takes a lot of time. (anecdotes)
   - The Dugout serves great food at great prices. (reasons and examples)
   - Teens need at least eight hours of sleep each night. (facts and statistics)
   - The bus ride was unpleasant. (sensory details)
   - The mayor has accomplished a lot. (facts and examples)
2. Select one of the topics to develop into a full paragraph. Write at least six sentences, using several methods of elaboration.

Copyright © 2014 by William H. Sadlier, Inc. All rights reserved.

D. Revising a Summary

Revise the paragraph below. Eliminate any sentences that disrupt paragraph unity. Add transitions to improve coherence.

[1]Charles Dickens's novel A Christmas Carol teaches the importance of kindness and generosity. [2]The story begins in the offices of Ebenezer Scrooge, one of the greediest and cruelest men in nineteenth-century London. [3]During this era, London was grimy and bleak. [4]It is clear that Scrooge abuses his employee, Bob Cratchit, dislikes Cratchit's family, and cares about money more than people. [5]Four different ghosts visit Scrooge. [6]Since the publication of A Christmas Carol, ghosts have become common in Christmas stories. [7]The first ghost is his old friend Jacob Marley, who warns Scrooge that if he does not change his ways, he will end up cursed for eternity. [8]He is visited by the Ghosts of Christmas Past, Present, and Future. [9]Each ghost reveals a lesson, and Scrooge becomes more aware of how he has allowed greed to destroy his life. [10]He becomes kinder and more generous. [11]This is one of Dickens's best stories.

CHAPTER

5

Writing an Essay

Copyright © 2014 by William H. Sadlier, Inc. All rights reserved.

LESSON 5.1

Parts of an Essay

An **essay** is a piece of writing composed of several paragraphs that are organized into a beginning, a middle, and an end.

Paragraphs are like smaller versions of the essays in which they appear.

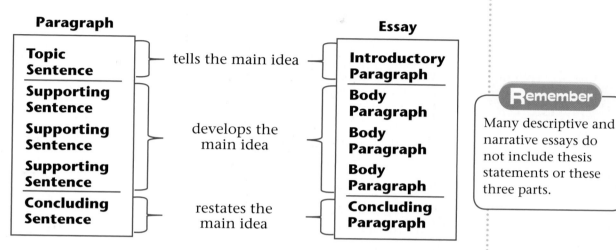

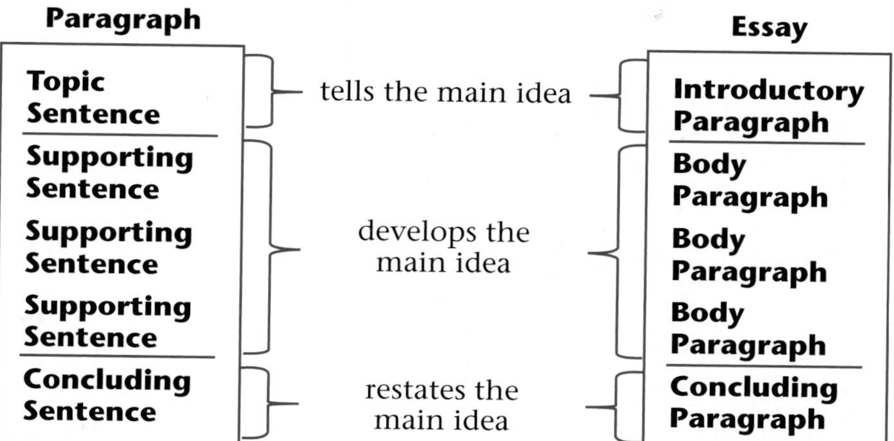

Expository and persuasive essays have three basic parts: an introduction, a body, and a conclusion.

- **Introduction** The introduction states the main idea. The introduction should also grab the readers' attention and may preview all of the essay's key points.
- **Body** Body paragraphs support the main idea with facts, examples, sensory details, and quotations. Many body paragraphs begin with a topic sentence, and other sentences in the paragraph should support that topic sentence.
- **Conclusion** The conclusion restates the main idea and gives a sense of completeness to the essay.

Remember

Many descriptive and narrative essays do not include thesis statements or these three parts.

Start a new body paragraph when:

- you express a new idea or change to a different subtopic or kind of detail
- a paragraph is so long and full of details that it overwhelms readers

EXERCISE Organizing an Essay

Read the following short essay. Break it into the three parts of an essay, and label each part. Underline the main idea in the introduction and the conclusion. Write ¶ to signal each paragraph. There are five paragraphs. Compare your paragraph breaks with those of a partner. Discuss the essay's strengths and weaknesses.

[1]Have you ever been walking in the woods and seen a mushroom growing? [2]Have you ever wondered what kind of mushroom it was or if it was poisonous? [3]While mushrooms are eaten all over the world and used in various other beneficial ways, many species are poisonous and should be avoided in the wild. [4]One of the most dangerous things about mushrooms is that, to the untrained eye, they all look alike. [5]Some very common cooking mushrooms, such as the portobello, are very similar in shape and size to their deadly cousins. [6]Even their coloring is the same. [7]Furthermore, the effects of poisonous mushrooms vary widely. [8]Some poisonous mushrooms produce sweating and abdominal pain. [9]Others, including the ominously named "destroying angel," can produce vomiting, fever, coma, and even death. [10]A major challenge faced by doctors is that the symptoms of the more deadly mushrooms take longer to appear. [11]Generally, a mushroom that is mildly poisonous will have an effect within two hours. [12]On the other hand, a person who has eaten a deadly mushroom may feel no symptoms for up to six hours. [13]You may see mushrooms in many places, and a lot of them are harmless and tasty. [14]However, if you encounter a mushroom in the woods, don't eat it. [15]It may be deadly.

Copyright © 2014 by William H. Sadlier, Inc. All rights reserved.

LESSON 5.2

Developing the Thesis

The **thesis,** or **thesis statement,** of an essay states the main idea. The thesis should be only one or two sentences long. It usually appears as the last sentence in the introductory paragraph. The thesis is sometimes called a **claim** or **controlling idea.**

➡ To draft an effective thesis, begin by examining your topic. Ask yourself, "What do I want to say about my topic? Do I have any strong opinions about it? What point do I want to communicate to my readers?"

➡ Follow these guidelines when developing a thesis statement:

1. The thesis should be one or more complete sentences.
2. The thesis should express an opinion or main idea. The thesis never simply restates the topic or expresses a fact.
3. The thesis should not be too broad nor too narrow.

TOO BROAD	Dogs are wonderful.
TOO NARROW	Your golden retriever dog is cute.
STRONG	Working dogs play an important role in everyday life.

It is often a good idea to include a preview of your essay's organization in your thesis. Mention the ideas in the order they will appear in the body.

> Golden retrievers make wonderful family pets because they are **friendly** and **good with children.**
> [The writer will discuss these two characteristics.]

> Working dogs play an important role in everyday life by **providing companionship, performing dangerous tasks,** and **helping those in need.**
> [The writer will discuss these three activities.]

Although you should have decided on your thesis before you begin writing, don't let it hold you back. If your writing leads you in another direction, you can revise your thesis.

Remember

The thesis tells the main idea of an essay just as the topic sentence tells the main idea of a paragraph. Think of the thesis as the roof and the body paragraphs as the beams that support it.

Exercise 1 Evaluating the Thesis, or Claim

Evaluate the following thesis statements for their use in a two- to three-page paper. Circle the letter of the strongest one. What do you predict the organizational pattern will be? Briefly describe what is wrong with the others.

EXAMPLE

A. I will discuss deep-sea diving. *restates topic*

B. Deep-sea diving is so much fun. *too broad*

(C.) Deep-sea diving is fun, educational, and healthy.

I predict one paragraph about fun, one about education, and one about health.

1. A. The coral reefs of Australia are beautiful.

B. Exploring Australia's coral reefs takes time and good equipment.

C. The clown fish is found in Australia's largest coral reef.

2. A. To save the coral reefs, we must clean up the atmosphere and stop polluting our oceans.

B. A reef can be made of rock or coral.

C. There are many beautiful coral reefs all over the world.

3. A. Baleen whales visit Australia's reefs every year.

B. Whales are interesting animals.

C. Whales are fascinating because of their intelligence and beauty.

Exercise 2 Writing Thesis Statements

With a partner, brainstorm a list of five or more topics.

See **Lesson 1.1** for tips about selecting a topic and deciding on your purpose.

1. Choose three topics, and write a different purpose for each one. Some purposes include to inform, to persuade, and to describe an experience.

2. For each topic, write a strong thesis statement that you could support in a two- to three-page paper. Be sure your thesis allows the reader to predict the organizational pattern.

Copyright © 2014 by William H. Sadlier, Inc. All rights reserved.

LESSON 5.3

Writing an Introduction

The first paragraph of an essay is called the **introduction.** The introduction has three main functions. It grabs your readers' attention, introduces the topic, and states the main idea, or **thesis.**

See **Lesson 5.2** for more about developing a strong thesis.

Always begin by catching the readers' attention. The chart below compares some effective and ineffective ways to begin.

Effective	Ineffective
• state an amazing fact • ask a question • offer a related quotation • tell an anecdote • describe a vivid image • provide an example • make an unusual comparison	• state: "This paper is about..." • state: "I am going to write about..." • begin with an unrelated or minor detail • make a vague or general statement

Let readers know what your topic is right away. Keep your introduction brief. Notice how the writer of the model below began with a question and moved toward a more specific thesis statement.

Writing Model

[1]Did you know that there are dogs all over the world that have jobs? [2]They are called working dogs. [3]For thousands of years, people have used these dogs in a variety of ways. [4]Saint Bernard dogs have worked as search and rescue animals, huskies have pulled sleds, and Seeing Eye dogs have helped the blind navigate city streets. [5]Working dogs play an important role in everyday life by providing companionship, performing vital and dangerous tasks, and helping those in need.

Strong opening

Topic

Thesis that previews three points

Statements in the introduction must be supported by the remaining paragraphs. You don't want to introduce material that won't be discussed in the rest of the essay.

Exercise 1 Creating Strong Introductions

Below is a list of essay topics.

1. With a partner, discuss different effective ways to begin an introductory paragraph for each one.
2. Write your best idea for an attention-grabbing opening for each topic.

EXAMPLE literary essay about a novel's theme

Begin with an important quotation.

- informative essay about a sports figure
- narrative essay about a time you felt proud
- persuasive essay about a new school rule
- descriptive essay about a person
- how-to essay about tips for making a science fair project

Exercise 2 Writing a Thesis, or Claim

Return to the list of essay topics in Exercise 1. Choose the topic that you would most like to write about in a two- to three-page paper.

1. Consider the topic and the purpose of the essay.
2. Write a thesis statement for an introductory paragraph that would begin an essay about this topic.
3. Remember, your thesis should express an opinion or main idea and provide a preview of the organizational pattern.

Copyright © 2014 by William H. Sadlier, Inc. All rights reserved.

Exercise 3 Writing an Introduction

Write an introduction of no more than five sentences for an essay about the topic that you selected in Exercise 2. Make sure you grab your readers' attention. Include a clear thesis statement. You may use or revise the thesis you wrote in Exercise 2.

Exercise 4 Revising an Introduction

Read the introductory paragraph below. On a separate sheet of paper, revise it using the information you learned in this lesson.

[1]In this paper, I am going to write about Australian coral reefs. [2]Coral reefs are important to our environment. [3]Coral reefs have thousands of species living in them. [4]Did you know that Australia's coral reefs are changing colors because of pollution? [5]Oceans can be amazing places. [6]They are a source of water. [7]Coral reefs are threatened by industrial pollution, and they are threatened by commercial fishing. [8]We need stricter laws.

Write What You Think

Draft an introductory paragraph for your response to the expository writing prompt below. Be sure to include a thesis statement that previews the organizational pattern.

What do you think is most important in a teenager's life: personal success, popularity, or friendship?

LESSON 5.4

Body Paragraphs

In an introductory paragraph, the writer presents a topic and **thesis,** or **claim.** This information leads into the body of the essay. The **body paragraphs** provide the details that support the thesis.

Each body paragraph develops one key idea. For a paragraph to have **unity,** every sentence should relate to or support that main idea. Use a **topic sentence** in each body paragraph to help you stay focused on the main idea and to help your readers understand what the paragraph is about.

One good way to make sure your essay has unity is to create an informal **outline** before you write your first draft. Check that the topic sentence of each body paragraph relates to the thesis.

The claim, or thesis, previews the three main ideas that the body paragraphs will develop.

Eliminate any ideas that do not relate to the claim (thesis).

Writing Model

Informal Outline

Claim: Working dogs play an important role in everyday life by providing companionship, performing vital and dangerous tasks, and helping those in need.

Body 1: Well-trained working dogs make great companions for handicapped or elderly people.

Body 2: Police and other authorities use working dogs in dangerous situations.

~~**Body 3:** Training working dogs is extremely expensive.~~

Body 4: Many kinds of dogs help thousands of handicapped people by performing a wide range of tasks.

Copyright © 2014 by William H. Sadlier, Inc. All rights reserved.

➡ To support the thesis effectively, **elaborate** on the ideas in each body paragraph with details that support and explain the topic sentence. Present a variety of details, such as **facts, examples, quotations, anecdotes,** and **statistics.** (See Lesson 4.2 for more about methods of elaboration.)

➡ Effective body paragraphs should have coherence. **Coherence** means that your essay flows smoothly and logically from one sentence and paragraph to the next. Help readers follow your ideas easily by using one of the following **patterns of organization:**

- **Chronological Order** Present events in the order in which they occurred.
- **Order of Importance** Arrange details or reasons from the least important to the most important—or the reverse.
- **Spatial Order** Present details in the order that they are arranged, such as from front to back or top to bottom.
- **Cause and Effect** Describe the relationship between what happens and why it happens.
- **Compare and Contrast** Explain the similarities and differences in people, places, objects, or ideas.

Choose an organizational pattern that matches your purpose. For example, chronological order probably makes the most sense for a narrative or autobiographical essay.

Remember

When you group together related ideas (such as causes and effects or similarities and differences), you are using **logical order.** See **Lessons 4.4** and **4.5** for more about organizing ideas and using transitions to give your writing coherence.

➡ Use **transitions** between sentences and paragraphs to clarify the relationships among your ideas.

Purpose	Examples
To show **time relationship**	after, later, shortly, then
To show **importance**	above all, most important
To show **spatial relationship**	around, beside, next to
To show **cause and effect**	as a result, because, since
To show **comparisons**	in the same way, similarly
To show **contrasts**	on the contrary, however

Exercise 1 Revising a Body Paragraph

Read the body paragraph below.

1. On a separate sheet of paper, revise the paragraph so that it has unity. The first sentence should be a clear topic sentence.
2. Add transitions, and improve the organization to give the paragraph more coherence.

[1]Polyps are tiny animals that build new coral. [2]They cannot survive in polluted water. [3]The dumping of poisonous waste and the exhaust from boats can result in polluted oceans. [4]One major cause of the destruction of coral reefs is various types of water pollution. [5]Global warming and overfishing are other things that damage fragile coral reefs. [6]When polyps die, coral reefs weaken and die. [7]Pollution can enter the ocean from acid rain and oil spills.

HINT

Use a variety of details, such as facts, examples, and quotations, to support your topic sentences.

Exercise 2 Supporting the Thesis, or Claim

Reread the introduction you wrote for Exercise 3 on page 133.

1. Write two body paragraphs to support the thesis that appears in your introduction.
2. Include topic sentences for each body paragraph, and make sure each paragraph is unified and coherent. Use transitions effectively.

Copyright © 2014 by William H. Sadlier, Inc. All rights reserved.

LESSON 5.5

Writing a Conclusion

The last paragraph in an essay is called the **conclusion.** It serves three main purposes. It restates the thesis, sums up the essay's main points, and provides readers with a sense of completeness.

1. **Restate your thesis, or claim, in new words.** By rephrasing your thesis at the end of your essay, you remind readers of your central idea.
2. **Summarize the main points.** This summary should be very brief. Keep your main points in the same order that you presented them in the body of your essay.
3. **Write an effective ending.** Your conclusion should give readers a sense of completeness and leave them thinking about your topic. The chart below lists effective and ineffective ways to conclude an essay.

Effective	Ineffective
• offer an opinion • make a call to action • make a prediction about the future • present a quotation • include an anecdote • ask a question • comment on the importance of the topic • answer a question posed in the introduction • repeat key words that were used in the introduction	• state: "That is all I know about..." • apologize that you cannot cover more information • contradict your thesis or any other main point • introduce an unrelated, new, or minor detail • repeat your thesis exactly as you stated it in your introduction

Keep your conclusion brief, usually no more than four or five sentences. The conclusion should balance the introduction. Remember, the body, not the conclusion, is the main part of your essay.

Read and compare two examples of a concluding paragraph. What makes the second paragraph strong? What makes the first paragraph weak?

DRAFT In general, dogs are really great. This is especially true of working dogs. Working dogs do many important things that I have not talked about. Dogs have been man's best friend for a long time.

REVISION Working dogs, such as Saint Bernard dogs and huskies, are critical to the lives of many people. These dogs offer lonely people companionship, perform dangerous tasks, and help those with special needs. There is no doubt that these amazing animals will be saving lives and offering hope for centuries to come.

Exercise 1 Evaluating Others' Writing

Find a conclusion that you have written in a paper for this or another class. Exchange papers with a classmate. As you read through his or her work, ask yourself the questions below. Write down your responses to these questions, and discuss them with your partner.

1. How effectively has the writer restated his or her thesis?
2. How effectively has the writer summarized the main ideas?
3. Has the conclusion caused you to think about the topic?
4. What suggestions can you offer to make this conclusion more effective?

Exercise 2 Analyzing a Conclusion

Read the following conclusion to a persuasive essay.

1. On a separate sheet of paper, write a short paragraph analyzing its effectiveness.
2. Offer the writer several specific suggestions for improving the conclusion.

Copyright © 2014 by William H. Sadlier, Inc. All rights reserved.

[1]Unfortunately, many things have been destroying coral reefs around the world at an alarming rate. [2]Some of those things people have control over, but others people cannot control. [3]If you let coral reefs continue to disappear without doing something, you are just as guilty as if you destroyed them yourself. [4]If I had more space and time, I could present more facts about how we are losing this precious resource and how time is running out. [5]People across the world need to realize that our natural resources are not limitless. [6]Earth's growing population means that we may run out of clean water. [7]We may not have enough farmland to grow crops to solve the world hunger crisis. [8]Also, various plants and animals become extinct or are added to lists of endangered species each year.

Exercise 3 Writing a Conclusion

Reread the introductory paragraph you wrote for Exercise 3 on page 133 and the body paragraphs you wrote for Exercise 2 on page 136.

1. Write a conclusion that might follow the last body paragraph.
2. Restate your thesis in new words.
3. Restate the main ideas presented in the body paragraphs.
4. Use one of the effective conclusion strategies listed on the first page of this lesson.
5. Keep your conclusion brief. Write no more than five sentences.

WRITER'S WORKSHOP

ONLINE MODEL
www.grammarforwriting.com

Persuasive Essay

How would you convince a friend to share your opinion of a favorite Web site? You might describe key details or compare and contrast it with other Web sites. By stating your opinion, providing strong reasons, and presenting evidence, you are making a persuasive argument.

When you write a **persuasive essay,** you try to convince readers to share your opinion or to take a particular action. There are many kinds of persuasive writing.

Book Reviews	Reviewer argues that a book is good or bad.
Editorials	Writer presents and defends an opinion.
Persuasive Letters	Sender presents opinion and calls for an action.
Speeches	Speaker presents and defends an opinion.

In your persuasive essay, include the features below.

Key Features

- strong thesis, or claim
- logically organized reasons and relevant supporting evidence
- transition words, phrases, and clauses that create coherence
- counterargument and response that refutes the counterargument
- formal style and reasonable tone
- conclusion that follows logically from the argument presented

ASSIGNMENT

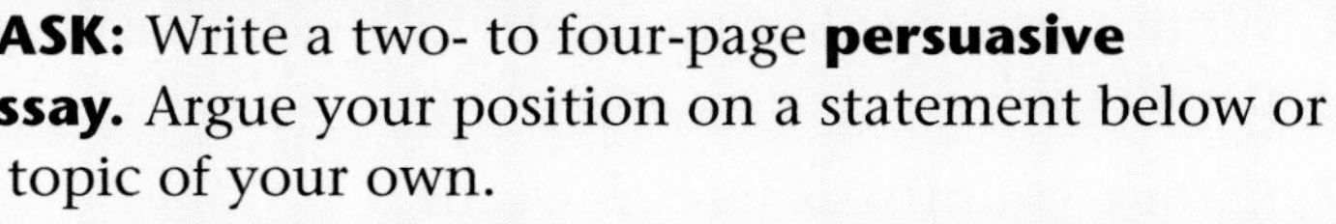

TASK: Write a two- to four-page **persuasive essay.** Argue your position on a statement below or a topic of your own.

- Teens should receive an allowance if they do chores.
- Students should do community service.

AUDIENCE: your teacher and classmates

PURPOSE: to persuade

Copyright © 2014 by William H. Sadlier, Inc. All rights reserved.

Prewriting

Select a Topic First, you will need to choose your topic. Begin by examining the options provided. Ask yourself:

- Which topic seems most interesting to me?
- Which topic will I be able to write about most effectively?

Create a list like the one below to help you decide your position.

Thesis, or Claim: Students should do community service.

Pros	Cons
Students will learn the value of work.	Students will have less time for schoolwork.
Students will gain a sense of pride in their communities.	Students already have demanding schedules.
Communities will benefit from large numbers of volunteers.	Students may be forced to give up extracurricular activities.

Make a Claim Next, draft your **thesis,** or **claim.**

1. Your thesis should clearly and concisely state your opinion. Avoid simply restating the topic of your essay or making your thesis too broad or too narrow.

   STATING TOPIC My paper will be about community service.

   TOO BROAD Students have a lot to do.

   TOO NARROW Students in my math class are too busy to do a community service project this school year.

2. Your thesis should be thought-provoking and engage readers. You should also be able to support it with reasons that can be backed up by evidence.

   STRONG While a community service project has some benefits, it will hurt students' studying and overload their schedules.

For more help with thesis statements, or claims, see **Lesson 5.2.**

Prewriting

Explain Your Reasons and Evidence Be sure that you can provide at least two strong reasons that support your position.

REASON 1 Mandatory community service projects mean less time for studying.

REASON 2 Many students' schedules are already filled with extracurricular activities and family obligations.

Then gather a variety of evidence to support each reason:

1. **Facts** are statements that can be proved true. They may include **statistics,** or data expressed in numbers.
2. **Examples** are particular instances that illustrate the point you are trying to make.
3. **Quotations** may include the opinions of specialists in the field that you are discussing. If you directly quote an expert, be sure to enclose the words in quotation marks.
4. **Anecdotes** are brief stories that you have heard about, read about, or seen.

For more help with elaboration and supporting a thesis, or claim, see **Lessons 4.2** and **5.4.**

Be careful when using evidence from the Internet. Use Web sites from educational institutions or the government. The URL addresses for these Web sites end in *.edu* or *.gov*.

Avoid Logical Fallacies When you support your thesis, or claim, avoid **logical fallacies,** or faulty reasoning.

- **Hasty generalizations** are broad statements that are based on few facts and use such words as *all, every,* and *never.*

  All students will agree that they are busy. [not one exception?]

- **Circular reasoning** includes arguments in which the evidence and the conclusion are the same.

  Students' schedules are packed because they are filled with many activities. [packed schedule = filled with activities]

Copyright © 2014 by William H. Sadlier, Inc. All rights reserved.

Drafting

Organize the Body Your essay should contain three basic parts: the **introduction,** the **body,** and the **conclusion.**

1. Your introduction should present your topic and thesis, or claim. It should also catch your audience's attention and immediately allow readers to grasp your position on the issue.
2. Your body paragraphs present reasons and evidence to support your thesis. Organize the body of the essay by **order of importance.** The strongest reason, and the evidence that supports it, should come either first or last. To connect one sentence or paragraph to the next, use **transitional words and phrases,** such as *above all, first, most important,* and *last.*
3. The conclusion sums up your arguments. It should restate the thesis, or claim, and main reasons.

TEST-TAKING TIP

On standardized tests you will often encounter writing prompts. To determine if you must write a persuasive essay, look for key words in the prompt, such as *argue, make a case, prove,* and *persuade.*

Use an Outline Refer to an outline to guide your writing. Below is the beginning of an outline.

See **Lesson 5.4** for more information about organizing body paragraphs.

Writing Model

Thesis, or Claim: While a community service project has some benefits, it will hurt students' studying and overload their schedules.

I. Mandatory community service projects mean less time for studying.
   A. Students are given an average of four hours of homework per night.
   B. Community service projects at Dale School were optional after students' grades began to decline.
   C. According to Dr. Abdul, "In addition to the time students need to spend on homework, they also need time to study."

The strongest reason is listed first.

A variety of evidence includes one statistic, one example, and one quotation.

Revising

Now, use the Revising Questions to improve your draft.

Revising Questions

- ❑ How clear and strong is my thesis, or claim?
- ❑ How well do my reasons explain my thesis?
- ❑ Where can I add evidence to support my reasons?
- ❑ How clearly did I organize details by order of importance?
- ❑ Do I maintain a formal style and reasonable tone?
- ❑ How fairly did I present and address counterarguments?

See the next page for information on tone and counterarguments. As you revise, keep in mind the traits of good writing. See **Lesson 1.3.**

Present counterargument.

Add transitions.

Refute counterargument.

Eliminate unrelated evidence.

[1]Some people might argue that by making students participate in community service projects, the community will grow stronger and be able to accomplish more. ^However,^ [2]Think of what students, as well as the community, will lose. [3]By overloading their schedules, students will be less likely to participate in extracurricular activities. [4]~~Students will also be stressed out.~~ [5]That means fewer school concerts, sporting events, and school plays. [6]These losses will have a negative effect on the community.

Copyright © 2014 by William H. Sadlier, Inc. All rights reserved.

Revising

Adjust Style and Tone Remember to maintain a formal style and reasonable tone. If your style is casual or your tone is harsh, readers will be less likely to accept your argument or even take it seriously. **Tone**, or attitude, is especially important when responding to **counterarguments**, or opposing points of view. By anticipating and responding to counterarguments reasonably, you show that you have considered other sides of the issue.

INAPPROPRIATE	Some people argue that mandatory service will give students pride in their communities. That's nonsense!
APPROPRIATE	Some people argue that mandatory service will give students pride in their communities. However, this reasoning is somewhat flawed.

Read the passage below from a famous speech. Examine the response to the counterargument and persuasive techniques.

Literary Model

[1]There are those who are asking the devotees of civil rights, "When will you be satisfied?" [2]We can never be satisfied as long as the Negro is the victim of the unspeakable horrors of police brutality. [3]We can never be satisfied as long as our bodies, heavy with the fatigue of travel, cannot gain lodging in the motels of the highways and the hotels of the cities. [4]We cannot be satisfied as long as the Negro's basic mobility is from a smaller ghetto to a larger one.

—Excerpt from "I Have a Dream" by Dr. Martin Luther King, Jr.

Reading as a Writer

1. What is the counterargument King presents? How does he respond to it?
2. What persuasive techniques does King use?

Use **persuasive techniques** to enhance your writing. Some techniques include:

- rhetorical questions, or questions asked for effect

Don't we all care about our students?

- repetition of key words and phrases

Fewer demands need to be made upon students. **Fewer demands** will help students succeed in school and in life.

CONNECTING Writing & Grammar

Pronouns must always agree in number with their **antecedents,** or the words they refer to. If the antecedent is singular and the gender is not clear, use the phrase *he or she* or *him or her*. See **Lesson 7.7.**

A **student** must have **his or her** parent sign the slip.

Proofreading Symbols

^ Add.

⊙ Add a period.

≡ Capitalize.

Editing and Proofreading

Use the checklist below to edit and proofread your draft.

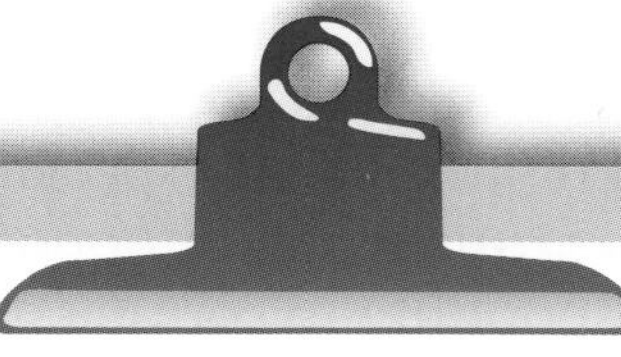

Editing and Proofreading Checklist

- ❑ Have I checked that all words are spelled correctly?
- ❑ Have I capitalized the first letter of every sentence?
- ❑ Have I avoided run-ons and fragments?
- ❑ Have I checked that all pronouns agree with their antecedents?

[1]A student may be forced to contribute extra hours toward a community service project. [2]But (he or she) will have to juggle or skip other obligations, such as band practice or family events⊙ as (a) result, students' schedules will be overloaded, and they and their families will feel frustrated.

Reflect On Your Writing

- Which of your reasons is the strongest? Why?
- Which part of your essay did you have the most trouble writing? Why?

Publishing and Presenting

Choose one of these ways to share your persuasive essay.

- **Give a speech.** Write your main ideas and key details on note cards, and share your opinion with classmates.
- **Write a letter.** Present your ideas as a letter to the editor in a school or local newspaper.

Copyright © 2014 by William H. Sadlier, Inc. All rights reserved.

Chapter Review

A. Practice Test

In the passage below, there is a question *for each numbered item.* Read the passage carefully, and circle the best answer to each question.

Vote Beckett!

I am going to explain why Shannon Beckett is the best candidate for student body president. [1] Many qualified students are running this year. Some have excellent grades. Others are highly motivated or have lots of experience. Shannon Beckett, however, is the only candidate with all of these characteristics. Shannon's record of academic excellence shows that she is intelligent enough to handle the responsibilities of student body president. [2] She has made honor roll for nine straight semesters. She did it while taking advanced math and English classes. Furthermore, Shannon is in both jazz and marching band. [3]

In addition, Shannon is highly motivated. She works a job after school. Shannon participates [4] in several extracurricular activities. In the summer, she volunteers, and this summer she will be working as a summer camp counselor.

1. What is the main problem with the underlined thesis?
A. It is too narrow.
B. It is too broad.
C. It is not attention grabbing.
D. It is not a sentence.

2. Which of the following best describes the underlined sentence?
A. It is a thesis statement.
B. It is a topic sentence.
C. It is a conclusion.
D. It is a controlling idea.

3. What change, if any, should be made to the underlined section?
A. NO CHANGE
B. Remove the transition.
C. Move it to the introduction.
D. Move it to the next paragraph.

4. What is the best replacement for the underlined part?
A. NO CHANGE
B. as a babysitter after school and participates
C. after school, however, Shannon participates
D. as a babysitter and

Finally, Shannon has experience. For two years, she has been student body treasurer. This position has provided her with a unique perspective.

Cast your vote for Shannon Beckett this Tuesday. She has the academics, the motivation, and the experience to lead our student body. Also, Shannon won the spelling bee last month. [5]

5. What is the main problem with the underlined sentence?

A. It introduces a minor, unrelated detail.

B. It restates the thesis in new words.

C. It states a fact, without the writer's opinion.

D. It is too broad.

B. Describing an Essay's Parts

Circle the best answer for each item below.

1. This part of the essay should grab the readers' attention and state the thesis.
(a) conclusion (b) body paragraphs (c) introduction

2. When you write this part of an essay, follow one pattern of organization, such as cause-effect order.
(a) body paragraphs (b) thesis (c) conclusion

3. Some writers often include a startling fact or a vivid image in this part of an essay to encourage their audience to continue reading.
(a) conclusion (b) introduction (c) body paragraphs

4. In this part of an essay, state all of the details that support the thesis.
(a) body paragraphs (b) conclusion (c) introduction

5. When you write a conclusion, you should:
(a) introduce several new details (b) tell readers "This is the end."
(c) restate your thesis

C. Writing Thesis Statements

For each set of topics and purposes below, write a thesis for a two- to three-page paper. In at least one, include a preview of your essay's organization.

1. young people and television (to persuade)

2. the strangest day of my life (to tell about an experience)

Copyright © 2014 by William H. Sadlier, Inc. All rights reserved.

3. a famous person (to inform)
4. my funniest friend (to describe)
5. Earth Day participation (to persuade)

D. Revising a Persuasive Essay

Revise the draft below by adding paragraph breaks, transitions, and improving paragraph unity and coherence. Label the three parts of the essay, and underline the thesis.

Proofreading Symbols

℣	Delete.	⊙	Add a period.	/	Make lowercase.	¶	Start a new paragraph.
∧	Add.	∧	Add a comma.	≡	Capitalize		

[1]Did you know that our town's oldest building is scheduled to be torn down? [2]The Crane Building, constructed in 1802, is a monument to our town's earliest years and must be protected from demolition.

[3]The Crane Building symbolizes our town's history. [4]It was built only thirty years after the Revolutionary War. [5]It is named after the Crane family. [6]The Cranes built the three-story house.[7]It has been home to at least fourteen different families. [8]It now stands empty. [9]There are many empty buildings on the same block. [10]Developers intend to tear the Crane Building down and also Wilson School.

[11]We must work together to stop its destruction. [12]We should write letters to our mayor and congressperson. [13]We should make our feelings known. [14]We should contact the developers. [15]We should demand a change. [16]The school is a historic landmark. [17]The Crane Building is our heritage we must prevent its destruction. [18]The Crane Building is over two hundred years old. [19]If we don't protect our past, who will?

CHAPTER 6

Parts of a Sentence

Copyright © 2014 by William H. Sadlier, Inc. All rights reserved.

Complete Sentences

LESSON 6.1

A **complete sentence** is a group of words that expresses a complete thought. Every complete sentence has a subject and a predicate. (See Lesson 6.2 for more about subjects and predicates.)

A **sentence fragment** is not a complete sentence. It may begin with a capital letter and end with an end punctuation mark, but it does not express a complete thought. A fragment may be missing a subject, a predicate, or both. (See Lesson 2.1 for ways to correct sentence fragments.)

FRAGMENT Folk singers in the 1960s.
[missing a predicate]

SENTENCE Folk singers in the 1960s recorded many classic songs.

FRAGMENT If you remember the words.
[The word *If* turns the words into a sentence fragment.]

SENTENCE If you remember the words, you should sing along.

There are four kinds of sentences.

1. **Declarative sentences** make a statement. They end with a period.

   Ethel Waters was a talented blues singer**.**

2. **Imperative sentences** make a command or a request. They end with a period or (if the command is strong) an exclamation point.

   Finish your music report by next Tuesday**.**

3. **Interrogative sentences** ask a question. They end with a question mark.

   When and where was Louis Armstrong born**?**

4. **Exclamatory sentences** show strong feeling. They end with an exclamation point.

   Oh, that CD sounds absolutely amazing**!**

Varying the length and kinds of sentences you use can add interest to your writing. For example, include a short interrogative sentence to break up a series of long declarative ones.

See **Lessons 3.1** and **3.2** for more about improving sentence variety.

ONLINE PRACTICE
www.grammarforwriting.com

Exercise Identifying Sentences and Revising Sentence Fragments

Identify each of the following word groups as either a sentence fragment (*F*) or a complete sentence (*S*). Label each complete sentence as *declarative*, *imperative*, *interrogative*, or *exclamatory*. Rewrite each fragment as a complete sentence, and then identify the sentence type.

HINT

As you rewrite the sentence fragments, you may need to add, delete, or change words, capital letters, and punctuation marks.

EXAMPLE F A scoop of seawater in a bucket.

Milo carried a scoop of seawater in a bucket. (declarative)

___ **1.** Some sea animals in deep water.

___ **2.** Have been to the Pacific Ocean.

___ **3.** When we went to the beach for two weeks.

___ **4.** Did you know that tiny living organisms can be found in deep and shallow water?

___ **5.** Was once running water in the canals of Mars.

___ **6.** Debate about whether there could be life on Mars.

___ **7.** Because I am curious about astronomy.

___ **8.** The largest crater on Mars, the Hellas impact basin.

___ **9.** The crater is wider than the United States.

___ **10.** That book about how asteroids crashed into Mars.

Write What You Think

Write a paragraph that explains your position on the question below. Support your opinion with evidence. Exchange paragraphs with a partner, and check each other's work for fragments.

Should the U.S. government fund another trip to the moon?

Copyright © 2014 by William H. Sadlier, Inc. All rights reserved.

Subjects and Predicates

LESSON 6.2

The **subject** of a sentence is the person or thing that performs the action. The **predicate** tells what the subject does, has, feels, or is. Sometimes it tells what happens to the subject.

➡ The **complete subject** includes all the words that describe the subject. The **simple subject (s)** is the main word or words in the complete subject.

> The **coach** (S) of the team swims backstroke.
> [The coach of the team = COMPLETE SUBJECT]

The simple subject may be compound.

> Thirteen-year-old **Randy** (S), his older **sister** (S), and his younger **brother** (S) all dive.

➡ The **complete predicate** includes all the words that tell what the subject does, has, feels, or is. The **simple predicate (v)** is the main word or words in the complete predicate. It is always a **verb** or a **verb phrase.**

> Randy **will swim** (V) in the meet next week.
> [will swim in the meet next week = COMPLETE PREDICATE]

The simple predicate may be compound.

> He **swims** (V) each day and **lifts** (V) weights twice a week.

Note: In this book, the term *verb* refers to the simple predicate and *subject* refers to the simple subject unless otherwise noted.

Remember

In many sentences, a prepositional phrase comes between the subject and the verb. Note that the subject is never in a prepositional phrase.

The relay **teams** (S) from our school **set** (V) a record.

For more about prepositional phrases and identifying subjects, see **Lessons 9.6** and **10.1.**

See **Lesson 8.1** for more about verb phrases, which consist of a main verb and one or more helping verbs.

EXERCISE 1 Identifying Subjects and Predicates

Read the sentences on the next page. Draw a line to separate the complete subjects and predicates. Underline the simple subject once and the simple predicate (verb) twice.

EXAMPLE The safety of products | is a huge concern for consumers.

ONLINE PRACTICE
www.grammarforwriting.com

Three sentences have a compound subject, and two sentences have a compound verb.

1. Parents must select toys for young children carefully.
2. Shopping for toys during the holidays can be exciting, fun, and frustrating.
3. Millions of toys from China have been banned recently.
4. Tests on many popular toys, dolls, trains, and cars revealed a variety of possible dangers.
5. Some of the ones with high levels of lead were recalled and removed from store shelves.
6. Certain amounts of lead can damage children's mental development, hearing, and vital organs.
7. Babies often put toys in their mouths and can easily choke on small pieces like magnets.
8. Parents and other caregivers should check every old toy for possible hazards.
9. Sharp edges, sharp points, and loud noises make some toys extremely dangerous for toddlers.
10. Since 1970, many hazardous toys and other items have been removed from stores.

Exercise 2 Writing a Paragraph

Study the photo to the right. Imagine you can see the scene from the hot air balloon's perspective.

1. Write at least six sentences describing what you might see.
2. Underline each simple subject once and each simple predicate twice.

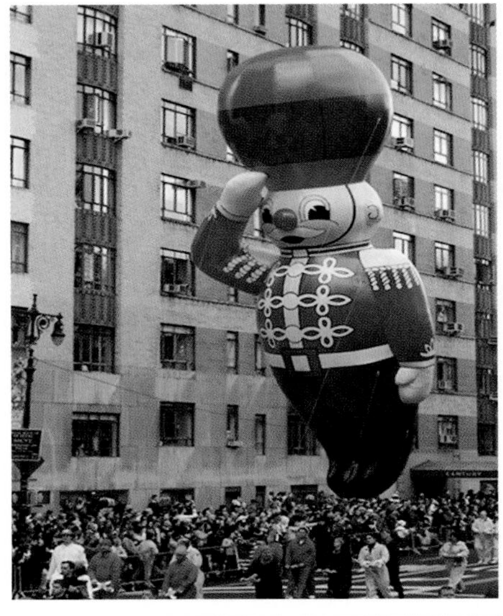

Copyright © 2014 by William H. Sadlier, Inc. All rights reserved.

LESSON 6.3

Identifying the Subject

Identifying the subject **(s)** is necessary so that you can make sure the verb **(v)** and the subject agree.

In **imperative sentences** (commands or requests), the subject is *you,* even though the word *you* does not appear in the sentence. *You* is called the **understood subject.**

[**You**] (s) Please read (v) the instructions.

Sometimes the subject is difficult to find because other words come between the subject and the verb. **Remember:** The subject is never in a prepositional phrase.

The **computers** (s) in the lab on the third floor are (v) available.

Last week, **one** (s) of the computers crashed (v).

In **inverted sentences,** the verb comes before the subject. Use the chart below to help you identify the subjects in three kinds of inverted sentences.

Sentence Type	How to Find the Subject	Examples
Interrogative sentence (question)	Turn the question into a statement.	**Is (v) the computer lab (s) open today?** [The computer lab is open today.]
Sentence that begins with a phrase	Put the sentence in normal order with the subject before the verb.	In the lab are (v) five **computers (s).** [Five computers are in the lab.]
Sentence that begins with *here* or *there*	Find the verb, and ask *who* or *what.* (*Here* and *there* are never subjects.)	Here comes (v) the **instructor (s).** [The instructor comes here.]

CONNECTING Writing & Grammar

Verbs must agree with their subjects in number. Use a singular verb with a singular subject.

In the offices **is** [not *are*] a new **system** of phones.

Use a plural verb with a plural subject.

There **are** [not *is*] **computers** in the lab on the third floor.

See the lessons in **Chapter 10** for more about subject-verb agreement.

Exercise 1 Identifying Subjects

Underline the subject once and the verb twice. Write *you* for an understood subject.

EXAMPLE Have you visited Chicago?

1. Along the east side of Chicago sits Lake Michigan.
2. There are boats galore during the summer months.
3. Relax on the beach, and enjoy the sights and sounds.
4. Why is Chicago called the "Windy City"?
5. There have been stories of long-winded politicians in history books.
6. Here is a city with a long and colorful past.
7. Ride the Ferris wheel at Navy Pier.
8. Visit the many museums around the city.
9. Among the city's many attractions are buildings rich in architectural history.
10. Can you think of Chicago without the Cubs?

HINT

Do not forget to underline helping verbs, such as *are, can, do,* and *is*. The subject in a question often comes between the helping verb and the main verb.

Do you know the address?

Exercise 2 Rewriting Sentences

Rewrite each inverted sentence below so that the subject precedes the verb. Underline the subject of each of your sentences.

1. Was the purpose of the Chicago World's Fair to highlight scientific discoveries?
2. Along Lake Michigan were four hundred acres of exhibits.
3. There were displays from cultures around the world.
4. Did many people attend the fair?
5. In the library are many books about the fair.

Copyright © 2014 by William H. Sadlier, Inc. All rights reserved.

LESSON 6.4

Compound Subjects and Verbs

Sentences may have compound subjects and compound verbs.

➠ A **compound subject** contains two or more subjects that share the same verb. Compound subjects are joined by coordinating conjunctions, such as *and, or,* and *nor*. They may also be joined by correlative conjunctions, such as *both…and, either…or,* and *neither…nor*. (See Lesson 9.7 for more about conjunctions.)

> **Walt Disney** and **Winston Churchill** had learning disabilities.
>
> Neither **Disney** nor **others** were ready to give up easily.

➠ A **compound verb** contains two or more verbs that share the same subject. Conjunctions like *and, or,* or *but* usually join the verbs.

> Churchill **was born** in 1874 and **died** in 1965.
>
> Disney **created** cartoons and **dreamed** of a theme park.

➠ Use compound subjects and compound verbs to combine sentences and make your writing less repetitive.

ORIGINAL Disney directed cartoons. Disney wrote for the screen. He followed his dreams.

REVISED Disney **directed** cartoons, **wrote** for the screen, and **followed** his dreams. [compound verb]

Sentences may have more than one subject or verb without containing a compound subject or a compound verb. (See Lesson 3.4 about four types of sentence structures.)

S V S V
I like to draw, but **I have** little talent.
[compound sentence]

S V S V
If **she could, Toni would become** an artist.
[complex sentence]

TEST-TAKING TIP

Many test questions ask you to correct subject-verb agreement errors. When a compound subject is joined by *or* or *nor,* the verb should agree with the subject closest to it.

Neither the book nor the articles **were** useful.

Neither the articles nor the book **was** useful.

For practice using compound subjects and compound verbs to combine sentences, see **Lesson 3.6.**

Exercise 1 Identifying Compound Parts

Underline the subjects once and the verbs twice. Write *CS* for a compound subject, *CV* for a compound verb, and *N* if the sentence has no compound subjects or compound verbs.

EXAMPLE *CS, CV* Jay and I like adventure and enjoy sports.

___ **1.** Bungee jumping and other extreme sports appeal to many and are growing in popularity.

___ **2.** Bungee jumping originated and became popular in New Zealand.

___ **3.** Bungee jumping is considered very dangerous.

___ **4.** Secure cables and safety gear are essential in ensuring the safety of a jumper.

___ **5.** After the adventurer jumped, she dangled at the end of the cable.

Exercise 2 Combining Sentences

Use a compound subject or compound verb to combine the groups of short sentences. You may add or delete words.

Remember

Do not use a comma before a conjunction that joins the parts of a compound subject or compound verb.

Haru enjoys skiing **and** likes excitement.

EXAMPLE Snowboarding is an Olympic sport. Snowboarding draws crowds of spectators.

Snowboarding is an Olympic sport and draws crowds of spectators.

1. Haru snowboards. So does his sister.

2. Today, skiing is popular in North America and Europe. Snowboarding is popular in North America and Europe.

3. Snowboarders dress in padded pants. They wear helmets.

4. Snowboarding is a lot like skateboarding. Both have freestyle competition. Skiing also has freestyle competition.

5. Top-rated snowboarders compete in a ten-month season. They draw crowds of fans.

Copyright © 2014 by William H. Sadlier, Inc. All rights reserved.

LESSON 6.5

Direct and Indirect Objects

Action verbs often need direct and indirect objects to complete their meaning.

A **direct object (DO)** is a noun, pronoun, or group of words that tells *who* or *what* receives the action of the verb. To find a direct object, ask *whom?* or *what?* after the action verb.

> DO DO
> Minutemen fought the **French** and the **British.**
> [Fought *whom?* Answer: *French* and *British*]
>
> DO
> They played key **roles** in many battles.
> [Played *what?* Answer: *roles*]

Sentences with direct objects may also contain an indirect object. An **indirect object (IO)** is a noun, pronoun, or group of words that tells *to what?* or *to whom?* (or *for what?* or *for whom?*) an action verb is done. An indirect object usually comes between a verb and a direct object.

> IO DO
> Veterans offered new **volunteers** useful **advice.**
> [Offered advice *to whom?* Answer: *volunteers*]
>
> IO DO
> The men gave the **map** a quick **look.**
> [Gave a look *to what?* Answer: *map*]

Neither direct objects nor indirect objects appear in a prepositional phrase. (See Lesson 9.6 to review prepositional phrases.)

> Patriots fought for their independence.
> [*Independence* is not a direct object. It is the object of the preposition *for.*]
>
> DO
> Mr. Ortiz discussed the **minutemen** with us.
> [*Us* is not an indirect object. It is the object of the preposition *with.*]

Remember

Like subjects and verbs, direct objects and indirect objects may be compound.

IO IO DO DO
Please give **Rob** and **me** the **book** and the **photo**.

Exercise 1 Identifying Indirect Objects and Direct Objects

In the sentences that follow, label each direct object *DO* and each indirect object *IO*.

IO DO
EXAMPLE The colonies gave settlers a new chance.

ONLINE PRACTICE
www.grammarforwriting.com

HINT

Be sure to use an object pronoun (such as *me*, *us*, or *them*) and not a subject pronoun (such as *I*, *we*, or *they*) as a direct or indirect object.

He showed Jesse and **me** (DO) [not *I*] the picture.

See **Lesson 7.4** for more about object pronouns.

1. King James I wanted land for England.

2. Colonization would solve many problems for the English.

3. King James granted the Virginia Company its first charter.

4. The charter gave the company the right to establish colonies.

5. Under this charter, English investors gave money.

6. Three ships made the voyage to the New World.

7. In 1607, the settlers sighted land in the distance.

8. Captain Christopher Newport commanded one of the ships.

9. He reached land on May 14, 1607.

10. Newport chose the site for Jamestown.

11. He brought the settlers supplies in later return voyages.

12. Newport inspired and led the early settlers.

13. The English met many Native Americans.

14. The settlers built themselves a church and a fort.

15. Few settlers survived the first winter.

Exercise 2 Writing a Story

Write the first paragraph of a story based on the people and events in the photo. When you have finished, underline direct objects, and circle indirect objects.

A MINUTE MAN PREPARING FOR WAR.

Copyright © 2014 by William H. Sadlier, Inc. All rights reserved.

LESSON 6.6

Subject Complements

A **subject complement (SC)** follows a **linking verb** and defines, renames, or describes the subject of a sentence. Without a subject complement, a sentence with a linking verb does not express a complete thought.

Jennifer Rodriguez is a speed **skater.** (SC)
[The noun *skater* renames the subject, *Jennifer Rodriguez.*]

Rodriguez feels **lucky.** (SC) [The adjective *lucky* describes *Rodriguez.*]

There are two kinds of subject complements: predicate nominatives and predicate adjectives. A **predicate nominative (PN)** is a noun or pronoun that identifies the subject. A **predicate adjective (PA)** is an adjective that modifies, or describes, the subject.

Predicate Nominative	Two of speed skating's biggest fans are **Andres** (PN) and **I.** (PN) [The noun *Andres* and the pronoun *I* identify the subject, *fans.*]
	Rodriguez is an Olympic **medalist.** (PN) [The noun *medalist* renames the subject, *Rodriguez.*]
Predicate Adjective	Rodriguez's father is **Cuban American.** (PA) [The adjective *Cuban American* describes the subject, *father.*]
	As a child, Jennifer became **interested** (PA) in roller skating. [The adjective *interested* describes the subject, *Jennifer.*]

Some verbs, such as *look, smell, sound,* and *grow,* may be used as linking verbs in some sentences and action verbs in others.

The racer **sounded** sad in her interview.
[*Sounded* is a linking verb. It links the predicate adjective *sad* to the subject, *racer.*]

Mr. Alioto, the referee, **sounded** his whistle.
[*Sounded* is an action verb. It is followed by the direct object, *whistle.*]

Remember

Subject complements follow linking verbs only.

All the forms of *be* are linking verbs. These other verbs can also be linking verbs:

appear	remain
become	seem
feel	smell
grow	sound
look	taste

For more about linking verbs, see **Lesson 8.1.**

HINT

Remember that both predicate nominatives and predicate adjectives may be compound.

Rodriguez is a top **athlete** (PN) and a speed skating **champion.** (PN)

EXERCISE 1 Using Subject Complements

On a separate sheet of paper, write a sentence with the subject complements listed below. Underline the complement(s).

EXAMPLE a predicate adjective after the verb *grew*

The lead singer grew tired.

1. a compound predicate noun
2. a predicate noun and a predicate pronoun
3. a predicate adjective after the verb *appears*
4. a predicate noun after the verb *were*
5. a compound predicate adjective

EXERCISE 2 Identifying Subject Complements

Itzhak Perlman

Underline each predicate noun or pronoun, and circle each predicate adjective in the sentences below. Some sentences have compound subject complements. One sentence has no subject complements.

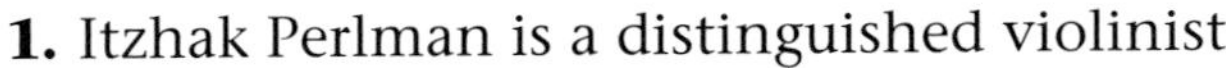

1. Itzhak Perlman is a distinguished violinist.
2. Born in 1945, Perlman contracted polio at the age of four.
3. Perlman is also an award-winning teacher and conductor.
4. His playing style is enthusiastic, expressive, and flawless.
5. When my friends and I listen to him play, we are amazed at his talent.

EXERCISE 3 Writing an E-mail

Write an e-mail of at least six sentences to a friend. Tell about one of your favorite musicians or musical groups. Use and underline either a predicate nominative or a predicate adjective in at least three sentences.

Copyright © 2014 by William H. Sadlier, Inc. All rights reserved.

WRITING APPLICATION

Business Letter

Suppose that you want to apply for a job or internship. How would you go about it? One of the first things you would need to do is draft a cover letter. Cover letters are one kind of business letter. **Business letters** are formal letters that request a particular action or express thanks. They can be written for a variety of purposes.

When you write a business letter, include the following features.

Key Features

- clear statement of purpose
- cohesive organizational pattern
- relevant details and supporting information
- formal style and professional tone
- parts of a business letter, including a heading, body, and closing

ASSIGNMENT

TASK: Apply for a summer volunteer position in a **business letter.**

PURPOSE: to persuade

AUDIENCE: manager of the business

KEY INSTRUCTIONS: Include your qualifications for the job using a formal style and tone.

Be Direct Begin the first paragraph of your letter with a clearly stated **purpose.** In this case, you are asking the business manager to offer the position to you.

Then, give at least two strong reasons why you should be hired. Brainstorm details that make you a good fit for the position.

Experiences and Accomplishments

- worked as a babysitter for two years
- have been a Girl Scout for five years
- made honor roll three semesters in a row

Qualities

- hardworking, smart
- fun, easy-going

Clear purpose in the first sentence

Two strong reasons for being hired

[1]I am writing to submit my application for the summer volunteer position advertised on your Web site. [2]My background makes me a strong candidate for this position. [3]I have several years of related experience, and I'm a hard worker.

See **Lesson 4.2** for more about elaboration.

Be Organized In the body paragraph(s) of your letter, elaborate on the reasons that you should be hired. Use the list you brainstormed to provide specific details to support each reason. Include only relevant details.

During my five years as a Girl Scout, I have learned responsibility and leadership. ~~I have also had many fun experiences.~~

Copyright © 2014 by William H. Sadlier, Inc. All rights reserved.

Be Formal You are trying to make a good impression, so use formal style and a professional tone. **Formal style** includes:

- standard rules of English and spelling
- complete sentences
- no slang
- few, if any, abbreviations or contractions

INFORMAL One more thing! Don't forget that I've made the honor roll three times in a row. I'm a hard worker—big time.

FORMAL Finally, I have made the honor roll for three consecutive semesters, which shows that I am a very hard worker.

Be Complete Make sure you include every part of a business letter.

- **Heading** The heading includes your address and the date. Add a comma between the date and year and between the city and state.
- **Inside address** This is the name and address of your letter's recipient. Add a comma between the city and state.
- **Greeting** Your greeting begins your letter. Use a formal greeting, such as *Dear Ms. Ruiz*. Follow your greeting with a colon.
- **Body** The body is the core of your letter.
- **Closing** Use a formal phrase, such as *Sincerely,* to end your letter. Place a comma at the end of your closing.
- **Signature** Write your name at the end of your letter.

Express your ideas in the fewest possible words. Replace phrases that have little or no meaning with single words that mean the same thing. See **Lesson 2.5.**

Wordy	**Concise**
at the present time	now
in order to	because
in spite of	despite
prior to	before

Fix any fragments in your letter. Fragments are missing a subject, a predicate, or both. See **Lessons 6.1** and **6.2.**

FRAGMENT The **children,** who were mostly under the age of six.

SENTENCE The **children,** who were mostly under the age of six, **were excited.**

Be Correct Use the checklist to review your letter.

WRITING CHECKLIST

Did you…

- ✔ clearly state your purpose?
- ✔ include all the parts of a business letter?
- ✔ write in formal style?
- ✔ include only relevant details and clearly organize them?
- ✔ write one page only and avoid sentence fragments?

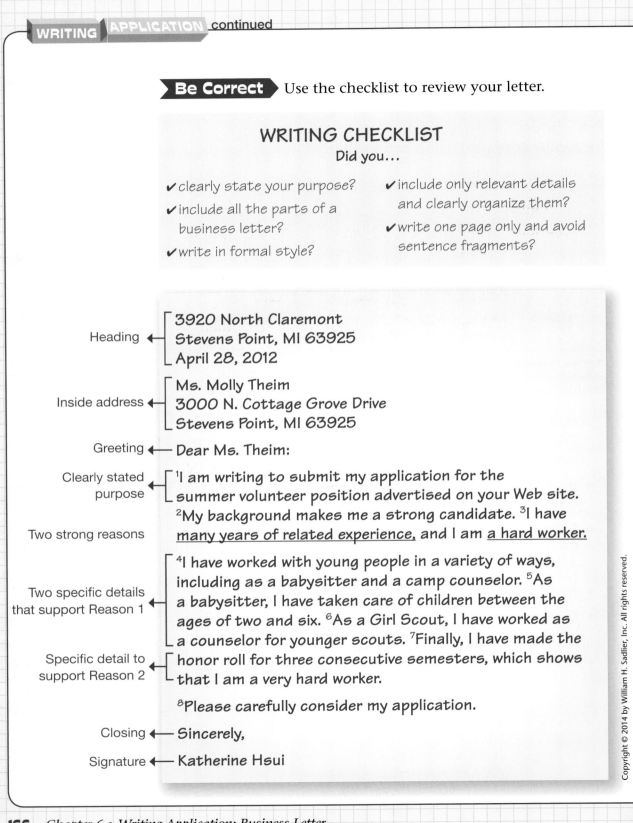

Heading ← 3920 North Claremont
Stevens Point, MI 63925
April 28, 2012

Inside address ← Ms. Molly Theim
3000 N. Cottage Grove Drive
Stevens Point, MI 63925

Greeting ← Dear Ms. Theim:

Clearly stated purpose ← [1]I am writing to submit my application for the summer volunteer position advertised on your Web site.

Two strong reasons ← [2]My background makes me a strong candidate. [3]I have <u>many years of related experience,</u> and I am <u>a hard worker.</u>

Two specific details that support Reason 1 ← [4]I have worked with young people in a variety of ways, including as a babysitter and a camp counselor. [5]As a babysitter, I have taken care of children between the ages of two and six. [6]As a Girl Scout, I have worked as a counselor for younger scouts.

Specific detail to support Reason 2 ← [7]Finally, I have made the honor roll for three consecutive semesters, which shows that I am a very hard worker.

[8]Please carefully consider my application.

Closing ← Sincerely,

Signature ← Katherine Hsui

Copyright © 2014 by William H. Sadlier, Inc. All rights reserved.

Chapter Review

A. Practice Test

Read the draft and questions below carefully. Fill in the corresponding circle for your answer choice.

(1) Born in 1973 in Newark, New Jersey, to the singer Yvette Glover, Savion Glover became a Broadway sensation in *The Tap Dance Kid* at just eleven years old. **(2)** Savion was always interested in rhythm. **(3)** As a young child, he used to line up kitchen pots and pans and bang on them to create different beats. **(4)** When he was four years old, Savion's mother got him drum lessons. **(5)** Savion then moved on to tap dancing lessons at age seven. **(6)** Savion says that when he began dancing, his mother couldn't afford to buy him tap shoes, so he used an old pair of cowboy boots instead. **(7)** The boots didn't sound quite right, but that didn't stop Savion from learning. **(8)** The famous dancer Gregory Hines said that Savion "was doing things as a dancer at ten that I couldn't do until I was twenty-five." **(9)** After gaining experience as a stage performer, Glover moved on to do television work, with recurring appearances on *Sesame Street*. **(10)** Then he returned to Broadway and starred in his original dance show *Bring in 'Da Noise, Bring in 'Da Funk*. **(11)** For his ingenious choreography in this production, Glover won Broadway's prestigious Tony Award in 1996.

Ⓐ Ⓑ Ⓒ Ⓓ Ⓔ **1.** What is the simple subject of sentence 1?
(A) *The Tap Dance Kid*
(B) Glover
(C) Yvette Glover
(D) Savion Glover
(E) a Broadway sensation

Chapter Review

ⒶⒷⒸⒹⒺ **2.** What is the indirect object in sentence 4?
(A) him
(B) he
(C) Savion's mother
(D) drum lessons
(E) There is none.

ⒶⒷⒸⒹⒺ **3.** What is the subject complement in sentence 7, and what type of complement is it?
(A) There is none.
(B) right (predicate noun)
(C) right (predicate adjective)
(D) from learning (predicate adjective)
(E) Savion (predicate noun)

ⒶⒷⒸⒹⒺ **4.** Which of the following is true of sentence 10?
(A) It does not state a complete thought.
(B) It has two direct objects.
(C) It has a compound subject.
(D) It has a compound verb.
(E) The simple predicate is *he returned*.

ⒶⒷⒸⒹⒺ **5.** What is the complete subject of sentence 11?
(A) ingenious work
(B) For his ingenious work on this production
(C) Broadway's prestigious Tony
(D) Tony Award
(E) Glover

B. Completing Sentences

Each group of words below is a sentence fragment. Turn each word group into a complete sentence by adding the missing sentence parts. In addition, add the item listed in parentheses.

1. Went ice-skating near Lake Devine. (compound verb)

2. My friends Sue, Carla, and Jake. (direct object)

3. In the next week. (compound subject joined by *or*)

4. The surface of the lake. (compound predicate adjectives)

5. Told the story. (indirect object)

Copyright © 2014 by William H. Sadlier, Inc. All rights reserved.

C. Analyzing and Editing a Business Letter

Read the draft of a business letter below.

1. Label each direct object *DO* and the one indirect object *IO*.
2. Circle each subject complement.
3. Use proofreading symbols to correct any uses of informal language, sentence fragments, or missing punctuation.

Proofreading Symbols			
^	Add.	/	Make lowercase.
℘	Delete.	^,	Add a comma.

To Whom It May Concern:

[1]I am writing to make a complaint about your EZ MP3 Player. [2]I bought it at my local electronics store. [3]Unfortunately it has never worked properly, and I am like totally frustrated. [4]There are several problems. [5]I went online and downloaded the latest software for the player, but it only made things worse. [6]When I called the support line, I was left on hold. [7]For thirty-five minutes. [8]Unbelievably, the technician didn't understand the stuff I complained about. [9]How can you justify such terrible service for such an expensive product?

[10]I am very unhappy with your product.

[11]Please give me a full refund. [12] Thanks.

Later

Bethany Jackson

Chapter Review

CHAPTER 7

Nouns and Pronouns

Copyright © 2014 by William H. Sadlier, Inc. All rights reserved.

LESSON 7.1

Using Nouns

A **noun** is a **part of speech** that names a person, place, thing, or idea. Nouns can be used in many different ways in a sentence, such as a subject, a predicate noun, or an object.

PERSONS Queen Elizabeth, doctor, great-grandson, goalie

PLACES island, Brazil, streets, Golden Gate Bridge

THINGS pencils, CD, snowflakes, dining room

IDEAS anger, self-confidence, success, happiness

You can classify nouns in several ways. For instance, all nouns are either common or proper, concrete or abstract, and singular or plural. (You will learn about other kinds of nouns in Lessons 7.2 and 7.6.)

1. **Common nouns** refer to general persons, places, things, or ideas. **Proper nouns** name specific persons, places, things, and ideas. Always capitalize proper nouns.

   COMMON author, river, country, restaurant

   PROPER Jack London, Nile River, Ethiopia, The Grill

2. **Concrete nouns** name things that you can see, hear, smell, taste, or touch. **Abstract nouns** name ideas, feelings, qualities, or characteristics.

   CONCRETE whistle, pizza, Saturn, Mr. Murawski

   ABSTRACT beauty, Buddhism, judgment, romanticism

3. **Singular nouns** refer to one person, place, thing, or idea. Nouns that refer to more than one person, place, thing, or idea are called **plural nouns.**

   SINGULAR picture, dress, army, half, child

   PLURAL pictures, dresses, armies, halves, children

Most nouns can be made plural by adding *-s* or *-es* to the end of the word. (See Lesson 12.7 for other rules about forming plural nouns.)

Use proper nouns and specific concrete nouns to make your writing more precise.

VAGUE The **girls** stood near the **people** at the **monument.**

CONCRETE **Kenna** and **Carli** stood near the **teenagers** at the **Vietnam Veterans Memorial.**

Exercise 1 Identifying Nouns

Remember

Nouns can be used in many different ways in a sentence, such as a subject, a predicate noun, a direct or indirect object, an object of a preposition, or an appositive.

Identify the underlined nouns in the passage below as either common or proper and singular or plural.

EXAMPLE Liyana—proper, singular

Literary Model

They flew to New York in steamy June, left their seventeen suitcases and Liyana's violin stored at the airport, and spent one day lugging stuffed backpacks around to the Empire State Building and riding up to the inside of the Statue of Liberty's head.

—Excerpt from *Habibi* by Naomi Shihab Nye

Exercise 2 Using Nouns

On a separate sheet of paper, write sentences using the types of nouns listed below. Underline them. **Hint:** Look around your classroom for ideas.

EXAMPLE one singular and one plural noun

Annie has five pencils.

1. two singular proper nouns
2. three common, concrete nouns
3. one abstract noun as a subject
4. one singular proper noun as a predicate noun
5. one abstract and two concrete nouns

Exercise 3 Writing Dialogue

Work with a partner to brainstorm a dialogue between two people looking for a lost item. Write at least three sets of sentences, and use several kinds of nouns.

EXAMPLE DAD: What did you do with your shoes, Donnie?

DONNIE: I put them on the chair in the kitchen.

Copyright © 2014 by William H. Sadlier, Inc. All rights reserved.

LESSON 7.2

Compound and Collective Nouns

A **compound noun** consists of two or more words used together as a single noun. A compound noun can be written as one word, as separate words, or as a hyphenated word.

One Word	airport, Greenland, keyboard, daydream, superhero, firewood, headaches, flashlight
Separate Words	post office, list price, New Yorkers, chief of staff, baseball bat, grizzly bear, Julia Alvarez
Hyphenated Word(s)	self-respect, sister-in-law, tip-off, know-it-all, fifteen-year-old

If you are uncertain about how to write a compound noun, look it up in a print or online dictionary.

To form the plural of a single-word compound noun, add *-s* or *-es* to most words.

headache**s** eyelash**es** wristwatch**es**

For compound nouns that are made up of two or more words or are hyphenated, make the main noun plural.

sister**s**-in-law wind chime**s** public-address system**s**

A **collective noun** names a group, or collection, of people, animals, or things. Collective nouns can be singular or plural. Use a singular verb when you think of the collective noun as one unit.

The **chorus sings** at its spring festival.
[The chorus as a unit is singing.]

Use a plural verb when you think of the separate individuals in the group.

After the program, the **chorus go** their separate ways.
[The members of the chorus go different ways.]

Some Collective Nouns

army, audience, band, chorus, class, club, committee, couple, crowd, faculty, family, flock, group, herd, jury, panel, team, troop

For more about subject-verb agreement with collective nouns, see **Lesson 10.4.**

Exercise 1 Identifying Nouns

Underline all of the compound nouns, and circle the three collective nouns in the passage below. Be sure that you identify nouns, not adjectives.

[1]In *The Land I Lost: Adventures of a Boy in Vietnam*, Huynh Quang Nhuong tells the true story of his boyhood in Vietnam during the 1950s. [2]The book's setting is the countryside near the village of Mytho, the author's hometown. [3]The author vividly describes its location on a riverbank, with houses scattered against the mountainsides.

[4]Huynh describes the animals his family feared most. [5]Among them are tigers, which he describes as man-eaters, snakes, and water buffaloes. [6]The buffalo herd was troublesome. [7]Huynh's job was to prevent a group of them from nibbling on rice plants when no one was watching.

Use a dictionary, or refer to **Lesson 12.7** for help with forming plurals.

Exercise 2 Forming Plurals

Use the plural form of each compound noun in a sentence.

EXAMPLE great-grandmother

Both of my great-grandmothers are alive.

1. horseshoe crab
2. mountain man
3. crybaby
4. do-it-yourselfer
5. merry-go-round

Copyright © 2014 by William H. Sadlier, Inc. All rights reserved.

Using Pronouns

LESSON 7.3

Pronouns are words that take the place of one or more nouns or pronouns. The word or phrase that a pronoun replaces is called its **antecedent.**

➡ A pronoun must agree with its antecedent in number, gender, and person. (See Lesson 7.7.)

> **Meg** choreographed a **dance**, and now **she** is teaching **it**. [The pronoun *she* replaces the noun *Meg*, and the singular pronoun *it* replaces the noun *dance*.]

➡ There are many different types of pronouns, and each type serves a different function in a sentence. (See Lesson 3.3 for information about relative pronouns.)

Type and Use	Examples
Personal pronouns refer to the person speaking, the person spoken to, or the one spoken about.	**We** gave the box to **him,** and **he** opened **it.**
Possessive pronouns show ownership or possession.	**His** letter came, but **mine** has not.
Indefinite pronouns express an amount or refer to an unspecified person or thing.	**Neither** of the guests had **any** of the food.
Demonstrative pronouns point out a person, a place, a thing, or an idea.	**This** is a funny card, but **that** is even funnier.
Interrogative pronouns begin a question.	**Who** are you, and **what** are you doing?
Reflexive pronouns refer to the subject. They function as an object or a predicate nominative.	He did not consider **himself** late.
Intensive pronouns emphasize a noun or another pronoun in the sentence.	I **myself** was impatient.

Possessive Pronouns

her, hers, his, its, mine, my, our, ours, their, theirs, your, yours

Some Indefinite Pronouns

all, any, both, few, none, several, some

Demonstrative Pronouns

that, these, this, those

Some Interrogative Pronouns

What?, Which?, Who?, Whom?, Whose?

Reflexive and Intensive Pronouns

herself, himself, itself, ourselves, themselves, yourself

EXERCISE 1 Identifying Pronouns

In each sentence below, underline the pronoun, and label the type of pronoun it is.

______ **1.** Everyone enjoyed the evening.

______ **2.** The band played its greatest hits.

______ **3.** Who requested that song?

______ **4.** She danced most of the evening.

______ **5.** That was an unforgettable party.

> **HINT**
>
> Sometimes a demonstrative or an interrogative pronoun is used before a noun and modifies the noun. In those cases, the pronoun functions as an adjective.
>
> **This** leash is old. [used as adjective]
>
> **This** is my dog. [used as pronoun]

EXERCISE 2 Revising with Pronouns

Revise the following wordy paragraph. Substitute pronouns for nouns to avoid repetition and to connect the sentences more smoothly. You may add or delete words and details as necessary. Check that your new sentences are punctuated correctly.

EXAMPLE Dog shows attract millions. Dog shows are fun.

Dog shows attract millions, and they are fun.

[1]The Westminster Kennel Dog Show is the "greatest" dog show in the world. [2]The Westminster Kennel Dog Show is the oldest dog show in America. [3]"Best in Show" is the top prize. [4]To win "Best in Show," a dog is judged as the best of all the breeds. [5]An English springer spaniel named Felicity's Diamond Jim won one show. [6]Four owners of the English springer spaniel were delighted with the win. [7]Diamond Jim's successor was a beagle named Uno.

Copyright © 2014 by William H. Sadlier, Inc. All rights reserved.

LESSON 7.4

Subject and Object Pronouns

Personal pronouns replace nouns, and like nouns, they act like subjects and as objects in sentences.

Subject Pronouns	I, we, you, he, she, it, they
Object Pronouns	me, us, you, him, her, it, them

A **subject pronoun** is used as the **subject (S)** of a sentence or a clause.

I (S) admire Jim Thorpe's athletic achievements.

Although **he** (S) played baseball, Thorpe liked football better.

A subject pronoun is also used as a **predicate nominative (PN)** following a linking verb. It renames the subject.

The tall men on the right are Brady and **he** (PN).

An **object pronoun** is used as a **direct object (DO)**, **indirect object (IO)**, or **object of a preposition (OP)**.

After winning two Olympic gold medals in 1912, Thorpe accepted **them** (DO) from King Gustav V of Sweden.

The news article gave **us** (IO) a **description** (DO) of Thorpe's life.

One town in Pennsylvania built a memorial to **him** (OP).

Pronouns in compound subjects, predicate nominatives, and objects can often cause problems. To help you choose the correct pronoun, try each pronoun separately in the sentence.

For my friends and (I, me), Thorpe is an American hero. [*For I* or *For me?*]

For my friends and **me,** Thorpe is an American hero. [object]

Exercise 1 Choosing Correct Pronouns

On the next page, underline the correct pronoun in parentheses. Then label it *S* for subject pronoun or *O* for object pronoun.

EXAMPLE He and (I, me) ride horses. S

For more about direct and indirect objects and predicate nominatives, see **Lessons 6.5** and **6.6.**

Remember

Although you might hear people say "It's me" or "That's Ben and him" in informal situations, the use of object pronouns after a linking verb is grammatically incorrect. On tests and in academic writing, use subject pronouns.

It is **I**. That's Ben and **he**.

ONLINE PRACTICE
www.grammarforwriting.com

1. Jack and (he, him) are reading about cowboys.
2. The presenters of our report are Lori and (her, she).
3. The favorite cowboy of Nyah and (I, me) is Bill Pickett.
4. Ellen gave (they and we, them and us) some books.
5. Now (she and I, her and me) have to write our reports.

Exercise 2 Editing a Paragraph

Work with a partner to correct errors with subject and object pronouns in the paragraph below.

Buffalo Soldier

[1]My classmates and me learned that Congress passed an act in 1866 to allow African-Americans in the regular army. [2]Our teacher wanted us to work in pairs, so he put Quinn and I together. [3]Her and me did research. [4]She and I shared our information with Thomas and them. [5]We and them studied the buffalo soldiers and Benjamin O. Davis, Sr. [6]The first African-American general in the U.S. military was him.

Exercise 3 Writing Paragraphs

Write two expository paragraphs about a person or event you have studied in science or history. Explain why this person or event interests you. Underline each subject and object pronoun when you have finished writing.

Copyright © 2014 by William H. Sadlier, Inc. All rights reserved.

LESSON 7.5

Who or Whom?

Many writers (and speakers) are uncertain about when to use the pronouns *who* and *whom*.

➠ *Who* is always used as a **subject** or **predicate nominative.**

Who is coming to the show?
[*Who* is the subject of the sentence.]

The girl **who** speaks first is Denise.
[*Who* is the subject of the adjective clause *who speaks first.*]

➠ *Whom* is always used as an **object.** It may be a direct object, an indirect object, or an object of a preposition in a sentence or in a clause.

The actor **whom** we met was nice.
[*Whom* is the direct object of the verb *met* in the adjective clause *whom we met.*]

With **whom** did the soloist train?
[*Whom* is the object of the preposition *with.*]

STEP BY STEP

When you need to choose between *who* and *whom* in a subordinate clause:

Ella is a singer (who, whom) I enjoy.

1. Find the subordinate clause. Focus only on it.

   (who, whom) I enjoy

2. Determine how the pronoun is used—as a subject, predicate nominative, or object.

   The subject is *I*. The pronoun is the direct object of the verb *enjoy*:

   I enjoy (who, whom)

3. If the pronoun is a subject or predicate nominative, choose *who.* If the pronoun is an object, choose *whom.*

   Ella is a singer **whom** I enjoy.

For help identifying direct and indirect objects and predicate nominatives, see **Lessons 6.5** and **6.6.**

Writers often confuse the contraction *who's* (*who* + *is*) with the pronoun *whose.*

INCORRECT **Whose** performing tonight?

CORRECT **Who's** performing tonight?

ONLINE PRACTICE
www.grammarforwriting.com

Frida Kahlo
and Diego Rivera

EXERCISE 1 Choosing *Who* or *Whom*

Underline the correct word in parentheses. Write *S* for subject pronoun or *O* for object pronoun to show how the word is used.

___ **1.** Diego Rivera, (who, whom) was born in Mexico, began studying art at the age of ten.

___ **2.** His father, (who, whom) first recognized his talent, encouraged him.

___ **3.** A government official, (who, whom) got Rivera a grant, made it possible for him to study in Europe.

___ **4.** Another artist, with (who, whom) he shared a studio in Paris, painted portraits of him.

___ **5.** Henry Ford, for (who, whom) Rivera painted a mural of industrial life, brought him to Detroit.

___ **6.** (Who, Whom) did Rivera marry?

___ **7.** Frida Kahlo, (who, whom) Rivera divorced later, was also an artist.

___ **8.** From (who, whom) did Rivera get inspiration for his public murals?

___ **9.** Rivera, (who, whom) explored the lives of working people, was well loved throughout his native country.

___ **10.** When he died, Rivera, (who, whom) was in Mexico City, was painting a mural about Mexican history.

www.CartoonStock.com

EXERCISE 2 Analyzing a Cartoon

Write a brief description that explains what point this cartoon makes and why it is, or is not, funny. Your answer should show you understand the purpose of this lesson.

Copyright © 2014 by William H. Sadlier, Inc. All rights reserved.

LESSON 7.6

Possessive Nouns and Pronouns

A **possessive noun** shows who or what owns or has something. Use the following rules to form possessive nouns. (See also Lesson 11.8 for more about apostrophes.)

Rule	Examples
Add an apostrophe and -*s* to singular nouns.	father**'s** pants Callie**'s** shoes great-aunt**'s** ring
Add only an apostrophe to plural nouns that end in -*s*.	girls' jackets Joneses' budget babies' blankets
Add an apostrophe and -*s* to plural nouns that do not end in -*s*.	women**'s** wardrobe children**'s** clothing people**'s** choice

Using possessive nouns can make your writing less wordy.

the boots that belong to Ryan

Ryan's boots

Possessive Pronouns

Singular	Plural
my, mine	our, ours
your, yours	your, yours
her, hers	their, theirs
his, its	

Possessive pronouns show ownership. (See list on the right.) Sometimes you may use the possessive pronoun before a noun.

This is **my** outfit, but here's **your** shirt.

Certain possessive pronouns may also be used by themselves.

Which cap is **his? Yours** is over there. Where is **mine?**

Unlike possessive nouns, possessive pronouns never include apostrophes. Do not confuse possessive pronouns with contractions, which always have apostrophes.

It's sad that **you're** going home.
[contractions for *It is* and *you are*]

Your suitcase is missing one of **its** handles.
[possessive pronouns]

Exercise 1 Completing Sentences

Underline the correct possessive form in parentheses.

National Palace in Haiti

1. (Haitis', Haiti's) capital is Port-au-Prince.
2. Mount La Selle is the (countries, country's) highest point.
3. One of the (Haitians, Haitians') official languages is French.
4. How is (their, they're) economy?
5. Is that stamp from Haiti (yours, your's)?
6. Write (your, you're) paper about Haiti.
7. (Its, It's) scenery is beautiful.
8. I saw photos at our (towns, town's) library.
9. Many Haitian (artist's, artists') works are on display there.
10. That book about the West Indies is (her's, hers).

Exercise 2 Proofreading a Paragraph

As you read the passage below, find and correct five errors in possessive nouns and pronouns.

Some test questions ask you to identify the correct spelling of possessive pronouns.

Remember that a possessive pronoun never has an apostrophe.

its hers theirs

For example, see question 5 in the Practice Test on page 195.

[1]Are you planning a vacation? [2]You might want you're plans to include a stop in Haiti. [3]It's on our familys list of great vacation trips. [4]Although the country is small, its also a land where you'll see vivid, richly colored art and hear energetic music. [5]Two Haitian artists are Wilson Bigaud and Georges Liautaud. [6]You can see the mens work in art galleries in the United States. [7]The work of their's that I've seen is unique.

Copyright © 2014 by William H. Sadlier, Inc. All rights reserved.

LESSON 7.7

Pronoun-Antecedent Agreement

Pronouns must agree with their antecedents. An **antecedent** is the word to which the pronoun refers.

Agreement	Examples
Use a singular pronoun with a singular antecedent and a plural pronoun with a plural antecedent.	The **U.S. Constitution** is short. **It** has just 4,400 words. The **writers** took **their** time drafting the document.
Use a singular pronoun when the sentence has a compound subject but refers to only one person.	My teacher and debate coach took **her** classes to the museum.
Use a singular pronoun to refer to two or more singular antecedents joined by *or.*	Either **Jason** or **Lance** left **his** history textbook on the round table in the corner.
Use a plural pronoun to refer to two or more nouns joined by *and.*	**George Washington** and **James Madison** signed the Constitution. **They** became presidents.

Indefinite pronouns do not refer to a specific person, place, or thing. (See Lessons 7.3 and 10.3.) As the lists on the right show, some indefinite pronouns always require singular pronouns, and others always require plural pronouns.

Neither of the girls brought **her** notebook. [singular]

Many had finished **their** tours. [plural]

All, any, most, and *some* can be singular or plural.

Most of the handwriting is legible, isn't **it?** [singular, refers to *handwriting*]

Most of the students had **their** chance to see the document. [plural, refers to *students*]

Some Indefinite Pronouns

Singular

anybody	no one
anyone	nobody
anything	nothing
each	one
either	somebody
everybody	someone
everyone	something
neither	

Plural

both	many
few	several

Remember

If you're not sure whether to use a singular or plural pronoun, look for prepositional phrases in the sentence. Sometimes the object of a preposition can give you a clue about which pronoun is correct.

Some of the **guides** raised **their** voices. [plural]

Some of the **trip** lost **its** appeal. [singular]

ONLINE PRACTICE
www.grammarforwriting.com

Exercise 1 Choosing Correct Pronouns

Underline the pronoun that agrees with its antecedent.

EXAMPLE One of the boys forgot (their, his) ticket.

1. Many of the students took (their, his or her) map printouts.

2. Neither Sue nor Pam has (their, her) camera.

3. Each of the mothers brought (their, her) younger children.

4. Did someone forget (their, his or her) ticket?

5. Somebody left (their, his or her) jacket on the bus.

> **HINT**
>
> When the antecedent of a singular indefinite pronoun refers to males and females, use *his* or *her*, or rewrite the sentence.
>
> **No one** should eat **his** or **her** lunch yet.
>
> No one should eat lunch yet.

Exercise 2 Editing a Paragraph

On a separate sheet of paper, edit the paragraph below to correct all errors in pronoun-antecedent agreement.

EXAMPLE No one in the girls' group had their cell phone.

No one in the girls' group had her cell phone.

The National Archives

[1]The tour of the National Archives was fabulous, and everyone had their favorite part of the day. [2]Maria and Robyn liked her tour guides. [3]Neither of the boys liked the Magna Carta room as much as the Public Vaults. [4]Both of them agreed that his favorite part of the tour was the exhibit of telegrams from Abraham Lincoln to his or her generals. [5]One of the teachers, either Ms. Miller or Mrs. Martinez, said they appreciated our good behavior on this trip!

Copyright © 2014 by William H. Sadlier, Inc. All rights reserved.

Clear Pronoun Reference

LESSON 7.8

When you use pronouns, make sure that the reference for the pronoun is clear.

Pronoun reference is confusing if a pronoun could refer to more than one **antecedent.** Sometimes you can revise the sentence and substitute a noun for the unclear pronoun.

UNCLEAR Charlie and Manuel play varsity soccer. **He** trains five days a week. [Who trains?]

CLEAR Charlie and Manuel play varsity soccer. **Manuel** trains five days a week.

UNCLEAR Manuel's mother asked his aunt if **she** could attend the game. [Who can attend?]

CLEAR Manuel's mother asked if **his aunt** could attend the game.

Pronoun reference can also be confusing if a pronoun's antecedent is not stated. Rewrite the sentence to eliminate the unclear use of a pronoun, such as *it, they, this, that, these, those,* or *which.*

UNCLEAR In the playbook, **it** says not to throw long passes early in the game. [Who is *it*?]

CLEAR In the playbook, the **coaches** say not to throw long passes early in the game.

WRITING HINT

There is often more than one way to rewrite a sentence to correct a pronoun reference problem. For example, consider these possible revisions of the last sentence in the comic strip below. Can you think of others?

My teachers say that writers should write about what they know.

People always tell writers to write about familiar topics.

CALVIN AND HOBBES © (1994) Watterson. Dist. By UNIVERSAL PRESS SYNDICATE. Reprinted with permission. All rights reserved.

ONLINE PRACTICE
www.grammarforwriting.com

Exercise 1 Identifying Pronoun Reference Problems

Underline the pronouns with unclear references. Then rewrite each sentence to make the reference clear.

EXAMPLE Aaron and a friend saw two children drowning. He jumped into the water.

When Aaron and a friend saw two children drowning, Aaron jumped into the water.

1. Aaron rescued both children, but it was exhausting.
2. In the Red Cross manual, they say to call for help.
3. Aaron and his friend ran to a nearby store where he worked.
4. Aaron is strong. This helped him rescue two children at once.
5. The officers spoke to the children, and they were relieved.

Exercise 2 Revising a Paragraph

Working Together

Work with a partner. On a separate sheet of paper, revise the paragraph to correct any unclear pronoun references. You may add or delete words, substitute a noun, or combine sentences.

EXAMPLE In the article, she writes about hope.

In the article, the reporter writes about hope.

[1]They say there is no cure for cystic fibrosis. [2]Emily Schreiber got the diagnosis of the disease at the age of nine. [3]It fills the lungs with mucus and leads to infections that can be fatal. [4]She had the idea for a fund-raiser for cystic fibrosis just six weeks later. [5]She got this from reading a book in which the main character raises money by participating in a bike-a-thon. [6]All over the world, they raise money for charities by doing special events like these. [7]This makes participants feel good.

Copyright © 2014 by William H. Sadlier, Inc. All rights reserved.

WRITER'S WORKSHOP

Literary Analysis

When you closely examine and discuss key aspects of a text, you are analyzing literature. In a **literary analysis** you analyze a piece of literature, such as a poem, a novel, a short story, or a play. A literary analysis often focuses on one or two of the following elements:

- theme
- setting
- characters
- plot
- point of view

When you write a literary analysis, remember to include the following features.

Key Features

- thesis, or claim, that clearly states your comparison
- logical organization
- brief summary of the two texts
- evidence from the texts that supports your claim
- transitions that connect evidence with your claim

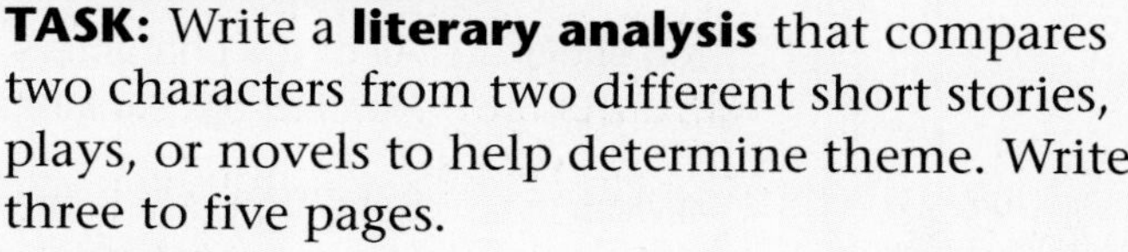

ASSIGNMENT

TASK: Write a **literary analysis** that compares two characters from two different short stories, plays, or novels to help determine theme. Write three to five pages.

AUDIENCE: people who have read both literary works

PURPOSE: to analyze the relationship between characters and theme in two pieces of literature, pointing to a deeper understanding of each

Remember

When you write about a literary work, always use the present tense.

Sam, the main character, **overcomes** difficult challenges.

Prewriting

Choose Your Works Make a list of literary works you've enjoyed. Briefly note the theme, characters, plot, and setting. Use the checklist to pick the two works you will compare:

- ✔ I have a strong opinion of both works.
- ✔ There are enough similarities to make a strong comparison.
- ✔ I can compare at least two characters.
- ✔ I can find enough text evidence to support my comparison.

Now, start thinking about which characters to compare.

- Which characters share common beliefs or attitudes?
- Do these characters change? How? Why?
- What do the comparisons point out about both books?

For more about developing a thesis, see **Lesson 5.2.**

What's Your Point? Organize your ideas into a **thesis,** or **claim,** that you will support in the rest of your essay. Include a reason for your comparison. Make your thesis neither too narrow nor too broad. Be concise, and write no more than two sentences.

TOO NARROW	The birds in *My Side of the Mountain* and *Hatchet* are mostly predators.
TOO BROAD	All of the characters in *My Side of the Mountain* and *Hatchet* are exciting.
REVISED	Sam, from *My Side of the Mountain,* and Brian, from *Hatchet,* both show independence and strength through determination and hard work. Their growth in the face of adversity reflects the theme of both books.

Copyright © 2014 by William H. Sadlier, Inc. All rights reserved.

Drafting

Organize the Details Review both books. Look for details about how the characters look and behave, what they say, and how they relate to other characters and the setting. Use a Venn diagram.

Use one of the types of organizations on the right to organize the body of your analysis.

Sam
• always wanted to live in the Catskill Mountains (p. 10)
• flees city to live in wilderness (p. 9)
• makes friends with a falcon (p. 44)
Both
• 13 years old
• determined, smart, independent
• struggle in the wild
• alone with limited resources
Brian
• struggling with parents' divorce (p. 2)
• stranded in Canadian wild (p. 33)
• has only a hatchet to help (p. 52)
• lives under rock overhang (p. 58)

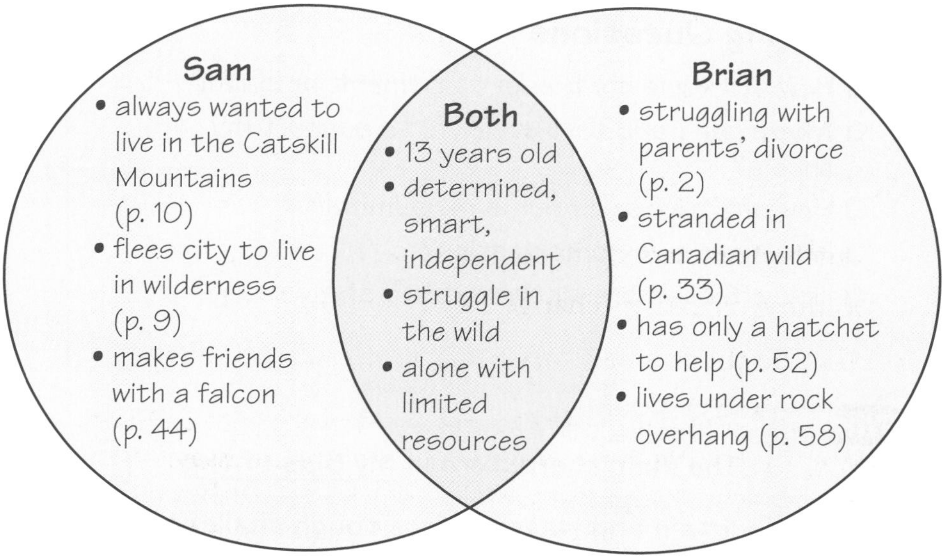

Include Every Part Include the three essay parts.

Introduction	Body	Conclusion
• includes thesis, or claim • catches readers' attention • includes a summary (no more than a few sentences long for each book) that states the titles, authors' names, key plot events, conflicts, and settings	• includes specific text evidence that supports the thesis • is logically organized • uses transitions between paragraphs and sentences	• restates the thesis • reviews the main points of the essay • leaves your audience with something to think about

Point-by-Point Organization

Focus on one feature at a time.

Feature 1: Independence
Subject A: Sam
Subject B: Brian

Feature 2: Strength
Subject A: Sam
Subject B: Brian

Block Method

Tell all the features about one subject first.

Subject A: Sam
Feature 1: Independence
Feature 2: Strength

Subject B: Brian
Feature 1: Independence
Feature 2: Strength

Revising

Use the Revising Questions to improve your draft. The model below shows the revision one writer made to an introduction.

See the next page for more about text evidence. As you revise, keep in mind the traits of good writing. See **Lesson 1.3.**

Revising Questions

- ❑ How strong is my thesis statement, or claim?
- ❑ Where can I add text evidence to support my thesis?
- ❑ How effective and brief is my summary?
- ❑ How clear is my organization?
- ❑ How effective are all three parts of my essay?

In the introduction, include a brief summary that mentions authors and titles.

Compare only two characters.

Include a clear and concise thesis statement, or claim.

Writing Model

[1]The main characters in My Side of the Mountain and Hatchet face tough challenges. [2]Sam, from ^Jean Craighead George's My Side of the Mountain, flees his home to live alone in the mountains. [3]Brian, from ^Gary Paulsen's Hatchet, is stranded in the wilderness after surviving a plane crash. ~~[4]They're like Julie, from Julie of the Wolves.~~ [5]While both are in the wild for different reasons, they share similar traits and experiences as they struggle to survive. ^Sam and Brian show independence and strength through determination and hard work.

Copyright © 2014 by William H. Sadlier, Inc. All rights reserved.

Revising

Include Text Evidence Your essay must include **text evidence,** or details from the texts you are analyzing. These details should be presented in the body of your essay and offered in support of your thesis, or claim. There are different ways to present text evidence. You can quote, summarize, or paraphrase.

Note the passage below. The chart that follows shows the three different methods for including text evidence.

Literary Model

[1]I was scared and thought maybe I'd never get out of my tree. [2]I had been scared for two days—ever since the first blizzard hit the Catskill Mountains. [3]When I came up to the sunlight, which I did by simply poking my head into the soft snow and standing up, I laughed at my dark fears.

—Excerpt from *My Side of the Mountain* by Jean Craighead George

Definition	Example
A **quotation** is the repetition of language from a source exactly as it was written. Place it in quotation marks.	Sam admits to being afraid and having "dark fears" the first two days.
A **summary** is a retelling in your own words. It should be at least two-thirds shorter than the original.	After several days, Sam explores outside and feels less frightened.
A **paraphrase** is also a retelling. However, a paraphrase can be as long as the original.	After the storm passes, Sam leaves his tree to explore the outside world. He is relieved to learn that his fears are unfounded.

Remember

Use a quotation when the wording is exceptionally strong and a paraphrase of it would lose its effect. However, avoid overloading your essay with quotations; use your own words most of the time.

Ask your teacher if you should include a page number in parentheses for a quotation or specific detail.

Editing and Proofreading

Use the Editing and Proofreading Checklist to check for errors in grammar, usage, mechanics, punctuation, and spelling. The model on the next page shows the corrections one writer made to the conclusion.

Editing and Proofreading Checklist

- ❑ Have I avoided sentence fragments and run-ons?
- ❑ Have I avoided pronoun reference problems?
- ❑ Have I checked that all pronouns agree with their antecedents?
- ❑ Are any words missing or run together?
- ❑ Is every paragraph indented?

For more help with pronoun reference, see **Lesson 7.8.**

Use Clear Pronoun Reference Pronouns, such as *she, it, they,* and *us,* are words that stand in for nouns. Pronouns must always refer to clear antecedents, or the nouns they are replacing.

UNCLEAR	Sam and his falcon sat silently. He looked at the sky. [Who looked?]
CLEAR	Sam and his falcon sat silently. Sam looked at the sky.
UNCLEAR	Brian explored and then decided to eat. This was good. [What was good?]
CLEAR	Brian explored and then decided to eat. This decision was good.

Copyright © 2014 by William H. Sadlier, Inc. All rights reserved.

Editing and Proofreading

Writing Model

[1]Brian and Sam are two very ~~curageous~~ courageous characters. [2]Both face dangerous obstacles with bravery and resolve. [3]Because of these challenges, Brian and Sam grow as people and learn about themselves and their families. [4]~~This~~ Growth in the face of adversity is the real theme of these two stories.

Proofreading Symbols

- Delete.
- ^ Add.
- ⊙ Add a period.
- # Add a space.

Publishing and Presenting

Choose one of these ways to share your literary analysis.

- **Interview classmates.** Ask those who have read the works you discuss to describe their opinions of the characters you compared.
- **Create a Web page.** Include your essay and other essays from your class. Invite students from other grades to look at your class's work
- **Illustrate your essay.** Draw the characters, settings, and the main actions from the texts you analyzed. Share your illustrated work with a family member.

Add your literary response to your **portfolio.** Before you do, ask yourself the following questions:

1. In what ways does this essay show clear improvements in my writing?
2. Compared to other pieces that appear in my portfolio, how successful is this essay?
3. What does this essay suggest about areas in which I could improve as a writer?

Reflect On Your Writing

- Which part or parts of your essay were easiest to write? Why?
- Which part or parts of your essay did you struggle with the most? Why?
- What have you learned about yourself as a writer?

CHAPTER 7

Chapter Review

A. Practice Test

Read each sentence below carefully. If you find an error, choose the underlined part that must be changed to make the sentence correct. Fill in the circle for the corresponding letter. If there is no error, fill in circle *E*.

EXAMPLE

Ⓐ Ⓑ Ⓒ Ⓓ Ⓔ When you plagiarize, <u>they</u> (A) use other <u>people's</u> (B) ideas in <u>your</u> (C) paper or project without <u>giving</u> (D) proper credit. <u>No error</u> (E)

Ⓐ Ⓑ Ⓒ Ⓓ Ⓔ **1.** If <u>they're</u> (A) not careful, <u>students</u> (B) may plagiarize unintentionally. <u>This</u> (C) is something <u>they</u> (D) need to watch out for. <u>No error</u> (E)

Ⓐ Ⓑ Ⓒ Ⓓ Ⓔ **2.** When <u>you</u> (A) use <u>your</u> (B) own words to paraphrase an <u>author's</u> (C) idea, it is necessary to give credit to <u>their</u> (D) idea. <u>No error</u> (E)

When identifying sentence errors, follow these tips:

1. Whenever you see a pronoun, look carefully for the word it replaces. Compare the two words, checking for agreement.
2. Remember that each item can contain no more than one error. If two underlined portions seem wrong, you need to read the sentence more carefully.

Copyright © 2014 by William H. Sadlier, Inc. All rights reserved.

Ⓐ Ⓑ Ⓒ Ⓓ Ⓔ **3.** However, if <u>you</u> [A] use facts that <u>are</u> [B] considered common knowledge, then <u>you don't</u> [C] have to cite <u>it</u> [D]. <u>No error</u> [E]

Ⓐ Ⓑ Ⓒ Ⓓ Ⓔ **4.** To see if a piece of information is common knowledge, ask <u>yourself</u> [A], "<u>Whom</u> [B] originally thought of <u>this</u> [C] idea?" Is <u>it something that most</u> [D] readers are likely to know? <u>No error</u> [E]

Ⓐ Ⓑ Ⓒ Ⓓ Ⓔ **5.** If <u>you</u> [A] are using an idea that is not <u>your's</u> [B], citing <u>its</u> [C] source is <u>your</u> [D] responsibility. <u>No error</u> [E]

B. Identifying Nouns and Pronouns

Read each sentence below. Label each underlined word with all the terms below that apply.

EXAMPLE Jake's <u>great-aunt</u> (CO) gave <u>him</u> (IO) a <u>basketball</u> (DO) for <u>his</u> (PP) birthday.

DO = direct object	IP = indefinite pronoun
IO = indirect object	PP = possessive pronoun
PN = predicate nominative	CO = compound noun
CN = collective noun	RP = reflexive pronoun

1. Armand gave <u>everyone</u> a <u>copy</u> of <u>his</u> notes.
2. Kay hurt <u>herself</u>, but <u>her</u> <u>team</u> won the <u>game</u>.
3. Clint Brennan is <u>my</u> <u>great-grandfather</u> and a <u>pilot</u>.
4. <u>Many</u> of the <u>five-year-olds</u> saw <u>their</u> <u>parents</u>.
5. <u>Both</u> of the boys gave the <u>cocker spaniel</u> <u>food</u>.
6. The <u>chorus</u> won several <u>awards</u>.
7. Lisa bought <u>Terri</u> new <u>earrings</u>.
8. Mr. Fox is the <u>chairman</u> of that <u>committee</u>.
9. <u>My</u> library doesn't have <u>either</u> of the books.
10. Ken asked <u>himself</u> where <u>everybody</u> went.

C. Choosing Nouns and Pronouns

In each sentence below, underline the correct noun or pronoun in parentheses.

1. Nate and Yolanda are throwing a surprise anniversary party for (they're, their) parents.
2. Cassie and (me, I) knew the plans were secret, but Nate let (us, him) in on the details.
3. Someone is going to call Mr. and Mrs. Rodriguez and invite (we and they, us and them) to dinner.
4. Mr. Taylor, (who, whom) I called yesterday, will help decorate.
5. Yolanda invited her (greats-aunt, great-aunts), and she hopes (they, them) come to the party.
6. (Whom, Who) will be bringing the flowers?
7. The (childrens', children's) table will look colorful.
8. Either Mary or Cassie will bring (their, her) camera.
9. From (who, whom) did the neighbors find out about the party?
10. The brains behind the celebration are Nate, Yolanda, and (we, us).
11. Are the gifts at our house or (yours, your's)?
12. The invitation says for each person to bring (his or her, their) favorite game.
13. Nate and Yolanda hope (their, they're) parents are happy.
14. Surprise (parties, party's) are always fun!
15. After the party, the (guests, guest's) will help clean up.

D. Proofreading a Literary Analysis

Use proofreading symbols to correct any errors in noun or pronoun usage in the draft on the facing page. Then answer the questions.

Proofreading Symbols	
ℽ Delete.	/ Make lowercase.
∧ Add.	≡ Capitalize.
⊙ Add a period.	∽ Switch order.

Copyright © 2014 by William H. Sadlier, Inc. All rights reserved.

Chapter Review

[1]*The Outsiders* was a pretty good book. [2]It is about two gangs, rich and poor, and how their hatred destroys some of his lives.

[3]One of the main characters names is Ponyboy. [4]Ponyboy has two brothers, and his names' are Darry and Sodapop. [5]The one thing my friend Sophie didn't like about the book was the nicksname the family members have for themselfs. [6]They asked my friend Jon and I to explain why the author likes such weird names. [7]They didn't bother he or I, though.

[8]One gang is made up of the rich kids, and them and the poor kids are always fighting. [9]By the end of the Books plot, a lot of peoples' lives are ruined or lost. [10]Ponyboy relates to a line from one of Robert Frosts poems. [11]He wrote, "Nothing gold can stay." [12]This symbolizes how the happy time of young peoples lives must make way for the difficult lessons of growing up.

1. What is the strongest part of this essay? On what should the writer elaborate more?

2. Aside from grammar, usage, and punctuation errors, what is the weakest part of this essay? What should the writer delete?

CHAPTER 8

Verbs

Copyright © 2014 by William H. Sadlier, Inc. All rights reserved.

Using Verbs

LESSON 8.1

A **verb** is a word used to express an action or a state of being. The two main types of verbs are action and linking verbs.

An **action verb (V)** tells what the subject does. It expresses an action that may be either physical or mental.

> That Ferris wheel **moves** (V) very quickly.
> [physical action]
>
> We **enjoyed** (V) the view from the top.
> [mental action]

Some action verbs take a direct object **(DO)**. (See Lesson 6.5 to review direct objects.)

> George Ferris **built** (V) his first giant **wheel** (DO) in 1893.

A **linking verb (LV)** joins, or links, its subject to a subject complement **(SC)**, a word or group of words that identifies or describes the subject. (For more about subject complements, see Lesson 6.6.)

> Ferris **was** (LV) a **bridgemaker** (SC) and a creative **thinker.** (SC)
>
> People **were** (LV) **amazed** (SC) by the thirty-six wooden cars.

Some verbs can function as action verbs in one sentence and linking verbs in another.

> When Angela **looked** (V) down, she **looked** (LV) nervous.

Remember that a sentence may have more than one verb. Some verbs consist of a **verb phrase,** which is made up of a **main verb (MV)** and at least one **helping verb (HV)**.

> When the structure **was** (HV) **finished,** (MV) it **stood** (MV) at 264 feet.
>
> **Have** (HV) you ever **ridden** (MV) a Ferris wheel?

Linking Verb:

Some Forms of *Be*

am	are	is
was	were	being
can be		have been
will be		should be
would have been		

Some Other Linking Verbs

appear	remain
become	seem
feel	smell
grow	sound
look	taste

Some Helping Verbs

be (is, am, are, was, were, be, been, being)
have (has, have, had)
do (does, do, did)

can	could	may
might	must	shall
should	will	would

Remember

Not or *n't* is never part of a verb phrase.

EXERCISE Identifying Verbs

Underline every verb and verb phrase in the sentences below, including helping verbs. Then circle all the linking verbs. **Hint:** Two sentences contain compound verbs. (See Lesson 6.4.)

1. Many people believe in good luck charms.
2. Haven't you ever worn a lucky shirt, carried a lucky coin, or avoided the number thirteen?
3. The horseshoe is a common symbol of good fortune.
4. Some people are certain that an acorn gives the gift of youth.
5. Friends gave President Theodore Roosevelt a rabbit's foot.
6. In many cultures around the world, superstitions are common.
7. My grandmother will not walk underneath an open ladder, step on a crack in the sidewalk, or place a hat on a bed.
8. Could a broken mirror possibly bring bad luck for seven years?
9. Superstitions about black cats seem ridiculous, but many people believe them.
10. However, I will not be discarding my lucky four-leaf clover!

Write What You Think

On a separate sheet of paper, write a brief paragraph that explains your answer to the question below:

Do you agree that two wrongs don't make a right? If yes, give a couple of examples. If not, explain why not.

1. Use a variety of linking and action verbs. After you have finished writing, underline each verb.
2. Exchange papers with a partner. Read each other's paragraphs, and check that all the verbs are underlined.

Copyright © 2014 by William H. Sadlier, Inc. All rights reserved.

LESSON 8.2

Regular and Irregular Verbs

All verbs have four **principal parts,** or basic forms.

Present	I **watch** old movies.
Present Participle	He is **watching** the game.
Past	They **watched** the dogs.
Past Participle	We had **watched** the show before.

Notice that helping verbs are used with the present participle and past participle. (See Lesson 8.1 for more about helping verbs.)

Most English verbs are regular. All **regular verbs** add *-d* or *-ed* to the present to form the past and past participle. They form the present participle by adding *-ing* to the present.

Present	Present Participle (Use with *am, is, are, was, were.*)	Past	Past Participle (Use with *has, have, had.*)
paint	(is) paint**ing**	paint**ed**	(had) paint**ed**
cry	(is) cry**ing**	cri**ed**	(had) cri**ed**
plan	(is) plan**ning**	plan**ned**	(had) plan**ned**

As the chart above shows, when you add *-ing* or *-ed* to the present form of a verb, you may need to change the spelling of some verbs. (See Lesson 12.6 for spelling rules.)

Irregular verbs do not form the past and past participle by adding *-d* or *-ed*. In some cases, the past and the past participle forms of an irregular verb are spelled the same. Often, however, the past and past participle are not the same. (See Lesson 8.3 for more about irregular verbs.)

Present	Present Participle (Use with *am, is, are, was, were.*)	Past	Past Participle (Use with *has, have, had.*)
teach	(is) teach**ing**	taught	(had) taught
go	(is) go**ing**	went	(had) gone
choose	(is) choos**ing**	chose	(had) chosen

TEST-TAKING TIP

Many standardized tests ask you to identify and correct errors in the past form of many verbs.

Be sure to add the *-d* or *-ed* ending of regular verbs.

Yesterday he use**d** up the paint.

ONLINE PRACTICE
www.grammarforwriting.com

EXERCISE 1 Identifying Verb Forms

On a separate sheet of paper, write *present, present participle, past,* or *past participle* for the verb form(s) underlined in the passage below.

Literary Model

[1]Principal Long was reading a newspaper. [2]She raised her head and peered through her glasses to see who had interrupted her. [3]"Principal Long, here is a note from my father." [4]Hastily I gave her the note, damp with sweat from my palm. [5]I hurried out of the office before she could look at it or ask me any questions.

—Excerpt from *Red Scarf Girl: A Memoir of the Cultural Revolution* by Ji Li Jiang

EXERCISE 2 Choosing Correct Verbs

Draw a line under the correct verb form in the parentheses. Label the verb as *R* (regular) or *I* (irregular).

HINT

Check an online dictionary if you are unsure about an irregular verb form.

The past and participle forms are listed after the present form and the pronunciation.

give (gĭv), **gave, given, giving**

If no verb forms are shown, the verb is regular.

1. The planning had (begin, begun) last September.
2. The town had (vote, voted) to fund the addition last year.
3. Everyone (knowed, knew) that the school was overcrowded.
4. School officials have (work, worked) with the architects before.
5. They (asked, had ask) for advice from many community residents.
6. They (made, have maked) the plans available online.
7. Have you (saw, seen) the size of the new auditorium?
8. Everybody in town has (trying, tried) to be patient.
9. Many have (come, came) to see how the construction was progressing, had progress).
10. Next month we are (planning, planned) a dedication.

Copyright © 2014 by William H. Sadlier, Inc. All rights reserved.

More Irregular Verbs

LESSON
8.3

Irregular verbs do not form the past and past participle by adding *-d* or *-ed*. They form their past and past participle forms in a variety of ways. Refer to this list of common irregular verbs, or consult a dictionary if you are unsure about the correct form.

Present	Present Participle (Use with *am, is, are, was, were.*)	Past	Past Participle (Use with *has, have, had.*)
become	(is) becoming	became	(had) become
break	(is) breaking	broke	(had) broken
bring	(is) bringing	brought	(had) brought
come	(is) coming	came	(had) come
drive	(is) driving	drove	(had) driven
eat	(is) eating	ate	(had) eaten
fall	(is) falling	fell	(had) fallen
give	(is) giving	gave	(had) given
grow	(is) growing	grew	(had) grown
lay	(is) laying	laid	(had) laid
make	(is) making	made	(had) made
put	(is) putting	put	(had) put
ride	(is) riding	rode	(had) ridden
run	(is) running	ran	(had) run
see	(is) seeing	saw	(had) seen
show	(is) showing	showed	(had) shown
sing	(is) singing	sang	(had) sung
speak	(is) speaking	spoke	(had) spoken
take	(is) taking	took	(had) taken
think	(is) thinking	thought	(had) thought
throw	(is) throwing	threw	(had) thrown
wear	(is) wearing	wore	(had) worn
win	(is) winning	won	(had) won

For more about irregular verbs, see **Lesson 8.2.**

Remember

To function as verbs, both present and past participles need a helping verb.

INCORRECT She seen Scott. He driving the convertible.

CORRECT She **had** seen Scott. He **was** driving the convertible.

Exercise 1 Correcting Verb Forms

On a separate sheet of paper, rewrite the paragraph to correct the incorrect forms of irregular verbs. Check a dictionary if needed.

EXAMPLE The coaches have already gave instructions.

The coaches have already given instructions.

[1]A question has arise about sports in our middle school. [2]Our soccer, wrestling, and football coaches have show their leadership ability over the years. [3]They have lead many successful individual athletes and teams. [4]After students have took a physical examination and choosed a sport, they may participate if their grades have not fell. [5]Students will not be allowed on a playing field or in the gym if they have forgot their signed permission form from a parent or guardian.

Exercise 2 Using Irregular Verbs

Write the correct form of the verb in parentheses.

1. The girls' team has (win) nineteen games in a row.
2. Yesterday Tyrus (lay) his football on his locker shelf.
3. Why hasn't Kenan (catch) a ball yet?
4. I have (do) my best to attend every practice.
5. When she (see) the score, Leila (run) to her friends.
6. After we (go) to the game, we (speak) to the coaches.
7. Before today, Ivan had (swim) that race two times.
8. The referee should have (give) us more time.
9. I (shake) Kerry's hand before the race (begin).
10. Samra had (drink) eight glasses of water right before she (break) the pole vault record.

HINT

Do not confuse the verbs *lay* and *lie*. *Lay* means "to place something," and *lie* means "to rest or to be located on a surface."

PRESENT	lay	lie
PAST	laid	lay
PAST PARTICIPLE	(had) laid	(had) lain

Copyright © 2014 by William H. Sadlier, Inc. All rights reserved.

Simple and Perfect Tenses

LESSON 8.4

The **tense** of a verb shows the time of an action, a condition, or a state of being.

English verbs have three **simple tenses** (present, past, and future) and three **perfect tenses** (present perfect, past perfect, and future perfect).

Tense	What It Shows	Examples
Present	action happening now, action that happens repeatedly	I **eat** lunch. I **eat** every evening at 5 P.M.
Past	action completed in the past	World War II **ended** in 1945.
Future	action that will happen in the future	Our class **will (shall) go** to Washington, D.C.
Present Perfect	action completed recently or in the indefinite past	We **have stayed** at the hotel before.
Past Perfect	action that happened before another past action	We **had left** before Al arrived.
Future Perfect	action that will happen before a future time or action	We **will have traveled** six hours by midnight.

Notice the simple and perfect tenses in the model below. The author uses the past perfect tense to show two things that happened before 1946.

Literary Model

[1]By 1946, fifty years after the Supreme Court's decision in *Plessy v. Ferguson*, both the Court and the people of the United States had changed. [2]The country had just emerged victorious from World War II, and there was a general sense of well-being and prosperity.

—Excerpt from *Freedom Rides: Journey for Justice* by James Haskins

CONNECTING Writing & Grammar

To show an ongoing action or state of being, use the **progressive form** of each tense. It consists of a form of the verb *be* plus the present participle (*-ing*) form.

PRESENT	(am, is, are) reading
PAST	(was, were) reading
FUTURE	(will, shall) be reading
PRESENT PERFECT	(has, have) been reading
PAST PERFECT	(had) been reading
FUTURE PERFECT	(will, shall) have been reading

ONLINE PRACTICE
www.grammarforwriting.com

Exercise 1 Identifying Tenses

Underline the verb in each of the following sentences, and label the tense. Remember to underline helping verbs. **Hint:** Four of the five sentences have a verb phrase with at least one helping verb.

EXAMPLE Katherine Dunham was a dancer. *past*

1. Bessie Smith's first record sold more than two million copies.
2. Josephine Baker had worked as a spy during World War II.
3. How long will jazz remain popular?
4. Mr. Gold has read many poems by Langston Hughes.
5. By next week, I will have read several of the poems.

Exercise 2 Changing Tenses

Work with a partner. Change each verb to a past perfect form, and rewrite the paragraph.

Langston Hughes

[1]Before the Harlem Renaissance in the 1920s, many African-American poets are not feeling comfortable writing about their experiences. [2]In fact, such expression is not possible. [3]The Harlem Renaissance changes things signficantly during that time. [4]It gives writers, musicians, and performers a chance to express themselves freely.

Use the past participle form with the helping verb *had* to form the past perfect tense.

Exercise 3 Using Verb Tenses

Imagine that you are writing the biography of a friend or family member. Write a paragraph that tells about an incident or experience from that person's childhood. Use strong verbs, and check your writing for verb tense correctness.

Copyright © 2014 by William H. Sadlier, Inc. All rights reserved.

Shifts in Tense

LESSON 8.5

Remember to keep **verb tenses** as consistent as possible.

➡ Use verbs in the same tense to describe events that occur at the same time. (See Lesson 8.4 for more about verb tense.)

INCONSISTENT The cars **are** clean. They **shone** in the sunlight. [*Are* is present tense, and *shone* is past tense.]

CONSISTENT The cars **are** clean. They **shine** in the sunlight. [*Are* and *shine* are present tense.]

➡ Sometimes, a shift in tense within a sentence or a paragraph is necessary. Use different tenses to make the order of events clear.

DIFFERENT TENSES The cars that **were** cleaned today **are** shiny now, but they **will be** dull after a few days. [The cars were washed in the past, they are shiny in the present, and their appearance will change in the future.]

➡ When you write about literary works, such as books or plays, use the **present tense** to describe the characters and their actions—even if the events took place in the past.

The main character, Juan, **washes** his father's car and **cleans** the interior.

➡ Shifts in mood are also common verb errors. **Mood** expresses attitude in a sentence. The **subjunctive mood** and the **conditional mood** often cause difficulty.

INCORRECT Carla wishes she **was** a car expert. [*Was* is in the indicative mood.]

CORRECT Carla wishes she **were** a car expert. [*Were* is in the subjunctive mood.]

WRITING HINT

Verbs have different moods. You probably use the first three quite naturally. Learn to use the last two correctly.

- Use the **indicative mood** to make a statement.
  The cars are valuable.
- Use the **interrogative mood** to ask a question.
  Are the cars valuable?
- Use the **imperative mood** to make a command or request.
  Show me that car.
- Use the **conditional mood** to express something hypothetical.
  If I could, I would buy rare cars.
- Use the **subjunctive mood** to express a statement (such as a wish) contrary to fact.
  I wish I were at a car convention instead.

Exercise 1 Making Tenses Consistent

On a separate sheet of paper, rewrite any of the sentences below that shift tenses needlessly. If a sentence is correct, write *C*.

EXAMPLE Keith was happy when he has won the contest.

Keith was happy when he won the contest.

1. Everyone congratulated Keith and wishes him well.

2. The crowd applauds and yelled his name.

ONLINE PRACTICE
www.grammarforwriting.com

3. Kerri will call Keith today and visited him tomorrow.

4. Because Keith has sung with the band for years, he will acquire a large following.

5. He plays the piano and writes the lyrics.

EXERCISE 2 Correcting Verb Tenses

On a separate sheet of paper, rewrite the paragraph below to correct needless shifts in verb tense.

EXAMPLE Omar's lessons had started before he is five.

Omar's lessons had started before he was five.

HINT

Several of the incorrect verbs are irregular. Review **Lesson 8.3**, and consult an online dictionary if you are not sure how to spell a verb form.

[1]His sisters' singing career begins in 1999 after they had graduated from high school. [2]They auditioned for many jobs, but they finally will become famous in 2003. [3]The trio had topped the charts for three years when they lose their lead singer. [4]After the group disbands in 2007, the members go their own ways. [5]Perhaps in the future, they will reunite, and crowds packed their concerts again.

EXERCISE 3 Writing About a Character

Choose a character from a favorite book. Write a short paragraph in present tense that tells what the character does. In your paragraph, include one sentence in the imperative and one in the subjunctive mood. Proofread and correct any shifts in tense or mood.

Copyright © 2014 by William H. Sadlier, Inc. All rights reserved.

LESSON 8.6

Active and Passive Voice

A verb is in the **active voice** when the subject performs the action of the verb. A verb is in the **passive voice** when the subject receives the action of the verb.

ACTIVE The soldiers **built** a fire.

PASSIVE A fire **was built** by the soldiers.

ACTIVE Anderson **told** his men stories.

PASSIVE His men **were told** stories by Anderson.

Use the active voice when you write because it gives your writing energy. It puts the focus on the subject and helps make your writing forceful. Active voice sentences are also less wordy.

ACTIVE In April of 1775, Paul Revere **warned** the patriots about the British soldiers. [13 words]

PASSIVE In April of 1775, the patriots **were warned** about the British soldiers by Paul Revere. [15 words]

Passive voice sentences are useful if you don't know who performed the action or if you don't want to emphasize the performer.

The American Navy **was organized** before the Declaration of Independence.
[The organizer is unknown.]

An error **was made** in our project about John Adams.
[The writer does not want to identify who made the error.]

To change a passive sentence into an active sentence, you can often turn the object of a preposition into the subject.

PASSIVE The map was studied by **Adri**.

ACTIVE **Adri** studied the map.

Maintain consistent voice (active or passive) as you write.

INCONSISTENT The Declaration of Independence was written by Thomas Jefferson, and Congress approved it.

CONSISTENT ACTIVE VOICE Thomas Jefferson wrote the Declaration of Independence, and Congress approved it.

WRITING HINT

The passive voice uses more words than the active voice. A verb in the passive voice always uses some form of the verb *be* as a helping verb. See **Lesson 2.5** for tips about eliminating wordiness.

ONLINE PRACTICE
www.grammarforwriting.com

Exercise 1 Using the Active Voice

Sitting Bull

On a separate sheet of paper, rewrite the sentences below using the active voice. If the passive voice is useful, explain why.

EXAMPLE Their old way of life was lost by the Sioux people.

The Sioux people lost their old way of life.

1. The Sioux tribe was given its name by Chippewa Indians.
2. Lives of freedom were once enjoyed by the Sioux.
3. Horses were introduced to the Sioux by the Spanish in the 1500s.
4. The Sioux lifestyle was destroyed by the loss of buffalo.
5. Better times were predicted by a Sioux prophet.
6. Much of the Sioux land was taken over.
7. During the Gold Rush, it was the belief of many people that gold was located on Sioux land.
8. A fierce battle was led by the legendary Chief Sitting Bull.
9. General Custer's troops were defeated by Sitting Bull's warriors in 1876.
10. Sitting Bull was killed in 1890 and was buried in North Dakota.

Exercise 2 Beginning a Story

Imagine you are writing a short story set in the 1800s—perhaps about a Sioux warrior, a pioneer family, or a soldier. Write with a partner, and check for inappropriate shifts in active and passive voice. Correct any errors you find.

1. Make up names, places, and details as necessary. Write at least seven sentences.
2. Use a variety of strong verbs in the active voice.
3. When you have finished writing, ask another group to read and respond to your opening. How effective are the verbs?

Copyright © 2014 by William H. Sadlier, Inc. All rights reserved.

LESSON 8.7

Participles and Participial Phrases

A **verbal** is a verb form that acts like a different part of speech. Participles, gerunds, and infinitives are the three kinds of verbals. (See Lessons 3.5, 8.8, and 8.9.)

A **participle** acts like an adjective and modifies a noun or pronoun. Participles have **present** and **past** forms.

	How to Form It	Examples
Present Participle	Add *-ing* to the present form of a verb.	The **yawning** cab driver opened the door. **Smiling** and **waving,** the candidate appeared.
Past Participle	Add *-ed* or *-d* to a regular verb, or use the past participle of an irregular verb.	With a **recognized** name, Jones is the party's **chosen** candidate. Sam handed Jones a packet of **written** notes.

A participle with modifiers makes up a **participial phrase.** Participial phrases may include prepositional phrases, modifiers, and objects. The whole phrase acts like an adjective.

Tired but determined, Sam worked hard.

The candidate, **knowing Sam's total dedication to the campaign,** thanked him.

To make your meaning clear, place a participial phrase as close as possible to the word it modifies. (See Lesson 9.5.)

CONFUSING We watched the debaters **eating our dinner.** [Were the debaters eating the dinner?]

CLEAR **Eating our dinner,** we watched the debaters.

Use a comma to set off a participial phrase that comes at the beginning of a sentence or that adds additional, nonessential information. See **Lesson 11.3.**

Standing by the microphone, William smiled.

Sam, **holding the phone in one hand,** looked exhausted.

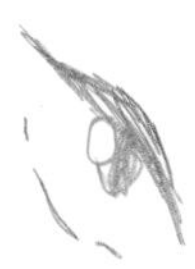

ONLINE PRACTICE
www.grammarforwriting.com

HINT

Remember to underline any prepositional phrases that are part of a participial phrase.

Exhausted **by our busy schedule,** we fell asleep.

Exercise 1 Identifying Participles and Participial Phrases

Underline the participle or participial phrase in each sentence. Then circle the noun or pronoun it modifies.

EXAMPLE Having lived in Europe, Mary Cassatt returned to the United States in 1855.

1. Cassatt's paintings received growing attention from critics.
2. Held in New York City in 1893, her first solo show was a success.
3. Abandoning needleworking, Grandma Moses turned to art in her seventies.
4. Her hidden talent surprised many art critics.
5. American painter John Singer Sargent, traveling throughout Europe, worked with great artists such as Pissarro and Monet.
6. Concentrating on portraits and landscapes, he enjoyed a successful career.
7. French artist Henri Matisse was a leading figure in modern art.
8. *La Danse* is one of his most inspiring paintings.
9. Jackson Pollock sometimes mixed sand and broken glass.
10. Much of Pollock's work features paint spattered on the canvas.

Remember

Check that you have used the phrases as adjectives, not as verb phrases. When you put a helping verb before a participle, you create a verb phrase. See **Lesson 8.1.**

PARTICIPIAL PHRASE **Grabbing a brush,** Claire was excited.

VERB PHRASE Farah **was grabbing** a brush.

Exercise 2 Writing a Paragraph

On a separate sheet of paper, write a narrative or descriptive paragraph using at least five of the following participles and participial phrases.

1. crouched under a tree
2. surprised
3. pointing to the door
4. surrounded by friends
5. moving quickly
6. running in circles
7. confused
8. laughing softly
9. leaning over
10. winning the race

Copyright © 2014 by William H. Sadlier, Inc. All rights reserved.

LESSON 8.8

Gerunds and Gerund Phrases

Like participles and infinitives, a gerund is a **verbal,** a word formed from a verb that is not used as a verb in a sentence.

A **gerund** acts like a noun. To form a gerund, add *-ing* to a verb. The chart below shows four ways that gerunds are commonly used.

Subject	Jana's **writing** is sloppy.
Predicate Noun	Her hobby is **running.**
Direct Object	We finished **eating.**
Object of a Preposition	I need advice about **cooking.**

A **gerund phrase** includes the gerund and its modifiers. The modifiers can be adjectives, adverbs, and prepositional phrases. The entire gerund phrase acts like a noun in the sentence.

Sasha likes **writing stories.** [direct object]

Biking long distances is great exercise. [subject]

The passage below include three gerunds. Two are used as subjects (*boasting, posturing*), and one is used as the object of a preposition (*winning*).

Remember

Like gerunds, present participles end in *-ing*. However, a participle acts like an adjective, and a gerund acts like a noun.

PARTICIPLE Jose's **editing** checklist is lost.

GERUND Your **editing** is good.

Literary Model

[1]In the eyes of her teammates, she was a brash and self-centered young woman, and she was judged harshly. [2]But her boasting, more than anything, was a display of the confidence she felt in her abilities and an expression of her joy in winning. [3]An athlete needs that kind of confidence to be a winner. [4]If Babe had been a young male athlete, her boastful posturing would have been considered healthy and natural. [5]As a young woman during the early 1930s, however, she was expected to be modest and demure.

—Excerpt from *Babe Didrikson Zaharias: The Making of a Champion* by Russell Freedman

Babe Didrikson Zaharias

ONLINE PRACTICE
www.grammarforwriting.com

HINT

Underline any prepositional phrases that are part of the gerund phrase.

Practicing **in the rain** frustrates me.

Exercise 1 Identifying Phrases

Underline each gerund and gerund phrase in the sentences below. Label each *S* for subject, *PN* for predicate noun, *DO* for direct object, or *OP* for object of the preposition.

___ **1.** My friends and I enjoy playing Ping-Pong on Saturdays.

___ **2.** Being an Olympic gymnast is Kirsti's long-term goal.

___ **3.** Barry likes lifting weights daily.

___ **4.** The coach is in charge of designing the plays.

___ **5.** Heather is tired of training.

___ **6.** Neil practiced making free throws.

___ **7.** Falling on ice caused Mary to break her arm.

___ **8.** The fan stopped the skater from crashing into the seats.

___ **9.** The hardest task for Sally was adjusting her goggles.

___ **10.** My teammates heard the loud ringing of the bells.

For more about direct objects, predicate nouns, and objects of a preposition, see **Lessons 6.5, 6.6,** and **9.6.**

Exercise 2 Writing from Notes

With a partner, write a paragraph based on the notes below. Include at least three sentences with a gerund or gerund phrase.

- physical benefits of aerobic exercise
  - —strengthens heart
  - —lowers blood pressure
- psychological benefits of aerobic exercise
  - —reduces tension
  - —promotes relaxation
- examples = running, walking, swimming, biking, dancing
- recommendation = 30 minutes a day

Copyright © 2014 by William H. Sadlier, Inc. All rights reserved.

Infinitives and Infinitive Phrases

An infinitive, like a participle and a gerund, is a **verbal,** a verb form that does not function like a verb in a sentence.

The word *to* plus a verb signals an **infinitive.** An infinitive acts likes a noun, an adjective, or an adverb.

NOUN	**To camp** can be difficult.
ADJECTIVE	One way **to cook** is over a fire.
ADVERB	The campers are ready **to leave.**

Do not confuse a prepositional phrase beginning with *to* with an infinitive. In an infinitive, a verb follows *to*. In a prepositional phrase, a noun or pronoun follows *to*.

INFINITIVE	We don't know where **to go**.
PREPOSITIONAL PHRASE	We went **to the drug store**.

Most infinitives begin with the word *to*. However, infinitives may appear without it, as the model below shows.

Literary Model

[1]The children pushed into the tent as if they were still outdoors. [2]Tripping over themselves, they were about to pull the tent down around them. [3]M. C. hurried in to organize them, motioning them not to speak, nor to touch or bump into anything.

—Excerpt from *M. C. Higgins, the Great* by Virginia Hamilton

In the last infinitive, *to* is understood: (*to*) *bump*.

An **infinitive phrase** is made up of an infinitive and all the words that complete its meaning. These words may include prepositional phrases, modifiers, or objects. The entire phrase functions as a noun, an adjective, or an adverb.

To go camping in August is Bianca's goal.
[noun, subject]

Wool socks will help **to keep us warm.**
[adverb modifying the verb *will help*]

ONLINE PRACTICE
www.grammarforwriting.com

Exercise 1 Identifying Infinitive Phrases

Not every *to* introduces an infinitive.

Underline each infinitive and infinitive phrase in the sentences below. Remember to underline the entire phrase, including any prepositional phrases and modifiers.

1. Some crocodiles can grow to be fifteen feet long.
2. Before Fido goes to the park, I need to find his leash.
3. When we open the door to the cage, the hamster tries to scurry out.
4. To the beach is where we like to take Muffy and Patches.
5. Blowing snow began to cover the coyote's paw prints.

Exercise 2 Writing About a Photo

On a separate sheet of paper, write five sentences based on the photo below. Use at least three infinitives.

Write What You Think

On a separate sheet of paper, write a brief response to the following question. Give reasons and evidence to support your opinion. Use at least three infinitives, and underline them.

Should pet owners be allowed to bring their dogs or cats into restaurants or shops? Why or why not?

Copyright © 2014 by William H. Sadlier, Inc. All rights reserved.

Poem

Poems, a kind of creative writing, contain words that are carefully chosen for their meaning, the way they look and sound, and the feelings they evoke in readers. Poems can take different shapes and use different techniques.

Poems...

- often evoke feelings
- contain striking images and details that appeal to the senses
- can be silly, sentimental, or action packed
- may include stanzas, or groups of lines
- have lines that can be a single word, a group of words, or a complete sentence
- may have a variety of musical sounds
- may have a specific form, such as a sonnet

When you write a poem, include the following features.

Key Features

- focus on a specific subject
- precise and original word choice
- sound devices
- figurative language and sensory details

ASSIGNMENT

TASK: Write a free-verse **poem** about something or someone you have seen. Free-verse poems do not use regular rhythms or rhymes. (See Writing Model on page 219.)

PURPOSE: to describe a person, an animal, an object, or an event

AUDIENCE: your family members and friends

KEY INSTRUCTIONS: Write at least ten lines.

WRITING HINT

Read your draft aloud to yourself. Include a sound device.

Alliteration is the repetition of consonant sounds at the beginnings of words.

a tower of tangled trees

Consonance is the repetition of consonant sounds in the middle or at the ends of words.

the broken rocks and bricks

Find a Subject Brainstorm a list of subjects. Your list could include events from your own life, specific feelings or ideas, or memorable people and places. Be creative! Use these guidelines to narrow your list:

1. You find your subject interesting and want to share your feelings or ideas about it.
2. You think an audience would enjoy reading about your subject.
3. You can easily think of colorful and vivid details to describe your subject.

Choose Your Words Carefully Compared to novels or short stories, most modern poems are very short. So, choose your words carefully.

- Pay attention to **denotation,** or a word's dictionary definition, and to **connotation,** or the feelings that a word evokes. (See Lesson 2.7.)
- Choose colorful words that best express the exact ideas you are trying to convey. Try repeating key words for emphasis.
- Choose specific **sensory details** that appeal to the five senses (touch, smell, sight, sound, and taste).
- Use strong verbs that emphasize the actor or action you are trying to describe. Passive or imprecise verbs will cloud your meaning. (See Lessons 2.6 and 8.6.)

WEAK The street was walked down by the cats.

STRONG The cats marched down the street.

Copyright © 2014 by William H. Sadlier, Inc. All rights reserved.

Use Your Imagination Make your descriptions vivid, detailed, and unique. Use the following types of **figurative language,** or language not meant to be taken literally.

Metaphor	A metaphor is a comparison between two unlike things that does not use the word *like* or *as.*	The dress **was a splash of blue and green.**
Simile	A simile is a comparison between two unlike things that uses the word *like* or *as.*	The bright kites were **like colorful stars in the daytime sky.**

Use the Writing Checklist to review your draft. The model below shows one writer's poem.

WRITING CHECKLIST

Did you...

- ✔ focus on a specific subject?
- ✔ use precise language and sensory details?
- ✔ use figurative language?
- ✔ use sound devices?
- ✔ write at least ten lines?

Writing Model

Through the fence, I spy
the polar bear sprawling on a slab of stone.
He places his paw to protect his face
as if to hide from the curious crowd.
His fur gleams white like computer paper,
and his eyes are like black buttons.
Four o'clock means feeding time.
The zookeeper lugs a bucket to the edge
of the fake Arctic atmosphere.
He flicks fish upwards, and the bear
lunges forward, tearing them apart with his teeth.
After lunch, the bear sprawls on a slab stone.

Alliteration

Similes

Consonance

Repetition of key words

CHAPTER 8

Chapter Review

A. Practice Test

Read each sentence below carefully. Decide which answer choice best replaces the underlined part, and fill in the circle of the correct letter of the sentence. If you think the underlined part is correct, fill in the circle for choice *A*.

EXAMPLE

Ⓐ Ⓑ Ⓒ Ⓓ Ⓔ In October 1972, a plane carrying an amateur rugby team has crashing in the Andes Mountains.
(A) has crashing
(B) had crashing
(C) crashing
(D) will crash
(E) crashed

Ⓐ ● Ⓒ Ⓓ Ⓔ **1.** The white plane landed in the snow, so it was not saw easily.
(A) landed in the snow, so it was not saw
(B) landed in the snow, so it was not seen
(C) was landing in the snow, so it was not seen
(D) was landing in the snow, so not being seen
(E) lands in the snow, so it was not saw

Ⓐ Ⓑ Ⓒ ● Ⓔ **2.** Thirty-three passengers were surviving the crash, but they have not prepared for exposure to subzero temperatures.
(A) were surviving the crash, but they have not prepared
(B) survive the crash, but they will not have prepared
(C) had survive the crash, but they will be unprepared
(D) survived the crash, but they had not prepared
(E) had survived the crash, but they have not prepare

Copyright © 2014 by William H. Sadlier, Inc. All rights reserved.

Ⓐ Ⓑ Ⓒ ● Ⓔ **3.** Little food was had by the survivors, and as days turning into weeks, a difficult situation got worse.

(A) Little food was had by the survivors, and as days turning into weeks,

(B) Little food was had by the survivors, and, as days turned into weeks,

(C) The survivors had little food, and as days will have turned into weeks,

(D) The survivors had little food, and as days turned into weeks,

(E) The survivors had little food, and as days will be turning into weeks,

● Ⓑ Ⓒ Ⓓ Ⓔ **4.** Without question, it must have taken great determination for so many passengers to survive.

(A) it must have taken great determination for so many passengers to survive.

(B) it had took great determination for so many passengers to survive.

(C) it must have took great determination for so many passengers to have survived.

(D) it must have taken great determination for so many passengers to survived.

(E) it taken great determination for so many passengers to survive.

Ⓐ Ⓑ Ⓒ Ⓓ ● **5.** In the end, officials rescued sixteen passengers and the amazing story is made into a book and a film.

(A) officials rescued sixteen passengers and the amazing story is made

(B) sixteen passengers are rescued by officials, and the amazing story had been made

(C) sixteen passengers are rescued, and the amazing story was maked

(D) officials rescued sixteen passengers, and the amazing story is making

(E) officials rescued sixteen passengers, and the amazing story was made

Chapter Review

B. Identifying Verb Tenses

For each sentence below, label the underlined verb or verb form *present, past, future, present perfect, past perfect,* or *future perfect.*

______ **1.** I will present a multimedia presentation on girl groups of the 1960s.

______ **2.** I will open with a recording by Diana Ross and the Supremes.

______ **3.** Once everyone has learned a bit about the era, I'll speak specifically about each group.

______ **4.** I can't wait until my classmates hear my favorite group, the Ronettes.

______ **5.** The Ronettes sang the hit "Be My Baby."

______ **6.** I had considered showing a video but decided on still photos instead.

______ **7.** I have given other multimedia presentations, but I think this will be the most interesting.

______ **8.** The girl group phenomenon gave women a voice in the culture of rock and roll.

______ **9.** During this groundbreaking era, women of color began dominating the Top 40 charts.

______ **10.** I hope that by the end of my presentation, my classmates will have learned something new.

C. Identifying Gerunds, Participles, and Infinitives

In each proverb below, underline and label each gerund (*G*), participle (*P*), and infinitive (*I*).

1. To talk without thinking is to shoot without aiming.

2. Let sleeping dogs lie.

3. Live to learn, and you will learn to live.

4. By learning to obey, you will know how to command.

5. Living well is the best revenge.

Copyright © 2014 by William H. Sadlier, Inc. All rights reserved.

D. Revising a Poem

On a separate sheet of paper, revise the draft of the free-verse poem below by following these directions.

1. Change all passive voice verbs to active voice.
2. Correct needless shifts in tense.
3. Replace incorrect verb forms.
4. Improve the overall poem. Add precise words, sensory details, and sound devices, such as alliteration and consonance.

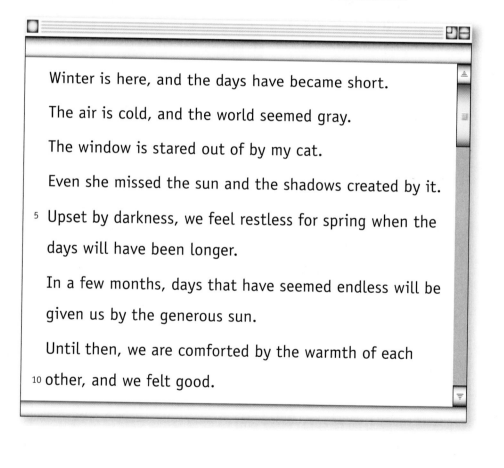

Winter is here, and the days have became short.
The air is cold, and the world seemed gray.
The window is stared out of by my cat.
Even she missed the sun and the shadows created by it.
Upset by darkness, we feel restless for spring when the
days will have been longer.
In a few months, days that have seemed endless will be
given us by the generous sun.
Until then, we are comforted by the warmth of each
other, and we felt good.

CHAPTER 9 Adjectives, Adverbs, and Other Parts of Speech

Copyright © 2014 by William H. Sadlier, Inc. All rights reserved.

Using Adjectives and Adverbs

LESSON 9.1

Adjectives and adverbs are **modifiers** that help writers add information and create vivid images.

Adjectives modify nouns or pronouns and answer questions like the ones below.

What kind?	**vine-ripened** tomato, **brown** eyes
Which one?	**third** row, **last** warning
How many?	**three** days, **numerous** people
How much?	**less** hope, **some** time

Proper adjectives are formed from proper nouns.

Honduran island **British** people

Adjectives often, but not always, come right before the noun they modify. **Predicate adjectives** follow a linking verb and describe the subject. (See Lesson 6.6.)

The bicycle is **old** and **rusted.**

Adverbs modify verbs, adjectives, and other adverbs. Adverbs may appear at various places in a sentence, and they answer the questions below.

When?	We took a field trip **yesterday.**
Where?	We drove **farther** than we expected.
How?	Four o'clock arrived **slowly.**
To what extent?	We were **exceptionally** tired.

Many adverbs end in the suffix *-ly* (*slowly, neatly, boldly*, for example), but many do not (*always, not [n't], soon*, and *also*, for example).

We **almost always** get **there very late.**

Remember

The **articles** *a*, *an*, and *the* are adjectives. *A* and *an* refer to any one of a group. *The* points to a particular noun.

To decide whether to use an adjective or an adverb, figure out which word you want to modify.

Use an adjective to modify a noun or a pronoun.

Stella seems **cautious.**

Use an adverb to modify a verb, an adjective, or another adverb.

Stella moves very **cautiously.**

ONLINE PRACTICE
www.grammarforwriting.com

Exercise 1 Identifying Words

Underline the adjectives, and circle the adverbs in the following paragraph. Omit the articles *a*, *an*, and *the*, but don't forget the predicate adjectives.

When a noun modifies another noun, it acts like an adjective.

summer breeze

corn muffins

One sentence contains a noun used like an adjective. Be sure to underline it.

[1]Offenders in a small town in Louisiana now face a possible fine or a jail sentence for wearing sagging jeans. [2]Such laws are raising constitutional issues, and today people are asking questions about appropriate dress in public places. [3]Do we really want laws about clothing styles? [4]Some communities have recently passed laws, and others are strictly enforcing existing ones. [5]Outrage at how teens dress is not new.

Exercise 2 Choosing Correct Modifiers

Think about the word that is being modified, and then underline the correct modifier in parentheses.

1. Clothing communicates many things (visual, visually).
2. That dress is (really, real) old.
3. The uniform of a surgeon appears (different, differently) from the uniform of a security guard.
4. Mr. Salvio dresses very (neatly, neat).
5. He (frequent, frequently) buys new clothes.

Exercise 3 Using Adjectives and Adverbs

Use four of the following adjectives and adverbs in a description of a typical school day morning. Write how the word is used.

1. groggy	**3.** harsh	**5.** hurriedly
2. healthy	**4.** lately	**6.** alert

Copyright © 2014 by William H. Sadlier, Inc. All rights reserved.

LESSON 9.2

Comparing with Adjectives and Adverbs

Adjectives and adverbs have three **degrees of comparison:** the **positive,** the **comparative,** and the **superlative.** The positive form describes one thing. The comparative form describes two things. The superlative form describes three or more things.

Positive	She is **strong.** She pitches the ball **forcefully.**
Comparative	She is **stronger** than I am. She pitches the ball **more forcefully** than I do.
Superlative	She is the **strongest** of everybody. She pitches the ball **most forcefully** of all of us.

One-syllable modifiers Add *-er* and *-est* to one-syllable modifiers.

tall, tall**er,** tall**est**

low, low**er,** low**est**

Two-syllable modifiers Add *-er* or *-est* to most two-syllable modifiers. When those endings sound awkward, use the words *more (less)* or *most (least).*

quiet, quiet**er,** quiet**est**

quickly, **more** quickly, **most** quickly

suddenly, **less** suddenly, **least** suddenly

Modifiers with more than two syllables For adjectives and adverbs of three or more syllables, use *more (less)* or *most (least).*

magnificently, **more** magnificently, **most** magnificently

easily, **less** easily, **least** easily

Sometimes you will need to change the spelling of a word when you add *-er* or *-est.* See **Lesson 12.6** for spelling rules.

big bigg**er** bigg**est**

pretty prett**ier** prett**iest**

ONLINE PRACTICE
www.grammarforwriting.com

Use *more (less)* and *most (least)* for all adverbs that end in *-ly*.

Exercise 1 Writing Sentences

Write the comparative and superlative forms of the following modifiers. Use each word in a sentence. You may use a dictionary to check spellings.

EXAMPLE bossy, *bossier, bossiest*

Shaylen is bossier than Rocky. She is the bossiest of everyone on the team.

1. calm	**3.** furious	**5.** tiny	**7.** gracefully	**9.** smoothly
2. tired	**4.** nervous	**6.** often	**8.** fragile	**10.** greedy

Exercise 2 Proofreading Sentences

Proofread the sentences below for incorrect comparative and superlative forms. Correct each incorrect form. If a sentence is correct, write *C*.

1. Racers, called mushers, and their dog teams race in the beautiful land you can imagine.
2. Temperatures drop extremely far below zero, and only the bravest mushers join the race.
3. Hazardous snow and wind are likely than mild weather.
4. The conditions vary from one day to the next, sometimes getting most unsafe from minute to minute.
5. The cool fact of all is that teams race over 1,150 miles.
6. Some mushers run most successfully during the night than during the day.
7. No competition is more exciting than the Iditarod.
8. Of all athletic competitions, the Iditarod has the more dedicated volunteer organizers.
9. Racers wear the warmer parkas and boots you can imagine.
10. Susan Butcher is among the most popular racers ever.

Copyright © 2014 by William H. Sadlier, Inc. All rights reserved.

Avoiding Comparison Problems

LESSON 9.3

The comparative and superlative forms of some adjectives and adverbs are **irregular.** They are not formed by the methods described in Lesson 9.2. Memorize the forms of these modifiers.

Positive	Comparative	Superlative
bad	worse	worst
good	better	best
well	better	best
far	farther	farthest
little	less	least
many	more	most
much	more	most

C. T. scored the **most** points of all. He played **better** than Billy.

Avoid **double comparisons.** When you use the word *more (less)* or *most (least),* do not also use the *-er* and *-est* endings.

INCORRECT The fire spread **more farther** than expected.

CORRECT The fire spread **farther** than expected.

Avoid confusing or illogical comparisons. Sometimes you may need to add one or more words (such as *other* or *else*) to make a comparison clear.

UNCLEAR Does Sandi like Jason more than Dan?

CLEAR Does Sandi like Jason more than Dan **does?**
Does Sandi like Jason more than **she likes Dan?**

WRITING HINT

The words *less* and *fewer* are often confused. *Less* tells "how much" and is used to describe a singular noun.

Ben had **less** time than Diane had.

Fewer tells "how many" and is used to describe a plural noun.

Diane read **fewer** pages than Jane did.

For a list of other commonly confused words, see page 325.

Snapshots

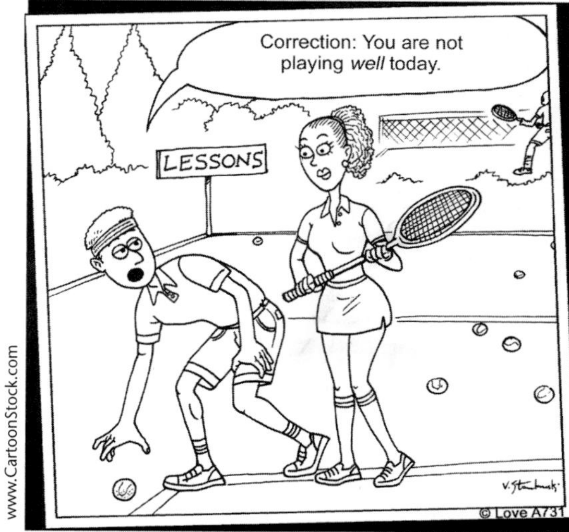

Bob would tack on $20 for the English lesson.

ONLINE PRACTICE
www.grammarforwriting.com

Exercise 1 Forming Irregular Comparisons

On a separate sheet of paper, write sentences that use the words below in a comparison. Write about your friends' interests and talents.

1. better (adjective)
2. better (adverb)
3. least (adverb)
4. worst (adjective)
5. more (adverb)

Exercise 2 Editing Sentences

HINT
A sentence may have more than one error.

Edit the sentences below for errors in how adjectives and adverbs have been used in comparisons. If you find an error, rewrite the sentence correctly on a separate piece of paper. If a sentence is correct, write *C*.

EXAMPLE Elliot cooks more worse than Chris does.

Elliot cooks worse than Chris does.

1. The food at Chez El tastes better than the food at La Vie.
2. Customers rate Rita's sandwiches as the goodest of all.
3. Why aren't the cherries more riper?
4. Elyse is more curious about cooking than Randi.
5. Tony's recipe is more spicier than mine is.

Exercise 3 Writing a Review

Working Together

Write a one-paragraph review of a movie, TV show, song, book, or magazine you have recently seen, heard, or read.

For help with writing a review, see the Writing Application in **Chapter 10.**

1. Explain two or three things that you like or dislike about it.
2. Use at least five comparative or superlative forms.
3. When you have finished, read your review to a classmate. Ask him or her to give you feedback on your review as well as to check for errors.

Copyright © 2014 by William H. Sadlier, Inc. All rights reserved.

Double Negatives

LESSON 9.4

A negative word, such as *no, none, never,* and *nothing,* expresses the meaning "no." A **double negative** is the use of two negative words to express a single negative idea. Avoid using double negatives in your writing and speech.

INCORRECT The rules do **not** allow **no one** to skateboard on the sidewalk. [double negative]

CORRECT The rules do **not** allow anyone to skateboard on the sidewalk. [one negative]

Remember that contractions such as *aren't, can't, don't, doesn't,* and *isn't* are negative words. They contain *-n't,* the shortened form of the word *not.* Many errors in using double negatives occur in sentences that have one of these negative contractions.

INCORRECT Erika **isn't never** late to school.

CORRECT Erika is**n't** ever late to school.

Many sentences with double negatives can be corrected in more than one way. Revise the sentence in a way that expresses your meaning and sounds natural.

INCORRECT All of those articles **can't hardly** be wrong.

CORRECT All of those articles can **hardly** be wrong.

CORRECT All of those articles ca**n't** be wrong.

CORRECT **Not** all of those articles can be wrong.

Common Negative Words

barely	none
hardly	not (n't)
neither	nothing
never	nowhere
no one	scarcely
nobody	

TEST-TAKING TIP

In multiple-choice tests, eliminate choices with more than one negative word. *Scarcely* is a negative word.

He **scarcely** ____ time to study.

(a) has no

(b) has any

(c) never has

Exercise 1 Editing Sentences

Rewrite each sentence to correct any double negatives. Eliminate or change words as necessary. If a sentence is correct, write *C.*

EXAMPLE I don't know ~~nothing~~ anything about stained glass.

1. I can't see none of the stained glass window.
2. Scarcely anybody knows who created that piece of art.
3. Nobody knows more about that glass than Dr. Franks does.

4. Haven't you never seen the window in our church?
5. Dr. Franks has never seen nobody photograph it.
6. Nowhere is there nothing as impressive.
7. Don't never ask me to draw the design myself.
8. Scholars haven't ever agreed on its title.
9. The article doesn't hardly spend time explaining how artists color the glass.
10. We haven't had no luck finding the name of a glass factory.

EXERCISE 2 Proofreading a Paragraph

Work with a partner to find and correct four sentences with double negatives in the paragraph below. Write the corrected sentences on a separate sheet of paper. **Note:** There is more than one way to correct each double negative.

Canterbury Cathedral

[1]Why haven't more people never heard of the Canterbury Cathedral? [2]Don't you know that it is one of the oldest and most famous structures anywhere in England? [3]Surprisingly, many tourists haven't made no plans to visit it. [4]Those who do visit can't believe the glorious stained glass windows. [5]The oldest window dates to the 1100s. [6]Through the years, some windows haven't survived with no damage. [7]It isn't scarcely believable that so much of the original glass remains.

Copyright © 2014 by William H. Sadlier, Inc. All rights reserved.

Misplaced and Dangling Modifiers

LESSON 9.5

A **misplaced modifier** is placed too far away from the word it modifies. To correct a misplaced modifier, move it as near as possible to the word it is meant to modify.

MISPLACED Meowing, Maria heard the kitten.
[The sentence says that Maria was meowing.]

CORRECT Maria heard the kitten meowing.

A **dangling modifier** does not logically modify any other word in the sentence. To correct a sentence that has a dangling modifier, reword the sentence. Add one or more words to refer to the dangling phrase or clause.

DANGLING Peering hard, Mars was visible.
[The sentence says that Mars was peering.]

CORRECT Peering hard, I saw Mars.

Real-World Writing

Misplaced and dangling modifiers can lead to unclear but humorous wording in newspaper headlines.

Officer with 200 Shoes Arrests Burglar

After 20 Years on TV Show Brothers Reunite

Young Divorcees Cut in Half

Exercise 1 Correcting Modifier Problems

Rewrite each sentence that has a misplaced or dangling modifier. If a sentence is correct, write *C*.

EXAMPLE Having a daydream, the bell rang.

He was having a daydream when the bell rang.

1. Javier looked up from his math book to see what time it was.
2. Hanging from the window, Javier spotted a huge spider.
3. He could see its fuzzy legs squinting in the sunlight.
4. To get Rita's attention, Javier kicked her chair.
5. Trying to disturb her concentration, the chair slid forward.
6. Startled and annoyed, her book dropped with a thud.
7. Rita noticed the spider while bending to pick something up from the floor.
8. It was scurrying along the bulletin board near the teacher's head with photo displays.

9. Calling "Watch out!" the spider continued to move.

10. Upon seeing the spider, the class erupted into shrieks and giggles.

Exercise 2 Editing a Paragraph

Work with a partner to correct misplaced and dangling modifiers in the paragraph below. Rewrite the paragraph on a separate sheet of paper.

[1]While researching famous Americans in the World War II era, many women's names are evident. [2]For example, Eleanor Roosevelt had many official and unofficial responsibilities. [3]Addressing the nation the day after the Pearl Harbor attack by radio the goal of Mrs. Roosevelt was to keep up the country's morale. [4]Frances Perkins nearly held the title of U.S. Secretary of Labor for twelve years. [5]Emerging after the war as a superpower, Perkins's lawmaking efforts helped America achieve economic success. [6]An African American, Mary McLeod Bethune urged the War Department as officers to hire black women. [7]I enjoy reading about women like these who have made history.

Eleanor Roosevelt

Copyright © 2014 by William H. Sadlier, Inc. All rights reserved.

Using Prepositions and Prepositional Phrases

LESSON **9.6**

Prepositions (P) show the relationship between words in a sentence. They are always part of a prepositional phrase.

A **prepositional phrase** begins with a preposition and ends with the **object of a preposition (O),** the noun or pronoun that follows the preposition.

Brazil is the largest country **in South America.** (P: in; O: South America)

To the west, Brazil shares a border **with Peru.** (P: To; O: west; P: with; O: Peru)

Some prepositions are **compound,** made up of two or more words. (See the list at the bottom right.) Some prepositional phrases may have compound objects, or two or more objects joined by *and* or *or*.

We ran **out of time due to flight delays.** (P: out of; O: time; P: due to; O: delays)

The countries **of Venezuela, Suriname,** and **French Guiana** are north of Brazil. (P: of; O: Venezuela; O: Suriname; O: French Guiana)

One or more modifiers may come between the preposition and the object.

Brazil has miles **of white sandy beaches along the magnificent Atlantic Ocean**. (P: of; O: beaches; P: along; O: Atlantic Ocean)

A **prepositional phrase** that describes a noun or a pronoun is an **adjective phrase.** Adjective phrases tell *what kind* or *which one*.

Rio de Janeiro is a city **of much beauty.**
[The adjective phrase modifies the noun *city*.]

A prepositional phrase that describes a verb, an adjective, or an adverb is an **adverb phrase.** Adverb phrases tell *how, where, when, why,* or *to what extent*.

Young people gather **at Brazil's many beaches.**
[The adverb phrase modifies the verb *gather*.]

Some Common Prepositions

about	from
above	inside
across	into
against	near
along	of
among	off
around	on
at	out
before	outside
behind	over
below	past
beneath	since
beside	through
between	to
beyond	under
by	until
down	up
during	with
except	without
for	

Some Common Compound Prepositions

along with	in front of
because of	instead of
due to	out of

Remember

A word may act like a preposition in one sentence and an adverb in another.

We played **inside.** [adverb]

The ball was **inside** the box. [preposition]

EXERCISE 1 Identifying Adjective and Adverb Prepositional Phrases

Underline the prepositional phrase(s) in each sentence. Label each phrase *ADJ* for adjective or *ADV* for adverb.

EXAMPLE Volleyball is popular <u>in Brazil.</u> (ADV)

1. Volleyball was invented in 1895.
2. At first, there was no limit on the number of players.
3. Simon tossed the ball up for the overhand serve.
4. The skills of spiking and blocking are important.
5. The match lasted for two hours.

EXERCISE 2 Recognizing Phrases

Underline the prepositional phrases in the following excerpt. Circle the objects of the prepositions.

HINT

Find ten prepositional phrases. One phrase has two objects.

Literary Model

[1]Kozienice is a small village in eastern Poland. [2]Here, on May Day, 1921, my mother went to the riverbank with her friends. [3]It was dusk, and the breeze carried the scent of lilacs. [4]The call of a cuckoo from the forest made the village girls laugh as they picked their way among the reeds and forget-me-nots at the water's edge, and the grasses brushed their ankles with dew as they passed.

—Excerpt from *In My Hands* by Irene Gut Opdyke

EXERCISE 3 Writing a Description

On a separate sheet of paper, write a description of a scene near a river, lake, or ocean. Use at least five prepositional phrases to add detail and create an interesting picture. Underline them.

EXAMPLE <u>From the shore</u> we saw sailboats <u>on the lake.</u>

Copyright © 2014 by William H. Sadlier, Inc. All rights reserved.

LESSON 9.7

Using Conjunctions and Interjections

A **conjunction** connects words, phrases, and clauses in a sentence. There are several types of conjunctions.

1. **Coordinating conjunctions** (*and, or, for, nor, yet, but, so*) join words, phrases, or clauses of equal importance. (See Lesson 3.6 for more about using coordinating conjunctions to combine sentences.)

   Plants **and** animals are made up of cells.
   [*And* joins two subjects.]

   Cells are tiny, **but** they have everything needed for life.
   [*But* joins two independent clauses.]

2. **Correlative conjunctions** are used in pairs to join words or phrases of equal importance.

   Either cells exist independently, **or** they are in clumps.
   [The correlative conjunction joins two clauses.]

   The experiment will focus **not only** on skin cells **but also** on hair.
   [The correlative conjunction joins two prepositional phrases.]

3. **Subordinating conjunctions** join subordinate clauses to independent clauses. (See Lessons 3.3 and 3.8 for more about adverb clauses and subordinating conjunctions.)

   If you had one cell, you wouldn't grow and change.

   We're studying cells in science **because** they are basic to life.

An **interjection** is a word or phrase that expresses emotion, such as *hooray, oh, ugh, well*, and *wow*. If an interjection expresses mild emotion, join it to the rest of the sentence with a comma. If an interjection expresses strong emotion, it may stand by itself. Follow it with an exclamation point.

Oh, you must learn these terms.

Oops! I forgot to study for this test.

Some Correlative Conjunctions

both...and	not only... but also
either...or	whether... or
neither...nor	

Some Subordinating Conjunctions

after	so that
although	than
as	though
as long as	unless
as soon as	when
because	whenever
before	where
even though	wherever
if	whether
since	while

ONLINE PRACTICE
www.grammarforwriting.com

EXERCISE 1 Identifying Conjunctions and Interjections

Underline each conjunction, and label it *C* for coordinating or *S* for subordinating. Circle each interjection.

1. Has the menu changed since we ate here?
2. The waiter recommends the salmon or the lemon chicken because they are fresh.
3. Even though the restaurant was busy, we were seated quickly. Yikes! The service was slow.
4. I can't tell if the meal comes with soup or fruit.
5. After customers and employees asked for recipes, the chef wrote a cookbook.

EXERCISE 2 Using Correlative Conjunctions

On a separate sheet of paper, write complete sentences for the starters. Include an appropriate correlative conjunction.

HINT

To help you decide which conjunction to add, review the list of correlative conjunctions on page 237.

EXAMPLE Both appetizers...*and meals here are great.*

1. Either the miso soup...
2. Both the cheese dish...
3. Not only will you like the salads,...
4. Neither the sandwiches...
5. Whether you choose soup...

Write What You Think

Write a paragraph that explains your answer to the question below. Support your opinion with at least two strong reasons and evidence. Use a variety of conjunctions and at least one interjection.

Should laws be passed that require fast-food restaurants to serve more healthy foods?

Copyright © 2014 by William H. Sadlier, Inc. All rights reserved.

Cause-Effect Essay

If you avoid studying for a test, you probably won't do well. If you don't do well, your grades will suffer. This is a chain of causes and effects. A **cause** is an event that makes something happen. An **effect** is the result of the cause. When you analyze causes and effects, you ask yourself: *Why did this happen?*

In this workshop, you will write a cause-effect essay. A **cause-effect essay** is a kind of **expository writing,** or writing that explains, instructs, or informs. Cause-effect essays can examine one or more causes with one or more effects.

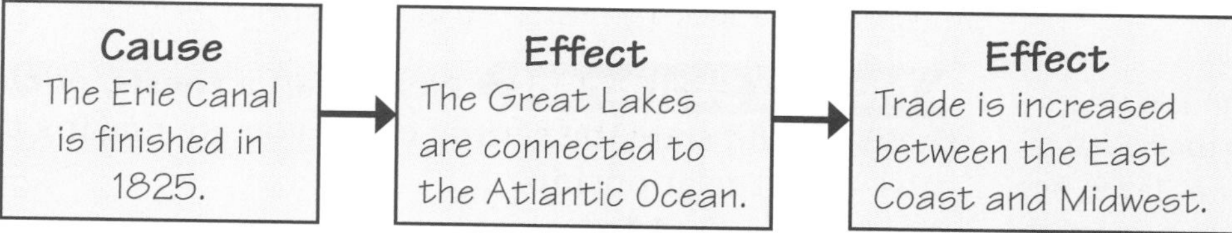

Cause
The Erie Canal is finished in 1825.
Effect
The Great Lakes are connected to the Atlantic Ocean.
Effect
Trade is increased between the East Coast and Midwest.

When you write a cause-effect essay, include the following features.

Key Features

- thesis, or claim, that gives a clear explanation of a cause-effect relationship
- organization that arranges causes and effects logically
- specific facts, details, and examples
- transitions that clarify the relationships among ideas
- conclusion that follows from the information given

ASSIGNMENT

TASK: Think about events or situations in the news or that you have studied in history, science, or social studies class. What sparked these changes? What are the effects of the change? Pick one, and explore it in a three- to four-page **cause-effect essay.**

AUDIENCE: your classmates

PURPOSE: to analyze causes and effects

Prewriting

Brainstorm a Topic Choose one or more general topics from this chart, or make up your own, to write about in three or four pages. Brainstorm specific details about the topic.

Science and Technology	History	Current Events	Personal Experience
• popularity of smart phones • causes of lightning	• American Revolution • key historical figures	• weather-related event • rising cost of gas or food	• a new rule at your school • a major change in your life

A thesis states the main idea of your essay in one or two sentences. See **Lesson 5.2** for more about developing a thesis.

Make a Statement Next, draft a **thesis,** or **claim.** Your thesis should state the central claim you are making about your cause-effect relationship.

1. Your thesis should be neither too narrow nor too broad.
2. Your thesis must state an opinion. It should never simply restate the topic of your essay.
3. Your thesis should state the key causes or effects.

The thesis, or claim, reveals that the essay will explore three effects.

Writing Model

[1]After fewer than ten years of construction, the Erie Canal opened in 1825. [2]The opening of the canal caused three major changes in the United States. [3]The Erie Canal connected the Midwest to the Atlantic, and it made trade with the center of the country easier and more profitable. [4]Perhaps most important, it turned small towns and forests into cities.

Copyright © 2014 by William H. Sadlier, Inc. All rights reserved.

Prewriting

Collect Evidence Provide details and evidence to support your thesis. If you are writing about a topic that calls for research, such as a historical event, use library and Internet resources, read newspapers, and interview experts. Record details in a Cause-Effect Chart.

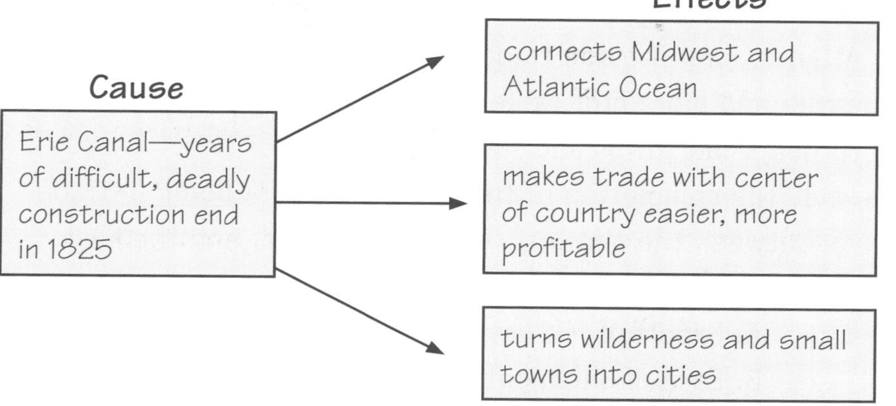

Effects
Cause
Erie Canal—years of difficult, deadly construction end in 1825
connects Midwest and Atlantic Ocean
makes trade with center of country easier, more profitable
turns wilderness and small towns into cities

WRITING HINT

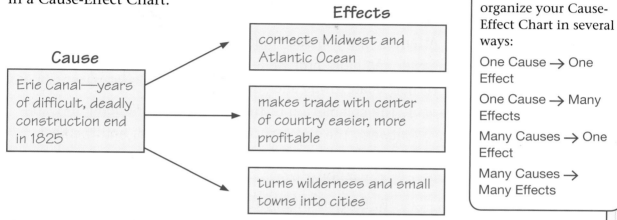

Depending on your topic, you can organize your Cause-Effect Chart in several ways:

One Cause → One Effect

One Cause → Many Effects

Many Causes → One Effect

Many Causes → Many Effects

Use a Variety of Details Include a variety of specific and relevant details from several different sources.

Type	Definition	Example
Facts	Facts are statements that can be proved true.	The Erie Canal was completed on October 26, 1825.
Examples	Examples are instances that illustrate the point you are trying to make.	Imagine what it must have been like to move goods from Illinois to New York without highways, jets, or trains.
Quotations	Quotations are spoken or written words from an expert.	President Jefferson called the project "a little short of madness."
Anecdotes	These are things that you have personally seen or experienced.	The Erie Canal's length amazed me.

Remember

A cause-effect chain is a series of events that has a domino effect. When a cause creates an effect, the effect becomes the cause for another effect.

WRITING HINT

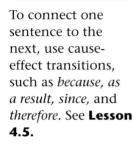

To connect one sentence to the next, use cause-effect transitions, such as *because, as a result, since,* and *therefore*. See **Lesson 4.5.**

Drafting

Organize Your Ideas Group ideas together as you draft. Refer to notes or an outline you created earlier.

Writing Model

Thesis: The Erie Canal connected the Midwest to the Atlantic, and it made trade with the center of the country easier and more profitable. Perhaps most important, it turned small towns and forests into cities.

One paragraph about one effect (boom in trade)

I. The completion of the canal created a boom in trade between the Midwest, on the one hand, and the East Coast and Europe, on the other.

Three specific examples

A. Export of Midwestern wheat to Britain increased.
B. Ease of shipment caused dramatic drop in cost.
C. Goods moved from East Coast to Midwest.

Write a Complete Essay Always include the three basic parts of an essay. The **introduction** includes the thesis, or claim, and grabs readers' attention. The **body** organizes details logically in paragraphs, each one containing a topic sentence. The **conclusion** restates your thesis and main points.

Body paragraph with topic sentence

Three examples

Transitions to connect ideas

[1]The canal created a boom in trade between the Midwest, on one hand, and the East Coast and Europe, on the other. [2]As a result of the canal's completion, Midwestern farmers could quickly ship their wheat to the East Coast and then on to Britain. [3]The ease of shipment also led to a dramatic drop in the cost of produce. [4]Finally, manufactured goods, such as farm equipment, moved easily from the East Coast to the Midwest.

Copyright © 2014 by William H. Sadlier, Inc. All rights reserved.

Revising

Use the Revising Questions to check and improve your draft. You may also participate in a peer review. Reviewers should read carefully and offer feedback to the writer. The model below shows revisions one writer made to one body paragraph.

Revising Questions

- ❏ How strong is my thesis statement, or claim?
- ❏ How clearly did I describe a cause-effect relationship?
- ❏ How specific and relevant are the details I included?
- ❏ Where can I add transitions to clarify the organization?
- ❏ How strong are my introduction, body, and conclusion?

As you revise, keep in mind the traits of good writing. See **Lesson 1.3.**

[1]The Erie Canal transformed small towns and wilderness regions across New York State and the Midwest into major cities. [2]*Because* ^ The canal project required many workers, ~~and~~ the populations of towns like Rochester and Buffalo exploded overnight. *In fact, Rochester doubled its population.* ^ [3]The increased trade and ease of travel caused towns in Ohio *, Illinois,* ^ and Michigan to grow.

Add cause-effect transitions.

Add specific details to support the topic sentence.

Editing and Proofreading

Use the tips below to guide your editing and proofreading.

1. Use an online dictionary to help you check your spelling.
2. Keep a proofreading log. Whenever you make a spelling or grammar error, make note of it. Keeping this log will help you avoid making these errors in the future.
3. Use the checklist to guide you as you check for errors in grammar, usage, mechanics, punctuation, and spelling.

Editing and Proofreading Checklist

- ❑ Have I checked that all words are spelled correctly?
- ❑ Have I used adjectives and adverbs correctly?
- ❑ Have I written only in complete sentences, avoiding run-ons and fragments?
- ❑ Did I run together or leave out any words?

For more help with double negatives, see **Lesson 9.4.**

Avoid Using Double Negatives Avoid using two or more negative words, such as *no, not, nobody, nothing,* and *never,* to express a negative idea. If more than one is used, the sentence will be confusing and incorrect. Remember, the contraction *-n't* is also a negative word.

Double negatives can usually be corrected in more than one way.

INCORRECT	There had **not** been **nothing** like the canal.
CORRECT	There had **not** been **anything** like the canal.
CORRECT	There **had** been **nothing** like the canal.

Copyright © 2014 by William H. Sadlier, Inc. All rights reserved.

Editing and Proofreading

Writing Model

[1]The Erie Canal has affected the United States in many important ways; the canal connected comunities communities on the East Coast with small towns and rural areas in the Midwest. [2]Because it allowed for the quick movement of goods across great distances, the canal changed the way Americans did Business at home and overseas [3]The canal also caused small towns in New York State andthe Midwest, including Syracuse, Cleveland, and Chicago, to grow rapidly and become major urban areas. [4]There hasn't been nothing anything that changed America as quickly as the Erie Canal did.

Proofreading Symbols

- ℘ Delete.
- ^ Add.
- ⊙ Add a period.
- / Make lowercase.
- ≡ Capitalize.
- # Add a space.

Publishing and Presenting

Choose one of these ways to share your cause-effect essay.

- **Make a display.** Use poster board, photographs, drawings, and charts to create a visual description of the causes and effects analyzed in your essay.
- **Create a short video.** As you record yourself, avoid reading directly from your essay. Instead, use note cards to prompt yourself.

Reflect On Your Writing

- Which part of your essay was most successful? Why?
- What have you learned about analyzing cause and effect?

CHAPTER 9

Chapter Review

A. Practice Test

In the passage below, there is a question *for each numbered item*. Read the passage carefully, and circle the best answer.

Boost Your Self-Esteem

Brian is about to try out for the school play, but he doesn't feel that his chances are very well for getting a part [1]. "I'm not near talented [2] enough to play this role," thinks Brian. Meanwhile, Fiona, who is also awaiting her audition, is thinking quite different. [3] "I may not be the most talentedest [4] singer in the world," she tells herself, "but my personality and sense of humor are great for musical comedy."

We all have a mental image of ourselves and who we are, including our strengths, our weaknesses, and our unique personalities. People with high self-esteem are able to value themselves because they accept their weaknesses and focus on their strengths, while people with low self-esteem tend to do the opposite. In which category are you? [5] If your train of thought is more similar

1. What is the best replacement for the underlined section?
- **A.** NO CHANGE
- **B.** feel that his chances are more better for getting a part.
- **C.** feel that his chances for getting a part are real well.
- **D.** feel that his chances for getting a part are very good.

2. What is the best replacement for the underlined section?
- **A.** NO CHANGE
- **B.** not nearly talented
- **C.** not hardly talented
- **D.** not barely talented

3. What is wrong with this sentence?
- **A.** It has a misplaced modifier.
- **B.** An adverb is used where an adjective is needed.
- **C.** An adjective is used where an adverb is needed.
- **D.** It contains a dangling modifier.

4. What is the best replacement for the underlined section?
- **A.** the most talented
- **B.** the more talented
- **C.** the talentedest
- **D.** better

Copyright © 2014 by William H. Sadlier, Inc. All rights reserved.

to Brian's perspective than Fiona's perspective, don't worry. There are things you can do to boost your self-esteem.

One thing to beware of is setting unrealistic goals for yourself. It is good to aim for excellence, but not for perfection[6]. If you try to be perfect, you will often disappoint yourself, or even worst[7], you may just stop trying. In addition, remember that everyone has different talents. If you are not good at one thing, you might be more better[8] at something else. Remember, too, that everyone makes mistakes. Try to think of them as learning opportunities.

Last, but certainly not least, try to think positive.[9] If you catch yourself thinking negative thoughts or being too critical of yourself, think of something that makes you proud. A good way to break the pattern of self-criticism is to keep a journal of accomplishments. At the end of each day, write down at least one thing you did that was a success. Chances are you'll be able to think of many more. Well, you may be surprised at just how quick you can boost your self-esteem![10]

5. What does this sentence contain?
A. a correlative conjunction
B. a prepositional phrase
C. an interjection
D. an adverb

6. What does the underlined section contain?
A. one interjection
B. a double negative
C. a dangling modifier
D. two prepositional phrases

7. What is the best replacement for the underlined section?
A. NO CHANGE
B. or even more bad
C. or even worse
D. or never even worst

8. What is the best replacement for the underlined section?
A. NO CHANGE
B. be gooder
C. more betterer
D. be better

9. What is the best replacement for the underlined section?
A. NO CHANGE
B. think positively.
C. think positiver.
D. think less positive.

10. What is true about this sentence?
A. It has two prepositions.
B. It contains a double comparison.
C. An adjective is used where an adverb is needed.
D. It contains a misplaced modifier.

B. Using Adjectives and Adverbs

Complete each sentence below by writing the correct form of the word in parentheses. Then label the word *adjective* or *adverb*, as well as *positive, comparative,* or *superlative.*

1. Many people today do most of their reading online, but in ________ cases I prefer books. (much)

2. The Internet can sometimes help you research a topic ____________ than books can. (rapid)

3. With a few clicks, you can ________ access information from countless sources. (easy)

4. However, the information you find may be ________ accurate than material found in books. (little)

5. Plus, it is ________ to snuggle up in bed with a laptop than with a great book! (bad)

C. Identifying Prepositions and Conjunctions

Read each sentence below. Underline each prepositional phrase. Circle each conjunction.

1. In a multifaceted book, there are many interpretations and aspects to discuss.

2. Book clubs allow readers to explore a book beyond their individual views, and they open a reader's mind to other readers' interpretations.

3. With the help of a successful book club, old classics can return to the top of a bestseller list, and people across the country can reconnect with a classic masterpiece.

4. Not only do book clubs inspire people to read, but book clubs also help readers keep a book alive beyond its last page.

5. Create a book club with the help of a few friends so that you can enjoy conversations about literature.

Copyright © 2014 by William H. Sadlier, Inc. All rights reserved.

D. Editing a Cause-Effect Essay

Read the draft of an introduction for a cause-effect essay below.

- On a separate sheet of paper, rewrite the passage to fix errors such as misplaced modifiers, double negatives, and double comparisons.
- Then answer the questions that follow.

[1]Baring its teeth and crouching on a rock, at the zoo we saw a tiger. [2]Its fur was a beautiful orange, and it looked very fierce. [3]If you've ever seen a tiger, no doubt its majestical beauty took your breath away; it is one of the magnificentest animals on the earth. [4]Unfortunately, tigers may not be around much longer. [5]Because of illegal hunting and a loss of habitats, the tiger population is dwindling, such as forests and jungles. [6]As humans, it is our responsibility to care much more better for the environment. [7]Unfortunately, people aren't doing nothing to save tigers from extinction.

1. What do you like best about the essay? Why?
2. What is the weakest part of this essay? How would you improve it?

CHAPTER 10

Subject-Verb Agreement

Copyright © 2014 by William H. Sadlier, Inc. All rights reserved.

LESSON 10.1

Agreement of Subject and Verb

A **verb (v)** must agree with its **subject (s).** To avoid a **subject-verb agreement** error, use a singular verb with a singular subject and a plural verb with a plural subject.

An **enchilada**[S] **is**[V] a popular Mexican dish. [singular]

My **brothers**[S] **prefer**[V] enchiladas with cheese. [plural]

In a **verb phrase,** which is made up of a main verb and at least one helping verb **(HV),** the first helping verb must agree with the subject. In a question, the first helping verb often comes before the subject. (See Lesson 8.1 for more about verb phrases.)

My mother is[HV] making enchiladas tonight. [singular]

Have[HV] the boys tasted enchiladas with seafood? [plural]

In many sentences, a **prepositional phrase** comes between a subject and its verb. However, the verb needs to agree with the subject, not with the object of a preposition. Remember that a subject is never in a prepositional phrase. (See Lesson 9.6 for more about prepositional phrases.)

One[S] of the restaurants **has**[V] a new chef.
[The singular verb *has* agrees with *one*, not *restaurants*.]

My **friends**[S] on the soccer team **are**[V] hungry after practice.
[The plural verb *are* agrees with *friends*, not *team*.]

Some Common Helping Verbs

am	has
are	have
been	is
can	may
do	was
does	were

Exercise 1 Choosing Correct Verbs

Underline the subject of each sentence and the verb in parentheses that agrees with the subject.

1. The main eating utensils in Chinese culture (is, are) chopsticks.
2. Food in Chinese dishes (is, are) often bite-sized.
3. (Do, Does) most people have an individual bowl of rice?
4. Chinese food from various regions (has, have) become popular.
5. A Chinese meal (does, do) not typically end with a dessert.

"My subject and verb have agreed to disagree."

Mark Anderson, Andertoons.com.

ONLINE PRACTICE
www.grammarforwriting.com

Remember

Remember that many sentences have more than one clause. Be sure that the verb in each clause agrees with its subject.

The best **dishes,** which my **mother** always **orders,** **are** the salads.

6. My mom's favorite recipes (come, comes) from her Italian relatives, whom she (visits, visit) every summer.
7. Many kinds of Italian bread (is, are) featured at holiday meals.
8. Towns throughout Italy (creates, create) their own special celebration breads.
9. Cooking with my little sisters (results, result) in a messy kitchen, which one of my parents (have, has) to clean.
10. Some great chefs (teach, teaches) at local cooking schools, but the cost of their classes (is, are) expensive.

Exercise 2 Editing Sentences

Work with a partner to edit the sentences below. Correct any errors you find in subject-verb agreement. If a sentence is correct, write *C*.

EXAMPLE My friends ~~likes~~ like to have fruit for an afternoon snack.

1. Jasmine eats bananas almost every day for lunch.
2. Wild forms of the banana comes originally from Malaysia.
3. Different types of bananas exist.
4. Is bananas a kind of tree or a type of plant?
5. Many fruits, like a peach or a banana, has a lot of vitamins.
6. The peel of red bananas are a mixture of green and red.
7. The reddest kind of bananas contain the most nutrients.
8. The basic food in many tropical countries are bananas.
9. Do the encyclopedia show pictures of various kinds of bananas?
10. The bananas in that bowl need to ripen before we use them to make banana bread.

Copyright © 2014 by William H. Sadlier, Inc. All rights reserved.

Compound Subjects

In a sentence with a **compound subject,** two or more subjects share the same verb. When compound subjects are joined by *and,* they usually take a plural verb.

My principal, teacher, **and** classmates **are** visiting the Museum of African-American History.

A teacher **and** a chaperone **guide** us through the exhibits.

When two singular subjects are joined by *or* or *nor,* the verb is singular.

Neither the book **nor** the article **has** photos of slave owners.

David, Harry, **or** Sari **is** going to research slave ships.

If a singular and a plural subject are joined by *or* or *nor,* the verb must agree with the subject closest to it.

The ship captain, the slaves, **or** the owners **are** in the index.

The slaves, the owners, **or** the ship captain **is** in the index.

CONNECTING Writing & Grammar

Use a singular verb with a compound subject that names only one thing or person. See **Lesson 6.4.**

The **professor and poet is** signing her book.

Mustard greens and ham hocks **was** a popular dish.

EXERCISE 1 Choosing Correct Verbs

Underline the verb in the parentheses that agrees with the subject.

1. Omar and I (was, were) discussing meat-eating plants.
2. The pitcher plant and the sundew (is, are) two carnivorous plants.
3. Either Venus flytraps or the pitcher plant (produce, produces) a honeylike juice.
4. Insects and spiders (finds, find) themselves attracted to the liquid.
5. After falling into the nectar, a spider or another insect (is, are) trapped and eaten.
6. Neither my sister, my brother, nor my brother's friends (believe, believes) that meat-eating plants exist.

ONLINE PRACTICE
www.grammarforwriting.com

7. A recent Web site posting or news article (show, shows) a picture of one.
8. Our science book and those encyclopedias (has, have) articles on unusual plants.
9. I have seen the play *Little Shop of Horrors*, but my sister and brother (has, have) not.
10. In that funny play, either Seymour or other characters (discover, discovers) a weird plant that eats more than tiny insects!

Exercise 2 Editing a Paragraph

Edit the paragraph below, correcting all mistakes in agreement between compound subjects and their verbs.

[1]Either a single rose or a dozen tulips makes an artistic display. [2]If you or your classmates wants to come up with a winning entry in the art show, consider an arrangement of fresh flowers. [3]Neither Mahala's group nor the other groups has such an unusual idea. [4]Since it's spring, tulips and roses are easy to find and not very expensive. [5]Be creative. [6]Several small containers or one large one work. [7]Either you, Natalie, or Eva probably have something stashed away that will work!

Remember

You can use compound subjects to combine short, choppy sentences and eliminate repetition. See **Lesson 3.6.**

My bedroom walls are green. My favorite T-shirts are green.

Exercise 3 Using Compound Subjects

Write a paragraph describing why you like or dislike two animals, colors, or seasons. Use at least three compound subjects. Check your sentences for subject-verb agreement.

Copyright © 2014 by William H. Sadlier, Inc. All rights reserved.

LESSON 10.3

Indefinite Pronouns and Inverted Sentences

Pronouns that do not refer to a specific person, place, thing, or idea are called **indefinite pronouns.** When used as subjects, some indefinite pronouns are always singular, and some are always plural. (See the lists on the right.)

SINGULAR **Each** of the drawings **is** wonderfully detailed.
Everyone has done a fantastic job.

PLURAL **Both** of the judges **are** art instructors.
Many of the pictures **show** mountains and rocky landscapes.

Depending on the word they refer to, the indefinite pronouns *all*, *any*, *most*, and *some* can be either singular or plural. Other words in the sentence (such as the object of a preposition in a prepositional phrase) can help you decide whether to use a singular or plural verb.

SINGULAR **Most** of his work **appears** in catalogs and magazines.
[*Most* refers to the singular word *work*.]

PLURAL The photographs are interesting. **Most are** black and white.
[*Most* refers to the plural word *photographs*.]

In **inverted sentences,** the subject follows the verb or part of the verb phrase. Regardless of the subject's position in a sentence, the verb must agree with it. (See Lesson 6.3 for more about inverted sentences.)

Here **are** the oil **paintings** that I told you about.

Near the big mural in the lobby **stands** the **statue.**

Under the box **are** the museum **maps.**

Why **have** the ceiling **lights** been flickering?

Some Singular Indefinite Pronouns

anybody	neither
anyone	no one
each	nobody
either	one
everybody	somebody
everyone	someone

Plural Indefinite Pronouns

both	many
few	several

EXERCISE 1 Proofreading Sentences

Remember

The subject of a sentence is never part of a prepositional phrase.

Neither of the trees **has** many leaves.

[*Trees* is the object of a preposition, not the subject.]

Proofread each of the sentences below for subject-verb agreement. If the sentence is correct, write *C*. If a verb does not agree with its subject, draw a line through the verb, and write the correct form.

1. There was dozens of birds in the pine tree.
2. One of the crows appear larger than the others.
3. Under the branches are a piece of stale bread.
4. Each of the birds makes lots of noise.
5. On some of their legs are a tiny metal band.
6. What do the bands do, and who put them there?
7. Both of my friends is trying to feed the crows.
8. There is many articles about birds' intelligence.
9. Do anyone want to take a photograph of the birds?
10. Here is two books about crows.

EXERCISE 2 Writing About a Photo

Work with a partner to write a descriptive paragraph of six to ten sentences based on the photo below. Use details from the photo and your imagination to describe a scene that could begin an adventure story.

1. Include at least one indefinite pronoun and at least one inverted sentence.
2. Use present tense verbs, and check that each one agrees with its subject.

Copyright © 2014 by William H. Sadlier, Inc. All rights reserved.

Special Nouns

Collective nouns refer to a group of people or things. If you think of the collective noun as a single unit, the noun takes a singular verb.

> The **jury decides** guilt or innocence.
> [Use a singular verb because *jury* refers to a single unit.]

If you think of the collective noun as individual members, the noun takes a plural verb.

> The **jury are** trying their best to listen.
> [Use a plural verb because *jury* refers to individual members in the group.]

Certain nouns that end in *-s* act as singular subjects and take singular verbs. However, some nouns that end in *-s* name singular subjects and take plural verbs. (See the examples on the right.)

> The **news spreads** quickly around the courtroom. [singular]

> Judge Lane's **eyeglasses are** in her coat. [plural]

Even if it ends in *-s*, the title of a creative work (such as a book, movie, song, or painting) and the title of an organization, city, or country usually take a singular verb.

> ***Great Expectations* was** written by Charles Dickens. [one book]

> **"No Regrets" has** a nice melody. [one song]

> **Cedar Rapids is** near my house. [one city]

Some Collective Nouns

audience	family
class	flock
club	group
committee	herd
crowd	jury
faculty	team

Singular

gymnastics	mumps
mathematics	news
measles	physics

Plural

binoculars	pliers
eyeglasses	scissors
pants	slacks

Exercise 1 Writing Sentences

On a separate sheet of paper, write a complete sentence that uses each noun below as the subject. Use present tense verbs. Share your sentences with a partner, and discuss why you have chosen either a singular or a plural verb for each sentence.

1. measles
2. team
3. scissors
4. the Netherlands
5. *Jaws* (a movie)

ONLINE PRACTICE
www.grammarforwriting.com

EXERCISE 2 Choosing Correct Verbs

Remember

Some nouns that end in *-ics* (such as *politics* or *statistics*) may be singular or plural, depending on their meaning.

Statistics is an interesting subject. Those **statistics show** a drop in crime.

Underline the subject of each sentence and the verb in parentheses that agrees with it.

1. *Little Women* (were, was) written by Louisa May Alcott.
2. The different statistics (come, comes) from two sources.
3. Mathematics (is, are) one of Tami's favorite subjects.
4. The pants with black stripes (has, have) to be packed.
5. (Is, Are) the Philippines located in the Pacific Ocean?
6. News about the economy (worry, worries) many consumers.
7. The group of tourists (has, have) finished buying souvenirs for themselves and their friends.
8. Politics (is, are) the one subject my grandparents never discuss.
9. The binoculars (belongs, belong) in the black case.
10. *Star Wars* (has, have) won many film awards.

Write What You Think

Read the statement below.

Because most of us are social and enjoy being with others, we like to join groups. However, being a member of a group can sometimes be difficult.

1. Write an expository paragraph that explains your view of the good and bad aspects of being a member of a group, team, or club.
2. Write at least seven sentences. Include details from your own experience.
3. Check your sentences for subject-verb agreement.

Copyright © 2014 by William H. Sadlier, Inc. All rights reserved.

Other Agreement Problems

LESSON **10.5**

A subject **(S)** and a predicate nominative **(PN)** may differ in number. One may be plural, and one may be singular. The verb **(V)** must agree with the subject, not with the predicate nominative.

Children's **books** (S) **are** (V) my grandmother's **passion** (PN).

The **focus** (S) of her collection **is** (V) **works** (PN) by Latino authors.

To review predicate nominatives, see **Lesson 6.6.**

Use a singular verb with an amount (such as a percentage, a measurement, or a period of time) when the amount is thought of as a single unit. Use a plural verb when the amount is thought of as individual items.

Nine months is a long time to be away. [single amount]

These last **nine months have** gone by quickly. [individual items]

Fifty percent of the CD **is** new material. [single amount]

Fifty percent of my grandmother's books **are** autographed. [individual items]

Measurements (such as length and weight) are generally considered a single unit. They take a singular verb.

Five pounds of flour **is** in the sack.

Use *don't* (a contraction for *do not*) with all plural subjects and with the pronouns *I* and *you.*

"The **librarians don't** have my wallet," sighed T. J. He whispered, **"I don't** have any money. **Don't you** have some, Eli?"

Use *doesn't* (a contraction of *does not*) with all singular subjects except the pronouns *I* and *you.*

"It doesn't matter," thought Eli. **"Doesn't T. J.** know that?"

Exercise 1 Choosing the Correct Verb

Underline the subject and the verb in parentheses that agrees with it.

1. Ten dollars (seems, seem) like a fair sale price.
2. The book (don't, doesn't) cost as much at the store on Elm Street.
3. The poet (doesn't, don't) discuss every idea she has.

4. Ms. Wilson's best present (were, was) dozens of flowers.
5. She (don't, doesn't) need to change her travel plans.
6. Janelle's favorite food (is, are) bunches of grapes.
7. (Doesn't, Don't) you need my signed permission slip?
8. Ninety percent of the food (has, have) been eaten.
9. The quarterback's legacy (were, was) two championships.
10. Two weeks (is, are) the time I have at camp.
11. One-half of the sandwich (were, was) eaten.
12. Bob (don't, doesn't) like cold weather.
13. Ten percent of the students (are, is) in their seats.
14. (Doesn't, Don't) you know my name?
15. Six yards of ribbon (is, are) missing.

Exercise 2 Writing Sentences

Work with a partner or small group to write five sentences (using present tense verbs) based on some of the information in the graph below. You may also write about your reactions to the weather conditions where you live.

1. One of your sentences should include the verb *don't* or *doesn't*.
2. Check that the verb in each sentence agrees with its subject.

Rockville's Daily High Temperatures January

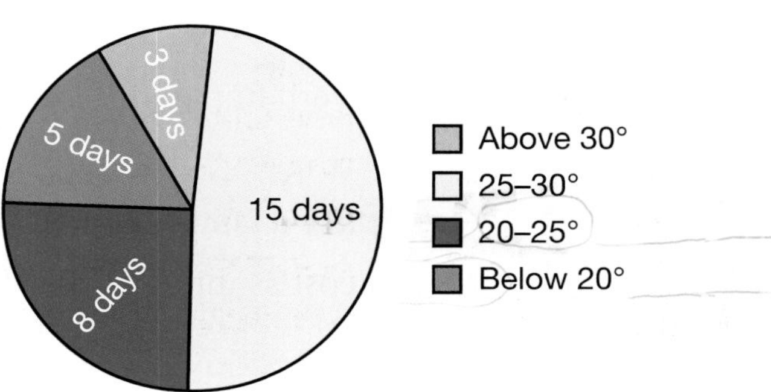

Copyright © 2014 by William H. Sadlier, Inc. All rights reserved.

Review

Have you ever left a movie with a very strong opinion? Did you talk to friends about it? If you wrote your opinion and supported it, you would be writing a review.

A **review** is a kind of persuasive writing that tries to convince readers to share an opinion. A review is a kind of persuasive writing, or **argument,** that is written in a formal style. An effective review states a claim, provides reasons to back up the claim, and supports the reasons with strong evidence.

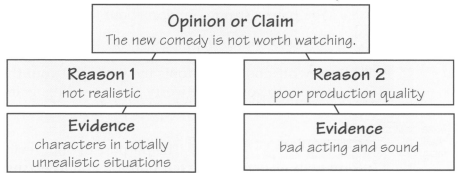

Opinion or Claim
The new comedy is not worth watching.

Reason 1
not realistic

Evidence
characters in totally unrealistic situations

Reason 2
poor production quality

Evidence
bad acting and sound

When you write a review, remember to include the following features.

Key Features

- clearly stated claim in the introduction
- logically organized reasons and evidence
- transitions that connect the reasons to the claim
- formal style
- conclusion that follows from the argument presented

ASSIGNMENT

TASK: Write a two- to three-page **review** of a new movie, television show, or Web site.

PURPOSE: to persuade readers to agree with your opinion of your subject

AUDIENCE: your classmates

KEY INSTRUCTIONS: Support your opinion with at least two reasons and specific evidence.

What Will You Review? Before you can begin writing your review, you will need to choose a topic. Follow these tips:

1. **Brainstorm ideas.** Use a chart, a Web, or other organizer to record ideas for possible topics.
2. **Rule out ideas.** Review your choices, and cross out any about which you don't have a strong opinion.
3. **Decide.** Choose the topic that fits the following criteria:
   - You find it interesting.
   - You have a strong opinion about it.
   - You remember enough details to support your opinion.

Next, freewrite about your topic by writing all your thoughts as they occur to you. Don't worry about spelling, grammar, or organization. Just get your ideas on the page.

State Your Opinion The purpose of your review is to inform your readers about your opinion and to persuade them to share it. Your opinion is your **thesis,** or **claim;** it gives the main idea of your review. Follow these guidelines to create an effective thesis:

See **Lesson 5.2** for more about developing a thesis, or claim.

- Clearly state your opinion in the introduction of your review.
- Avoid simply restating your topic.
- Make your opinion clear and concise.
- Briefly give at least two reasons for your opinion.

NO OPINION	I will discuss *The Lord of the Rings* films in this review.
NO REASON	I was very impressed by *The Lord of the Rings* films.
UNCLEAR; SLANG	There were a couple of things that were pretty cool in the three *The Lord of the Rings* films.
REVISED	*The Lord of the Rings* is an exciting film trilogy that is full of adventure and originality.

Copyright © 2014 by William H. Sadlier, Inc. All rights reserved.

Support Your Opinion Provide at least two strong reasons for your opinion. Support each reason with evidence.

- **Quotations** Use quotations from others who share your opinion, or use quotations directly from the movie, television program, or Web site you are reviewing.
- **Facts** Include statistics, dates, or any other relevant facts that support your opinion.
- **Anecdotes** Describe your own experience or others' personal experiences with your subject.
- **Comparisons** Compare the subject of your review with other subjects like it.

Organize reasons and evidence in an outline. Part of one writer's outline is shown below.

Claim: *The Lord of the Rings* is an exciting film trilogy that is full of adventure and originality.

Reason 1: The film is full of adventure.

Evidence 1: watching the film—audience on edge of their seats during action scenes — Anecdote

Evidence 2: many elaborate special effects — Facts

Evidence 3: part of a critic's review — Quotation

Organize Your Details Your review must include an introduction, a body, and a conclusion. The **introduction** states your opinion and includes a brief summary. The **body** presents your reasons and evidence. The **conclusion** restates your opinion and main points and brings your essay to a close.

CONNECTING Writing & Grammar

A sentence with a compound subject has two or more subjects sharing the same verb. If a compound subject is joined by the coordinating conjunction *and*, the verb is usually plural. See **Lesson 10.2.**

INCORRECT Frodo and Bilbo **is** both Hobbits.

CORRECT Frodo and Bilbo **are** both Hobbits.

Check Your Essay Use the checklist to review your essay. The model below shows the beginning of one review.

WRITING CHECKLIST

Did you…

- ✔ include a clearly stated claim supported by reasons and evidence?
- ✔ write a brief summary?
- ✔ include a clearly organized introduction, body, and conclusion?

Brief summary

Clear claim

First reason

Anecdote to support Reason 1

Facts to support Reason 1

Quotation to support Reason 1

[1]If you want excitement, I recommend that you watch *The Lord of the Rings* trilogy. [2]These films star Elijah Wood as Frodo. [3]Frodo is a Hobbit, a small elflike creature. [4]Frodo must carry a magic ring across many dangerous terrains and face people and creatures who are trying to kill him and steal his ring. [5]*The Lord of the Rings* is an exciting film trilogy that is full of adventure and originality.

[6]The adventures in the trilogy captivate the audience from beginning to end. [7]For example, the action scenes are incredibly entertaining. [8]When I saw the film, many in the theater were on the edge of their seats during each scene. [9]Their reaction was justified. [10]Elaborate special effects, including lifelike Orcs and dragons and swarming armies that crash across the screen, make the adventure come alive. [11]As one movie critic wrote, "The *Rings* films are packed with emotion and excitement."

Copyright © 2014 by William H. Sadlier, Inc. All rights reserved.

Chapter Review

A. Practice Test

Read each sentence below carefully. Decide which answer choice best replaces the underlined part, and fill in the circle of the corresponding letter. If you think the underlined part is correct, fill in the circle for choice *A*.

EXAMPLE

Ⓐ Ⓑ ● Ⓓ Ⓔ Reggaeton, a style of music that blends hip-hop with Jamaican and Latin American sounds, are popular in many urban areas.

(A) that blends hip-hop with Jamaican and Latin American sounds, are popular
(B) that blend hip-hop with Jamaican and Latin American sounds, are popular
(C) that blends hip-hop with Jamaican and Latin American sounds, is popular
(D) that blends hip-hop with Jamaican and Latin American sound, being popular
(E) that blends hip-hop with Jamaican and Latin American sound, popular

Ⓐ ● Ⓒ Ⓓ Ⓔ **1.** Many popular reggaeton musicians and singers comes from Puerto Rico and the Dominican Republic.

(A) musicians and singers comes
(B) musicians and singers come
(C) musician nor singer come
(D) musicians or singer come
(E) singers or musicians comes

Ⓐ Ⓑ Ⓒ ● Ⓔ **2.** The unique reggaeton beat, characterized by energetic drum tracks, get its name from a hit song.

(A) beat, characterized by energetic drum tracks, get its name
(B) beats, characterized by energetic drum tracks, gets its name
(C) beats, characterized by energetic drum track, gets its name
(D) beat, characterized by energetic drum tracks, gets its name
(E) beat get its name

Ⓐ Ⓑ Ⓒ Ⓓ Ⓔ **3.** Instruments, such as the bass, synthesizer, and drum machine, produces the reggaeton sound.

(A) Instruments, such as the bass, synthesizer, and drum machine, produces
(B) Instruments, such as the basses, synthesizers, and drum machines, produces
(C) Instrument, such as the bass, synthesizer, and drum machine, produces
(D) The bass, the synthesizer, and the drum machine producing
(E) Instruments, such as the bass, synthesizer, and drum machine, produce

Ⓐ Ⓑ Ⓒ Ⓓ Ⓔ **4.** Many of reggaeton's most popular stars lives in New York.

(A) Many of reggaeton's most popular stars lives
(B) Many of reggaeton's most popular star lives
(C) One of reggaeton's most popular stars live
(D) Many of reggaeton's most popular stars live
(E) Some of reggaeton's most popular star lives

Ⓐ Ⓑ Ⓒ Ⓓ Ⓔ **5.** Have anyone heard of a reggaeton band named after a Puerto Rican street?

(A) Have anyone heard of a reggaeton band
(B) Have everybody heard of a reggaeton band
(C) Has many of you heard of a reggaeton band
(D) Does you and your friends know about a reggaeton band
(E) Has anyone heard of a reggaeton band

B. Choosing the Correct Verb

Underline the correct verb(s) in each sentence below.

1. Your body's muscular system (is, are) a complex, hardworking machine. (Doesn't, Don't) you know that?
2. There (exists, exist) over 630 muscles in the human body, and several (act, acts) in groups.
3. One group of muscles in your face (controls, control) expressions, such as smiles and frowns.
4. Some muscles in the body (acts, act) voluntarily, but many (act, acts) involuntarily.
5. Neither walking nor talking (occur, occurs) without the use of muscles.

Copyright © 2014 by William H. Sadlier, Inc. All rights reserved.

C. Editing and Analyzing a Review

Edit this excerpt from a review, correcting any errors in subject-verb agreement. Then analyze the strengths and weaknesses of the draft by answering the questions below.

> [1]The DVD boxed set of the television series *Gilmore Girls*, which lasted seven seasons, are very entertaining. [2]Starring in the show is Lauren Graham and Alexis Bledel. [3]They play a mother and daughter.
>
> [4]The series take place in the fictional Connecticut town of Stars Hollow. [5]Many funny and interesting characters populates the town, including Luke, Kirk, and Miss Patty.
>
> [6]The element that makes *Gilmore Girls* different from other television shows are the way that it portrays teens. [7]The writers of *Gilmore Girls* sees teens as intelligent and witty. [8]*Gilmore Girls* never talk down to its viewers. [9]It presents realistic situations.

1. What are one or two strengths of the draft?

2. What are one or two weaknesses?

3. What suggestions can you give the writer about how to make the draft more effective?

CHAPTER

11

Punctuation

Copyright © 2014 by William H. Sadlier, Inc. All rights reserved.

LESSON 11.1

End Marks and Abbreviations

Periods, question marks, and **exclamation points** are **end marks,** punctuation marks used at the end of a sentence.

➡ Use a period at the end of a statement (declarative sentence) or a command or request (imperative sentence).

Seedlings grow into mature plants**.**

Put the flowers by the window**.**

See **Lesson 6.1** to review the four kinds of sentences.

➡ Use a question mark at the end of a direct question (interrogative sentence). Use a period after an indirect question.

When will the plant be fully grown**?**

The teacher asked if the flowers needed water**.**

➡ Use an exclamation point at the end of an exclamation (exclamatory sentence) and after an interjection.

That bloom is huge**!** Wow**!**

➡ Use periods after initials and many **abbreviations.** If you are uncertain about whether to use a period with an abbreviation, consult a dictionary.

Category	Examples			
Initials and Titles	Mr. J. M. Kahan, Jr.	Pat McCann, M.D.		
Addresses and Organizations	Ave.	Rd.	P.O. Box	
	Acme Co.	Bray Corp.	Treen Inc.	
Calendar Items and Time	Tues.	Fri.	Feb.	Oct.
	A.M.	P.M.	A.D.	B.C.
Other	etc.	vs.	in.	i.e.

An **acronym** is a word formed from the first letter(s) of several words. Acronyms are written without periods, as are postal abbreviations for states.

DVD MVP NFL
mph FL NE

Avoid using abbreviations or acronyms that may not be familiar to your readers.

Exercise 1 Proofreading a Paragraph

Proofread the paragraph below to add end punctuation marks and periods for abbreviations.

EXAMPLE Ms Lester says that education gives us choices

Ms. Lester says that education gives us choices.

ONLINE PRACTICE
www.grammarforwriting.com

Remember

When an abbreviation with a period ends a sentence, do not use a second period. However, do use a question mark or an exclamation point after an abbreviation.

School starts at 7:45 A.M.

Can you leave at 3:30 P.M.?

[1]Our principal, Dr Alma A Thomas, came to
talk to our class about education [2]She said
that education makes it possible for us to take
charge of our lives [3]She and Ms. Lester said that
education is not just good for us, but for our
families, too [4]In fact, they said that it's even good
for the world [5]I wondered how that is possible
[6]Then Dr Thomas explained that, around the world,
more than 115 million children of school age are not
in school [7]More than half of those children are girls
[8]My friend B J asked how the problem could be fixed

Exercise 2 Writing Sentences

Work with a partner to write four sentences about the graph below and your reactions to it. Include at least one period, question mark, and exclamation point as an end mark.

EXAMPLE Not many classmates have more than four siblings.

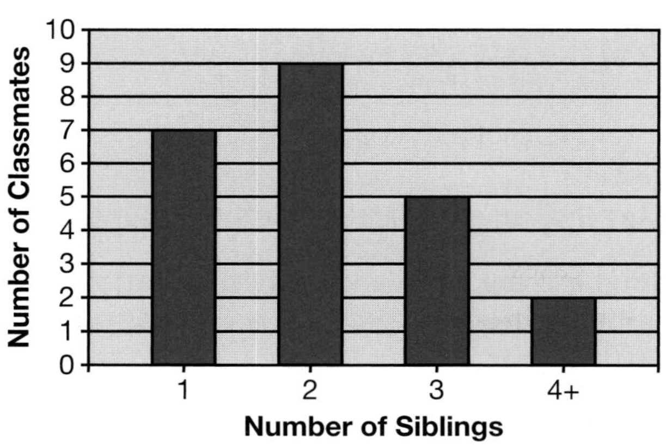

Copyright © 2014 by William H. Sadlier, Inc. All rights reserved.

LESSON

11.2

Commas I

Commas (,) are punctuation marks that indicate a pause or a break in thought. In the next several lessons, you will review the most important rules for using commas.

	Rule	Example
Items in a Series	Use a comma to separate words, phrases, or clauses that appear in a series of three or more. *Note:* Do not use a comma to separate two items.	We saw elephant tracks on the road, in the grass, and near the bush. We also saw a giraffe and a gazelle.
Adjectives Before a Noun	Use a comma to separate two or more adjectives that come before and modify the same noun.	The large, stampeding animal rushed closer.
Compound Sentences	Use a comma before a coordinating conjunction (*and, or, but, for, so, nor, yet*) that joins two independent clauses.	Kim's knees shook**,** but she never made a sound or moved.
Direct Quotations	Use a comma to separate a direct quotation from the rest of the sentence.	"Elephants**,**" Mr. Neri said**,** "are extremely intelligent."

To decide if you should use a comma between two adjectives before a noun, put *and* between them. If *and* makes sense, use a comma.

I watched the long**,** [and] boring film.

If *and* sounds awkward, do not use a comma.

I wore the heavy ~~and~~ black sweater.

See **Lessons 3.4** and **3.6** for more about compound sentences.

Exercise 1 Proofreading for Commas

Proofread the following sentences, adding commas where they are needed. Write *C* if the sentence is correct.

1. Dr. Connie Chou is an expert on brothers and sisters but she is an only child.
2. She gives lectures on sibling rivalry writes about families and testifies in court cases.
3. According to Chou "Parents should not compare their children or encourage competition between them."
4. *Who Knows You* is a fascinating well-researched book.

Remember

Do not use a comma before a coordinating conjunction that joins two compound subjects or verbs.

INCORRECT Von**,** and Jeff live in Texas**,** but work in Louisiana.

CORRECT Von and Jeff live in Texas but work in Louisiana.

5. I gave copies to my three brothers: Connor Lee and Dwayne.
6. Connor and I have an especially strong close relationship but we are not at all alike.
7. My older sister calls every week and sends e-mail every day.
8. Beth gives me advice but she doesn't expect me to follow it!
9. Competition between brothers, sisters parents or friends can sometimes be healthy but it can also cause problems.
10. Beth, Dwayne, and I used to compete in several sports.
11. We had long tough battles in tennis and basketball.
12. Nobody wanted to lose and nobody ever gave up.
13. My parents were huge sports fans and cheered for us all.
14. Beth and I talk often but we rarely see each other.
15. Dr. Chou wrote "Getting along with your siblings can be a complicated, rewarding challenge."

Exercise 2 Writing a Family History

Suppose that you've been asked to write a short history of a family member for a magazine profile.

1. Before writing, develop a list of points to cover, such as birthplace, education, jobs, family, personality traits, and interests.
2. Write one or more paragraphs.
3. Include sentences that illustrate several of the comma rules in the chart on the previous page. Be sure to proofread your paragraphs carefully.

Copyright © 2014 by William H. Sadlier, Inc. All rights reserved.

Commas II

LESSON
11.3

The chart below shows several important rules for using a **comma.** (See Lessons 11.2 and 11.4 to review other rules.)

	Rule	Examples
Introductory Words	Use a comma to set off *yes, no, well,* and single-word adjectives that begin a sentence.	Relieved**,** the boy hurried home. Yes**,** I saw him.
Introductory Phrases	Use a comma after one or more participial, infinitive, or prepositional phrases that begin a sentence.	Leaning against the wall**,** Jacob smiled. In a few minutes**,** he left.
Introductory Adverb Clauses	Use a comma after a subordinate adverb clause that begins a sentence.	If the storm passes**,** we will go to the beach.
Dates and Addresses	Use a comma to separate the date and the year. Use a comma between the city or town and the state or country.	Miguel's birthday is April 11**,** 1996. The office is near Nashville**,** Tennessee.
Letters	Use a comma after the greeting of a friendly letter and after the closing of any letter.	Dear Nora**,** Yours truly**,**

Remember

If you are unsure if you should use a comma, try reading the sentence with and without pauses. At the points where you pause naturally, you may need a comma.

Use a comma after the year or the state or country if a sentence continues after a date or address.

She gave the speech on May 30, 2005**,** to hundreds of people.

Her hometown of Penfield, New York**,** is a suburb of Rochester.

Exercise 1 Adding Commas

Add commas where they are needed in the sentences below. Write *C* if the sentence is correct.

1. Excited but nervous the last twenty campers spilled off the bus at Camp Owanka in Nisswa Minnesota.

2. In just under three hours, the August 12 camp session would officially begin.

HINT

Do not use a comma to separate a month from a year if the date is not given.

January 7, 1986

January 1986

3. When it was founded on July 4 1976 Camp Owanka consisted of only three buildings on two acres.

4. At the beginning of the 2013 season there were fourteen buildings on fifty acres.

5. To guarantee a spot for next year campers must complete their applications by March 1 2014.

Exercise 2 Proofreading a Friendly Letter

Rewrite the following letter on a separate sheet of paper, adding or deleting commas as necessary.

414 Lark, Avenue
North Rock MA 01267
July 24 2013

Dear Uncle John

1 When I was at your house last month do you remember the picture I showed you? 2 It was of a music camp in Bennington Vermont. 3 Well I just found out I will be going there. 4 My session starts August 20 2013 and lasts until August, 27. 5 Yes I am extremely excited! 6 In the past several days I have discovered that three of my best friends will also be going.

7 Before I leave I will call you. 8 If you have time, I would like to go fishing some Saturday. 9 Dad says Gull Lake is a nice spot, so maybe we could go there.

Sincerely
Ted

Copyright © 2014 by William H. Sadlier, Inc. All rights reserved.

Commas III

LESSON 11.4

Commas are used to set off **sentence interrupters,** words or phrases that interrupt, or break, the flow of thought in a sentence. Sentence interrupters, such as nonessential clauses and phrases, add extra information to a sentence. (See Lessons 11.2 and 11.3 for more comma rules.)

	Rule	Example
Direct Address	Use a comma to set off the name of a person being spoken to.	Ramon, did you see the space shuttle launch?
Appositives	Use a comma to set off nonessential appositives and appositive phrases. An **appositive** identifies a person or thing preceding it. (See Lesson 3.5.)	Yuri Gagarin, a Russian cosmonaut, was the first man in space.
Parenthetical and Transitional Expressions	Use a comma to set off a word or a phrase that interrupts a sentence.	The mission, in fact, lasted for ten days.
Nonessential Adjective Clauses and Phrases	Use a comma to set off a nonessential adjective clause or phrase.	The Kennedy Space Center, which is in Florida, employs thousands.

Some Parenthetical and Transitional Expressions

as a result	incidentally
by the way	in fact
for example	moreover
for instance	nevertheless

Nonessential phrases or clauses can be left out without changing a sentence's meaning. Use commas to set them off.

NONESSENTIAL CLAUSE

That woman**, who just flew in from Atlanta,** nearly missed her flight.

Essential clauses are necessary to a sentence's meaning. Do not use commas to set them off.

ESSENTIAL CLAUSE

The man **who is on the left** is the pilot.

Exercise 1 Adding Commas

Add commas where they are needed in the sentences below. If the sentence is correct, write *C*.

1. Valentina Tereshkova the first woman in space was also an expert parachutist.
2. Tereshkova who was born in 1937 journeyed into space in 1963.
3. The first American woman in space Sally Ride was a mission specialist in 1983.
4. At that time in fact Ride became the youngest American to enter outer space.

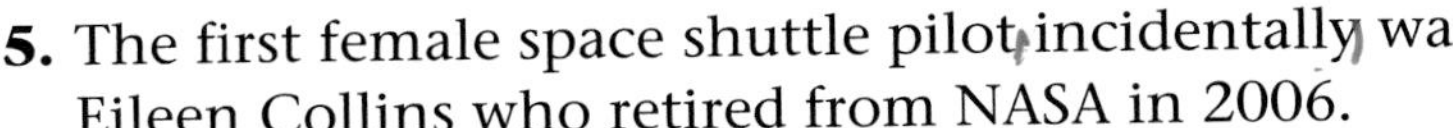

Remember

If a sentence interrupter comes at the beginning or end of a sentence, set it off with one comma.

Claudia finished her project early**, of course.**

If an interrupter comes in the middle of a sentence, set it off with two commas.

Claudia**, of course,** finished her project early.

5. The first female space shuttle pilot incidentally was Eileen Collins who retired from NASA in 2006.
6. Moreover Collins a colonel in the air force became the first woman to command a U.S. spacecraft.
7. The person who was selected from more than 10,000 applicants to be the first teacher in space was Christa McAuliffe.
8. A native of Boston McAuliffe was one of several astronauts who died in the 1986 *Challenger* disaster.
9. By the way you must be a U.S. citizen to apply for the astronaut training program; however payload specialists need not be American citizens.
10. It's too bad Andy that NASA has no plans to send children into space.

Exercise 2 Writing from Notes

Work with a partner to write an expository paragraph based on some of the notes below. Use at least one nonessential clause and one appositive. Proofread it for correct comma use.

Ellen Ochoa

Life of Ellen Ochoa

- born in Los Angeles (May 1958)
- Ph.D. in electrical engineering (1985)
- first Hispanic female astronaut
- became astronaut—1991
- veteran of four space flights
- logged over 978 hours in space
- first mission—1993—mission specialist
- last mission—2002—flight engineer
- expert on operating the RMS (Remote Manipulator System) robot arm

Copyright © 2014 by William H. Sadlier, Inc. All rights reserved.

Semicolons and Colons

LESSON 11.5

People often confuse **semicolons (;)** and **colons (:)**, but their functions are very different.

Semicolons join sentences or sentence parts.

1. Use a semicolon to join two independent clauses when you do not use a coordinating conjunction.

   Secondhand smoke can be fatal**;** experts believe it causes many deaths.

2. Use a semicolon before a conjunctive adverb or a transitional expression that joins two independent clauses. Use a comma after the conjunctive adverb or transitional expression.

   Ad campaigns warn about the dangers of secondhand smoke**; unfortunately,** many people do not heed the warnings.

3. Use a semicolon to join items in a series if one or more of the items already have commas.

   Secondhand smoke culprits include tar, a byproduct of smoke**;** nicotine, a carcinogen**;** and people who choose to smoke.

A **colon** signals that something follows.

1. Use a colon before a list of items at the end of a sentence.

   The effects of secondhand smoke are serious**:** cancer, heart disease, and respiratory infections.

2. Use a colon to introduce a long or formal quotation.

   One report reached a chilling conclusion**:** "Secondhand smoke, even at a low level, is a tremendous threat."

3. Use a colon between the hour and minutes, between a title and subtitle, and after the greeting of a business letter.

   10**:**42 A.M.   *Smoking***:** *The Facts*   Dear Store Manager**:**

Some Common Conjunctive Adverbs

accordingly	meanwhile
also	moreover
besides	nevertheless
consequently	otherwise
furthermore	still
however	then
indeed	therefore

Some Common Transitional Expressions

as a result
for example
for instance
in addition
in fact
in other words
on the other hand
that is

Exercise 1 Proofreading Sentences

Insert semicolons and colons where they are needed in the sentences below. If a sentence is correct, write *C*.

1. These items are shown in evidence a plate, a piece of broken glass, and a ticket stub.
2. The suspects include Thomas, a car mechanic Miranda, a business tycoon and Miranda's sister, Eva.
3. The author describes the trial in detail in fact, there is a diagram of the courtroom on the book's cover.
4. Detective Garcia is clever he is also funny.
5. Unique characters, funny dialogue, and a surprise ending make this mystery novel exciting. C

Remember

Do not use a colon with a list that follows a main verb or a preposition.

The officers showed the photo to: Robyn, Donnie, and Tina.

Exercise 2 Using Semicolons and Colons

Combine each pair of independent clauses by using semicolons and colons. Write the new sentences on a separate sheet of paper. You may add or delete words as necessary.

EXAMPLE Four people stayed in the hotel. They were Donnie, Mike, Robyn, and Tina.

Four people stayed in the hotel: Donnie, Mike, Robyn, and Tina.

1. The robbery probably occurred before midnight. However, it could have happened as late as 2:30 A.M.
2. The desk clerk discovered the empty vault. He called the police immediately after that.
3. Among the missing items were five paintings and a small steel safe. In addition, a diamond necklace was missing.
4. Police suspected several people, including Donnie, an architect, and Robyn, a lawyer. They also suspected Tina, an electrician.
5. After a thorough investigation, the police released all the suspects. The police have not given up.

Copyright © 2014 by William H. Sadlier, Inc. All rights reserved.

LESSON 11.6

Quotation Marks and Italics

Use **quotation marks (" ")** at the beginning and end of a direct quotation. When the quotation is an entire sentence, begin it with a capital letter. (See Lesson 11.7 for more about using quotation marks with dialogue.)

> According to Michael Crichton, **"B**ooks aren't written; they're rewritten.**"**

When only a word or phrase is quoted, use a lowercase letter if the quoted words do not begin the sentence.

> Thomas Edison described genius as **"o**ne percent inspiration, ninety-nine percent perspiration.**"**

When a quotation is made up of more than one sentence, place quotation marks only at the beginning and at the end of the entire quotation.

> Cathy explained, **"**People often misspell my name. They insist on using a *K* instead of a *C*.**"**

Use quotation marks to enclose the titles of short works, such as poems, short stories, songs, articles, book chapters, and episodes of TV programs.

> "Fire and Ice"   "The Beginning"   "Clouds"

Use *italics* for the titles of longer works, such as books, magazines, newspapers, plays, movies, and TV or radio series. (If you are writing by hand, use underlining to indicate italics; do not use both underlining and italics.)

> *Bud, Not Buddy*   *Sports Illustrated*   *Romeo and Juliet*

Also use italics for the names of works of art, ships, planes, trains, and spacecraft, as well as words, letters, and numbers referred to as such.

> *The Mona Lisa*   *Air Force One*   *Titanic*
>
> What is the difference between *affect* and *effect*?

Remember

Do not use quotation marks to set off an **indirect quotation,** a restatement of what someone said.

DIRECT Dennis asked, **"**Where is my CD case?**"**

INDIRECT Dennis asked where his CD case was.

Exercise 1 Proofreading Sentences

On a separate sheet of paper, rewrite the following sentences to correct errors in the use of quotation marks and italics. If a sentence is correct, write *C*.

1. I have always liked the folktale The Emperor's New Clothes.
2. My favorite Beatles song is "Eleanor Rigby."
3. The short story Charles has a surprising ending.
4. My teacher asked, What does dilapidated mean?
5. Ernesto Galarza's book Barrio Boy is autobiographical.
6. Do you like Georgia O'Keeffe's painting Oriental Poppies?
7. That reviewer described *Apollo 13* as a "movie masterpiece."
8. One chapter of the novel The Hound of the Baskervilles is titled *Death on the Moor*.
9. We read Gary Soto's poem "Oranges" in school today.
10. Ralph Waldo Emerson wrote, "Every hero becomes a bore at last.

See **Lesson 12.3** to review the rules for capitalizing words in a title.

Exercise 2 Writing Sentences

Write a sentence about each topic listed below. Be sure to check that you have used quotation marks and italics correctly.

1. a song or poem you dislike
2. a favorite book or story
3. a TV show you don't know much about
4. an article in a newspaper
5. a silly quotation from a made-up person

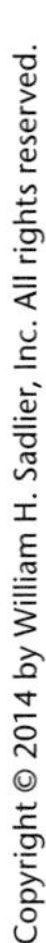
Copyright © 2014 by William H. Sadlier, Inc. All rights reserved.

Punctuating Dialogue

LESSON 11.7

Dialogue is a conversation between two or more people. The words that tell who is speaking are the **speech** (or dialogue) **tag.** When you write dialogue and direct quotations, follow these rules.

Rule 1: Use quotation marks before and after a person's exact words. If the words are a statement or a command, put the period inside the closing quotation mark.

> Kessy said, **"**The crowds at the airport were huge**."**

Rule 2: Place a question mark or an exclamation point inside the quotation marks if the question or exclamation is part of the quotation. Place the punctuation marks outside if the entire statement is a question or exclamation.

> "How much time do we have**?"** asked Robin.

> I can't believe she said, "Four hours**"!**

Rule 3: Use a comma to set off the speech tag from the rest of the sentence. Put the comma inside the quotation marks.

> "I've never seen it this crowded**,"** Kessy's father noted.

Rule 4: Use quotation marks around each part of a **divided quotation.** If a speech tag interrupts a quoted sentence, begin the second part with a lowercase letter.

> **"**Honestly**,"** said Kessy**, "f**lying makes me nervous.**"**

If the second part of a divided quotation is a complete sentence, begin the second part with a capital letter.

> **"**Flying is safer than riding in a car,**"** Robin answered with a smile. **"Y**ou shouldn't worry.**"**

Rule 5: Start a new paragraph every time the speaker changes. Note that not every quoted sentence contains a speech tag.

> "Can I stop and buy a magazine?" Robin said.

> "You'll miss the flight." Kessy's reply was quick.

Remember

Use a comma, question mark, or exclamation point to separate a quotation from a speech tag that follows it. Do not use a period.

"We're late**,**" sighed Reggie.

"How late are we**?**" asked Lynda.

"Oh no**!**" Corey exclaimed.

ONLINE PRACTICE www.grammarforwriting.com

Exercise 1 Punctuating Dialogue

On a separate sheet of paper, edit the following dialogue. Correct errors in how quotation marks and other marks of punctuation are used. You may need to add, delete, or move punctuation marks. Start a new paragraph each time the speaker changes.

In most writing, try to avoid sentence fragments. However, fragments can occasionally be effective in dialogue because they are typical of the way people talk in a conversation.

Josh asked, "Why are you late?"

"Because I overslept!" I responded.

[1]For me, a school uniform levels the playing field, explained Hank. [2]In what ways? asked Maddie. [3]"No one gets hung up on fashion Hank continued, and we can just be who we are. [4]Nobody tries to impress anyone. [5]That's silly! exclaimed Maddie. [6]"Clothes don't make us who we are, Hank. [7]That is simply not true". [8]"Well, said Hank," they let us know whether or not our parents allow us to spend a ton of money on fashion or—" [9]"Maybe" Maddie interrupted, "but I still think you're wrong. [10]It doesn't take a lot of money to dress in your own style." [11]Can't you show your own style in what you wear after school or on the weekends?" asked Hank, shrugging his shoulders. [12]Maddie snapped "That's not the point. [13]Don't I have a right to choose my own clothes?" [14]"I don't know about that Hank replied with a sigh." [15]Let's continue this debate over lunch, Maddie.

Exercise 2 Writing Dialogue

Work with a partner to write a dialogue between two people who have different points of view on a subject.

1. Follow the rules in this lesson for punctuating dialogue.
2. Try to write dialogue that sounds like the way people really talk. Use a variety of verbs besides *said* in the speech tags.

Copyright © 2014 by William H. Sadlier, Inc. All rights reserved.

Apostrophes

LESSON 11.8

Use **apostrophes (')** to show where a number or letter has been left out, to make nouns and some pronouns possessive, or to form certain plurals.

Use an apostrophe to form a **contraction,** a shortened form of a word, a numeral, or a group of words. The apostrophe shows where letters or numerals have been left out.

it is = it**'**s 2009 = **'**09 cannot = can**'**t

Use an apostrophe to make nouns and some pronouns show **possession.** Study the rules in the chart below.

Possessives	Rule	Examples
Singular nouns	Add an apostrophe and *-s.*	story**'s** ending great-aunt**'s** name
Plural nouns that end in *-s*	Add an apostrophe.	cities**'** streets parents**'** cars
Plural nouns that do not end in *-s*	Add an apostrophe and *-s.*	men**'s** sweaters people**'s** choice
Joint possession, when two or more persons or things share possession	Add an apostrophe and *-s* to the last noun.	Laura, Anne, and Alison**'s** art project
Indefinite pronouns that can show possession	Add an apostrophe and *-s.*	somebody**'s** coat anyone**'s** guess

Remember

Do not use an apostrophe in the possessive forms of personal pronouns. See **Lesson 7.6.**

INCORRECT The book is their**'**s.

CORRECT The book is thei**rs.**

Use an apostrophe and *-s* to form the plurals of letters, words, numbers, and some symbols. In general, however, do not use apostrophes to form the plurals of nouns. (See Lesson 12.7 for more about plural nouns.)

several *b***'s** many *so***'s** two *4***'s** *&***'s** and *$***'s**

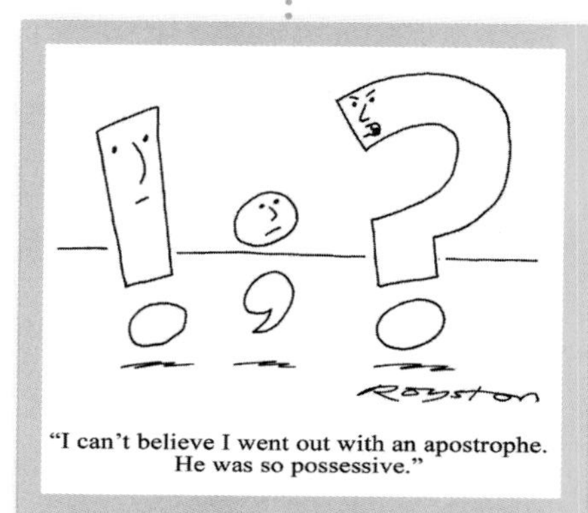

"I can't believe I went out with an apostrophe. He was so possessive."

ONLINE PRACTICE
www.grammarforwriting.com

Remember

Do not confuse *it's* with *its*. The contraction *it's* means "it is." *Its* is the possessive form of *it*.

It's my cat that injured **its** paw.

EXERCISE 1 Correcting Apostrophe Errors

Use proofreading symbols to add (^) or delete (ℽ) apostrophes as needed. Not every sentence contains an error. Some sentences have more than one.

1Stress can really take a toll on your bodys physical health and on your minds ability to focus. 2In a survey, fourteen-year-olds didnt mind listing why they worry. 3The stress caused by long hour's of homework topped the lists, along with demanding after-school activities. 4Its surprising, perhaps, but some peoples lists included families. 5Many of the teens even listed their friend's as a source of stress. 6Ten years ago, the list wasnt very different. 7Those fourteen-year-olds worries included siblings, too. 8However, theres some good news in the surveys conclusion. 9Experts say that you can do something about stress.

Working Together

EXERCISE 2 Writing a Paragraph

Write a paragraph describing something that causes you stress or something you do to try to relax.

1. Include details of at least one specific experience.
2. Use a variety of contractions and possessive nouns.
3. Ask a classmate to help you check for correctness.

Copyright © 2014 by William H. Sadlier, Inc. All rights reserved.

Other Marks of Punctuation

LESSON 11.9

A **hyphen (-)** is used to make some compound words, including compound nouns, compound adjectives that come before a noun, compound numbers between twenty-one and ninety-nine, and some fractions.

president-elect	one-third cup of milk	fifty-five
old-fashioned dress	twelve-year-old boy	ex-wife

Compound adjectives require hyphens when they come before the noun they modify, but usually not when they come after the noun.

a well-known actor
[but "an actor who is well known"]

Use a hyphen to divide a word at the end of a line. Always divide a word between syllables. Never divide a one-syllable word, and do not divide a word so that one letter stands alone.

hand-ker-chief	shame-less	mu-si-cal

A **dash (—)** is longer in length than a hyphen. Use a dash to show a sudden or dramatic break or change of thought. Also use it to set off an explanation or a list with commas.

"Bradley, please tell me where—oh, what's that noise?"

Dora—she's in eighth grade—won the spelling bee.

Use **parentheses ( )** around material that is added to a sentence but is not considered of major importance. These words might include definitions, facts, or short examples. A short sentence in parentheses may stand by itself.

The best players **(**Natalie and Mari, for example**)** should win the coaches' award.

An **ellipsis (...)** is used to indicate a pause or break in a sentence.

"I was wondering..." Maya began.
An ellipsis can also show where some words have been omitted from a quotation.

The Preamble states, "We the people . . . establish this Constitution for the United States of America."

Remember

Consult a dictionary if you're unsure whether a compound word is hyphenated or written as one or two words.

great-uncle

brand-new

pickup truck

For more about compound nouns and adjectives, see **Lesson 7.2.**

Avoid using too many dashes or parentheses in your writing. They can distract readers from your main idea.

ONLINE PRACTICE
www.grammarforwriting.com

Exercise 1 Adding Hyphens

Edit the phrases below, adding hyphens where needed. If the phrase is correct, write *C*. You may consult a dictionary.

1. sixty seven cents
2. sugar free cookie
3. bad jet lag
4. brand new car
5. large fireplace
6. two thirds majority
7. opinion that is pro uniforms
8. first rate restaurant
9. one hundred three pages
10. self confidence

Jim Abbott

Exercise 2 Editing Sentences

On a separate sheet of paper, edit the sentences below to add or delete hyphens, dashes, and parentheses where needed.

1. Jim Abbott the famous athlete is speaking tonight.
2. He is best-known for pitching in Major League Baseball, despite having been born without a right-hand.
3. Abbott (born in 1967) was an All American pitcher at Michigan and won a gold-medal in the Olympics.
4. In the early 1990s, Abbott was one of the best young left handers in baseball throwing a no hitter in 1993.
5. Abbott retired from baseball in 1999 with eighty seven wins and 888 strikeouts an amazing achievement.

Exercise 3 Writing a Paragraph

Work with a partner to write a paragraph about a person or place in the news that you find interesting.

1. You may use a newspaper, an encyclopedia, the Internet, or a textbook to find topic ideas and facts.
2. Include at least one hyphen, one dash, and a pair of parentheses.

Copyright © 2014 by William H. Sadlier, Inc. All rights reserved.

ONLINE MODEL
www.grammarforwriting.com

Research Report

You have probably read books or articles that describe the life of a famous person, a historical period or event, or a process in the natural world. Writing articles or books like these requires a lot of research. In this workshop, you will learn how to write a research report.

A **research report** is a type of expository writing, or writing that explains or informs. Research reports present information from a variety of reliable sources in support of a central idea. They differ from other types of essays because they require you to

- conduct research at the library and on the Internet
- locate credible sources that contain information on your topic
- gather important details, and take notes
- use research questions to form a thesis, or main idea
- present information from a variety of sources, and use standard citation format

Your research report should include the features below.

Key Features

- strong thesis, or claim
- clear organizational structure
- information from several credible print and digital sources
- supporting details from both primary and secondary sources
- transition words that clarify the relationships among ideas
- formal style
- Works Cited list

ASSIGNMENT

ASSIGNMENT: Write a four- to five-page **research report** on a woman who made a significant contribution to U.S. history, science, or literature.

AUDIENCE: your teachers and classmates

PURPOSE: to inform

Prewriting

Choose a Topic To guide research, generate a focused research question, such as: "How did Elizabeth Eckford help desegregate schools?" Use the following tips to find answers.

1. **Research Online.** Identify reliable search engines and online databases from educational (.edu) and government (.gov) Web sites. Use effective search terms related to your topic to help gather relevant information.
2. **Use the library.** Check the electronic database at your library, or ask a librarian for help with your search.

Make sure there are multiple print and digital sources on your topic. Also make sure these sources are accurate and up-to-date.

Write a Thesis Statement As you conduct preliminary research at the library and on the Internet, use the *5-W and How?* questions *(Who? What? When? Where? Why?* and *How?)* to focus your research question and to find information specific to your topic.

Then use the information you find to draft a possible **thesis,** or **claim.** Your thesis is your controlling idea, and it appears in your introductory paragraph. Follow the guidelines below.

Do	Don't
State an opinion or main idea about your subject.	Don't simply identify the topic of your report.
Write your thesis in one or two clear and concise sentences.	Don't make your thesis more than two sentences long.
Preview the main points you will make in your essay.	Don't introduce ideas that you will not discuss further.

CLAIM Elizabeth Eckford's upbringing gave her the courage to help desegregate schools. Her efforts helped change America for the better.

Topic Ideas

- Elizabeth Eckford, first African-American teen in a desegregated school in Arkansas
- Sandra Day O'Connor, first woman to serve on the Supreme Court
- Mae Jemison, first African-American female astronaut
- Jane Addams, 1931 winner of Nobel Peace Prize
- Maya Lin, architect of two national monuments

You can always change your thesis, or claim. See **Lesson 5.2** for more about developing a thesis.

Copyright © 2014 by William H. Sadlier, Inc. All rights reserved.

Prewriting

Locate Sources To support your thesis, or claim, you will need to present details from a variety of primary and secondary sources. **Primary sources** are original texts or documents. A **secondary source** presents a writer's interpretation of a primary source. Use the checklist on the right to evaluate your sources.

Take Notes As you research, record key words and phrases that relate to your thesis. You may use one of these three ways to record information:

- **Summarize it.** Restate main ideas and key details in your own words. A summary must be shorter than the original.
- **Paraphrase it.** Restate the passage in your own words. A paraphrase can be as long as the original.
- **Use quotations.** State facts, details, and other information in the exact words of the original. Use quotation marks.

Use index cards or an electronic document to keep track of the information you gather.

1. **Sources** On each source card—or in each entry of your electronic document—list the author, title, publisher and location, and date of publication. For online sources, include the Internet address and the date you accessed the site. (You'll need this information later when you create your Works Cited list.) Number each card or entry.
2. **Notes** On separate cards or entries, record the details you gather from your sources. Number the notes so that each one corresponds to a source card or entry.

Eckford's Childhood 3

• born October 4, 1941 • father—mechanic

• mother—teacher of blind and deaf children (p. 1)

Primary Sources

autobiography
diary
interview
letter
speech

Secondary Sources

article
biography
encyclopedia
textbook

SOURCE CHECKLIST

✔ **Up-to-date** Check that the source has been recently updated.

✔ **Accurate** Avoid Web sites that contain factual errors.

✔ **Reliable** Avoid personal Web pages and blogs.

Drafting

Avoid Plagiarism Using someone else's words or ideas without giving credit is called **plagiarism.** Plagiarism is a kind of stealing, and it is a serious issue. You must cite, or credit, all information that is not common knowledge. Common knowledge refers to facts that most people know or could find easily, such as the name of the current president. Avoid plagiarism by following the guidelines below.

1. In the body of your report, add **in-text citations** after summaries, paraphrases, and quotations. Follow these tips:
   - For information from print sources, such as books, list the author's last name and the page number of the source on which the information appears. Use parentheses.

     Later, Eckford served in the U.S. Army (Bates 87).

   - If an online source lacks page numbers, give the author's name. If it lacks an author, state the title of the Web site.

     Eckford was not aware of the revised plan (Beals).

     According to the National Park Service Web site, citizens in Little Rock voted 19,470 to 7,561 against integration.

2. At the end of your report, include a **Works Cited list**, which lists complete information for each of your sources. Alphabetize the list. For each entry, indent all turnover lines one-half inch.

Works Cited

Margolick, David. *Elizabeth and Hazel: Two Women of Little Rock*. New Haven, CT: Yale University Press, 2011. Print.

Williams, Juan. "The Legacy of Little Rock." *Time Magazine Archive*. *Time Magazine*, 20 Sept. 2007. Web. 28 Sept. 2012.

Works Cited List

Follow the style of documentation your teacher requests. Listed below are the kinds of information and the order required by MLA (Modern Language Association) style. Consult the latest edition of the *MLA Handbook* for complete information on citing sources.

Book

Author's Last Name, First Name. *Title*. Place of *Publication*: Publisher, Year Published. Print.

Web Site

Author's Last Name, First Name. *Title of Web site*. Version number. Name of institution/organization affiliated with the Web site, Date of Publication. Web. Date of access.

Copyright © 2014 by William H. Sadlier, Inc. All rights reserved.

Drafting

Organize Your Ideas The details you present in the body of your report must be clearly and consistently organized.

1. **Organize details.** Because your research report will present information about a person's life and accomplishments, organize details chronologically. To organize **chronologically,** present details in the order they happened. (See Lesson 4.4.)
2. **Use topic sentences.** Each body paragraph should begin with a **topic sentence.** A topic sentence is like a paragraph's thesis statement.
3. **Maintain paragraph unity.** All sentences that follow the topic sentence in a paragraph should support that topic.

As you draft, refer to any notes, such as an outline, you made during prewriting. Keep your thesis, or claim, in mind, and group related details into body paragraphs that have clear topic sentences. Below is the beginning of one student's outline.

WRITING HINT

Use transition words and phrases, such as *first, next, then, before,* and *after*, to connect sentences and paragraphs and clarify your organization.

Writing Model

THESIS, or CLAIM: Elizabeth Eckford's upbringing gave her the courage to help desegregate schools. Her efforts helped change America for the better.

I. Elizabeth Eckford's childhood shaped her into a person who was committed to change.
   A. Eckford was born in Little Rock, Arkansas. She attended segregated schools and faced racism.
   B. Eckford's mother, Birdie, worked at a school for blind and deaf African American children.
   C. Her parents encouraged her to go to college, but Eckford felt that segregated schools did not offer enough opportunity.

Clear topic sentence

Details that relate to and support topic sentence

Drafting

Start Out Strongly You can't just throw facts at your readers. One purpose of your introductory paragraph is to get your readers interested in what you have to say. Use the guidelines below to create a strong introduction.

1. **Grab attention.** It's important to grab your readers' interest right away. Try beginning with a quotation, exciting fact, or vivid description. Ask a question, or make a startling claim. By catching their attention, you will keep them reading.
2. **Stay focused.** State your thesis, or claim. It is often the last sentence in the introduction. Avoid introducing ideas or arguments that you will not address in your essay.

For more about writing strong introductions and conclusions, see **Lessons 5.3** and **5.5.**

End with a Bang Your concluding paragraph is just as important as your introduction. You should always leave your readers with a strong and positive impression of your work. Follow the guidelines below when drafting your conclusion.

1. **Recall your thesis, or claim.** Your conclusion should restate your thesis in new words. By restating your thesis, you will remind your readers of your report's main point and create a sense of completeness.
2. **Summarize key ideas.** You should briefly recall in a sentence or two all of the main points in your essay.
3. **End forcefully.** Always leave your readers with something to think about. Ask a question that reinforces your main point, or end with a prediction or an interesting quotation.

Copyright © 2014 by William H. Sadlier, Inc. All rights reserved.

Revising

Use the Revising Questions to improve your draft. The model below shows the revisions one writer made to an introduction.

Revising Questions

- ❑ How strong is my thesis, or claim, and where can I add details?
- ❑ How clear is my organization, and how effective are my transitions?
- ❑ How strong are my introduction and conclusion?
- ❑ Did I avoid plagiarism and cite my sources properly?

As you revise, keep in mind the traits of good writing. See **Lesson 1.3.**

[1]In the 1950s, the South was segregated. [2]African Americans faced racism, even at school. [3]Then the Supreme Court ruled that public education could not be segregated. ~~[4]This was a great ruling.~~ [5]In 1957, in Little Rock, Arkansas, nine students, including Elizabeth Eckford, faced harassment and violence as they became the first African American students to attend Central High School. [6]Eckford's upbringing gave her the courage to help desegregate schools. [7]Her efforts helped change America for the better.

Facts

Unrelated detail

Restatement of thesis, or claim

Editing and Proofreading

Use the checklist to edit and proofread your report.

Editing and Proofreading Checklist

- ❏ Have I checked that all words are spelled correctly?
- ❏ Have I used quotation marks and italics correctly?
- ❏ Have I used commas correctly with quotations?
- ❏ Did I run together or leave out any words?
- ❏ Have I used the correct format for in-text citations and the Works Cited list?

For more about quotation marks and titles, see **Lessons 11.6** and **12.3.**

Use Quotation Marks Correctly The titles of short works should be set inside of quotation marks. Use *italic* type (or underlining) to set off the titles of longer works.

"To Relive the Moment" [article]

The Long Shadow of Little Rock [book]

Be sure to use quotation marks when directly quoting from a source. Place a comma at the end of a speech tag if it precedes the quotation.

Dr. Key explains in his article**,** **"**The photograph permanently captured Eckford's courage**"** (14).

Place a comma at the end of the quotation if it precedes the speech tag.

"The photograph permanently captured Eckford's courage**,"** Dr. Key explains in his article (14).

Copyright © 2014 by William H. Sadlier, Inc. All rights reserved.

Editing and Proofreading

Writing Model

[1]Elizabeth Eckford's childhood shaped her into a person committed to change. (Canning) [2]Eckford was born in Little Rock, Arkansas, in 1941. [3]At the time, Little Rock, like the rest of the South, was segregated. [4]Even at a young age, she knew that the opportunities offered to her, as an African American, were fewer than those offered to whites. [5]In a 2004 interview with CNN, Eckford explained, "I'd always been told that I ought to, should, and would go to college. [6]And, in a segregated environment I knew that what was available to white students was more than, and better than, what was available in a Negro school."

Publishing and Presenting

Choose one of these ways to share your research report.

- **Read it to a group of other students in your class.** Ask them to explain whether they believe that the subject of your report qualifies as a hero.
- **Add it to your portfolio.** Include a one-paragraph cover sheet in which you state the title and topic of your report and summarize its main ideas.

Reflect On Your Writing

- What did you learn about researching?
- If you had to do the assignment again, what would you do differently?

CHAPTER 11

Chapter Review

A. Practice Test

Read each sentence below carefully. Decide which answer choice best replaces the underlined part, and fill in the circle of the corresponding letter. If you think the underlined part is correct, fill in the circle for choice *A*.

EXAMPLE

Ⓐ Ⓑ Ⓒ Ⓓ Ⓔ She was born on November 13 1955, and Whoopi Goldbergs given name was Caryn Johnson.

(A) She was born on November 13 1955, and Whoopi Goldbergs
(B) She was born on November 13, 1955, and Whoopi Goldbergs
(C) She was born on November 13, 1955, and Whoopi Goldberg's
(D) She was born on November 13, 1955, and Whoopi Goldbergs'
(E) She was born on November 13 1955, and Whoopi Goldberg's

Ⓐ Ⓑ Ⓒ Ⓓ Ⓔ **1.** Whoopi began her show business career at the age of eight; she performed with the Helena Rubinstein Children's Theatre in New York City.

(A) eight; she performed with the Helena Rubinstein Children's Theatre in New York City.
(B) eight-she performed with the Helena Rubinstein Childrens Theatre in New York City.
(C) eight, she performed with the Helena Rubinstein Childrens Theatre in New York City!
(D) eight: she performed with the Helena Rubinstein Childrens' Theatre in New York City.
(E) eight—she performed, with the Helena Rubinstein Children's Theatre, in New York City

Copyright © 2014 by William H. Sadlier, Inc. All rights reserved.

ⒶⒷⒸⒹⒺ **2.** Playing to sold-out audiences Goldberg starred in a one-woman show on Broadway in 1984.

(A) Playing to sold-out audiences Goldberg starred in a one-woman

(B) Playing to sold-out audiences, Goldberg starred in: a one-woman

(C) Playing, to sold-out audiences', Goldberg starred in a one-woman

(D) Playing to sold-out audiences; Goldberg starred in a one woman

(E) Playing to sold-out audiences, Goldberg starred in a one-woman

ⒶⒷⒸⒹⒺ **3.** Goldberg won an Oscar nomination for her role in "The Color Purple", Steven Spielbergs' film.

(A) "The Color Purple", Steven Spielbergs'

(B) "The Color Purple," Steven Spielberg's

(C) *The Color Purple*, Steven Spielberg's

(D) *The Color Purple* Steven Spielberg's

(E) "The Color Purple," Steven Spielbergs'

ⒶⒷⒸⒹⒺ **4.** Goldberg made several disappointing films but then she won the Academy Award for her role in Ghost.

(A) several disappointing films but then she won the Academy Award for her role in Ghost.

(B) several, disappointing films but then she won the Academy Award for her role in "Ghost"!

(C) several disappointing films, but then she won the Academy-Award for her role in *Ghost*.

(D) several disappointing films, but then she won the Academy Award for her role in *Ghost*.

(E) several (disappointing) films, then she won the Academy Award for her role in *Ghost*.

ⒶⒷⒸⒹⒺ **5.** Along with perseverance Whoopi Goldberg's talent has brought her a very long way from her childhood in the housing projects of Manhattan.

(A) perseverance Whoopi Goldberg's

(B) perseverance: Whoopi Goldberg's

(C) perseverance, Whoopi Goldberg's

(D) perseverance, Whoopi Goldbergs

(E) perseverance; Whoopi Goldberg's

Chapter Review

B. Punctuating Sentences

On a separate sheet of paper, rewrite each sentence below. Add periods, commas, question marks, colons, quotation marks, hyphens, and apostrophes as needed.

1. I've been volunteering at the community center this year said Charles.
2. Sams school is located in Oberlin Ohio.
3. Dean made a list of three items shampoo milk and tea
4. Because gas prices rose we postponed our trip
5. We did in fact mail the huge heavy boxes.
6. Dr Lauren said "Yes the homework is due today.
7. The left handed bowler did well however he didnt win.
8. I wonder where both boys bikes are
9. Mr and Mrs Gomez who are from Texas bought Kyle's house.
10. Marie Curie 1867–1934 was a well known chemist.
11. His fathers full name is Edward A Shelby, Jr
12. In the opening scene is the hero alone on the stage
13. Adams was the second president and Jefferson was the third.
14. The capital of Egypt, Cairo is a delightful fascinating city.
15. "Eve and Marys project is about Jupiter and Saturn said the teacher, "and they will present it tomorrow.

Copyright © 2014 by William H. Sadlier, Inc. All rights reserved.

C. Understanding Punctuation Marks

Match each punctuation mark below with the correct usage. Write the letter of your choice in the space provided.

___ **1.** hyphen

___ **2.** dash

___ **3.** colon

___ **4.** apostrophe

___ **5.** comma

___ **6.** ellipsis

a. to show a shift in thought

b. to follow a friendly letter's greeting

c. to join compound words

d. to introduce a long or formal quotation

e. to show where a letter has been left out

f. to show words have been omitted

D. Proofreading a Research Report

Read the body paragraph below from a research report. On a separate sheet of paper, rewrite the paragraph, correcting any punctuation errors. You may add, delete, or rearrange words.

[1]Anne Frank a German Jew spent two years during World War II hiding in an attic. [2]She recorded her experience's in her journal which became the basis of many books and plays [3]Her and her familys hiding place was discovered by German security police on August, 4 1944. [4]Sadly Anne Frank died: of typhus in the Bergen-Belsen concentration camp. [5]Nevertheless the life and tribulation's of Anne Frank will forever be remembered; through her powerful journal.

Chapter Review

CHAPTER 12

Capitalization and Spelling

Copyright © 2014 by William H. Sadlier, Inc. All rights reserved.

LESSON 12.1

Names and Titles of People

As is true of other **proper nouns,** the names of individuals are capitalized. So are many of the titles that are used with them. (See Lesson 7.1 for more about proper nouns.)

Type of Word	Examples
Names of individual people and animals	**A**lexander the **G**reat, **L**assie, **M**artin **L**uther **K**ing, **J**r.
Titles and abbreviations before names	**D**r. Brown, **G**eneral Eisenhower, **M**r. and **M**rs. Ramirez, **P**rofessor Chung
Abbreviations of academic degrees after a name	Gary Middlecoff, **D.D.S.,** Christy Cale, **Ph.D.**
Titles of heads of state and royalty before a name	**Q**ueen Elizabeth, **C**hief **J**ustice Jay, **P**resident **O**bama
Words indicating family relationships used as names or before a name	**A**unt Judy, **G**randpa Smith, "Is that your car, **U**ncle Chris?"

Remember

In general, do not capitalize titles that come after a proper name or are used alone.

Bill Frist is a **s**enator and a **d**octor.

For other rules of capitalization, see **Lessons 12.2, 12.3,** and **12.4.**

EXERCISE 1 Capitalizing Names and Titles

Most of the sentences below contain at least one error in the capitalization of names and titles. On a separate sheet of paper, write the corrected word or words. If a sentence is correct, write *C*.

EXAMPLE Rudolfo anaya is a writer of novels for young readers. Anaya

1. Rudolfo Anaya, ph.d., is also an excellent teacher.
2. He has been a Professor at several schools.
3. The birthplace of dr. Anaya is in New Mexico.
4. Martin and Rafaelita, his Parents, moved the family to another town soon after his birth.
5. Anaya enjoyed spending time swimming with his Sisters.
6. He married his wife, Patricia Lawless, in 1966.
7. His first novel tells the story of Antonio, a six-year-old boy, and his friendship with a kindly older woman, Ultima.

Rudolfo Anaya

Remember

Do not capitalize a word showing a family relationship when a possessive noun or pronoun precedes it.

We asked Tim's **m**other and his **b**rother to dinner.

8. The boy's name is Antonio Márez.

9. Antonio's Father and Mother try to give him advice.

10. My teacher, mr. Jason Bernard, jr., once met mr. Anaya.

Exercise 2 Proofreading a Paragraph

Proofread the following sentences for the correct use of capital letters. Use the proofreading symbols on the left to make the necessary corrections.

Proofreading Symbols

≡ Capitalize.

/ Make lowercase.

[1]Novelist louisa may alcott, author of Little Women (a book I truly enjoy), was born in 1832. [2]Her Father and Mother were prominent people in their hometown. [3]her uncle, Samuel j. may, was a noted abolitionist. [4]For mr. and mrs. alcott, education was extremely important. [5]Young Louisa received hours of tutoring from family friends, including Ralph waldo Emerson and henry david thoreau. [6]In 1868, miss alcott wrote Little Women, a semi-autobiographical account of her Childhood Years with her sisters in Massachusetts. [7]unlike jo, the main character in Little Women, Louisa never married. [8]Wilma Howard, ph.d., called Alcott a "marvelous storyteller." [9]I definitely agree with her opinion.

Copyright © 2014 by William H. Sadlier, Inc. All rights reserved.

Geographical Names

LESSON 12.2

Capitalize each word in the name of a specific geographical place, except for articles (*a*, *an*, and *the*) and prepositions (such as *to* and *from*).

Types of Words	Examples
Towns, cities, and states	Hanover, New Hampshire, Portland, Oregon
Countries, counties, and continents	Israel, Cook County, Guatemala, Greenland, Asia
Bodies of water	Pacific Ocean, Bay of Fundy, Lake Ontario, Turtle Pond
Streets, highways, and roads	Fifth Avenue, Highway 5, Ocean Drive, Main Street
Islands, deserts, mountains, valleys, and other landforms	Jamaica, Grand Canyon, the Sahara, Meteor Crater, San Luis Valley, Petrified Forest
Regions	the West, Northern Hemisphere, Southeast Asia
Planets, stars, constellations, and other celestial bodies	Saturn, the Milky Way, the Big Dipper, the North Star
Parks and monuments	Central Park, Statue of Liberty, Washington Monument
Buildings, bridges, and other structures	Willis Tower, the White House, Jin Mao Building, Lincoln Tunnel

Remember

The words *north*, *south*, *east*, and *west* are written with lowercase letters when they refer to directions. Capitalize them when they refer to a region.

The sun comes up in the **e**ast. [direction]

He lives in the **S**outhwest. [region]

For other rules of capitalization, see **Lessons 12.1, 12.3,** and **12.4.**

Exercise 1 Adding Capital Letters

As you read the article on the next page, add a proofreading symbol (≡) under each letter that should be capitalized.

EXAMPLE The caribbean is a top travel destination.

ONLINE PRACTICE
www.grammarforwriting.com

HINT

Common nouns like *lake*, *river*, and *park* are capitalized only when they are part of the name of a proper noun.

The **l**ake near my house is **L**ake **H**uron.

See **Lesson 7.1** to review common and proper nouns.

Top Travel Spots in the World

[1]On a vacation in trinidad, an island in the caribbean sea, you're likely to see mountains, forests, and beaches. [2]Other popular islands in the caribbean include st. lucia, st. thomas, and barbados.

[3]Paris, france, where you must see the famous eiffel tower, is still one of the world's most popular travel spots. [4]Other cities in france, like lyon and marseille, are filled with wonderful museums and flower gardens.

[5]Many think rome, italy, is one of the most beautiful cities in europe. [6]The food, museums, churches, and palaces can't be beat. [7]The appian way leads south from rome and is the oldest of the country's paved roads. [8]Italy's lake como (with the alps in the background) is one place travelers should not miss.

[9]Ah, hawaii! [10]There you'll find some of the most spectacular beaches in the world. [11]Kilauea volcano is live and continues to erupt. [12]The state capital, honolulu, is probably the best-known city in hawaii.

[13]Then there is New york city. [14]If you vacation there, you might want to visit central park and times square. [15]Don't forget to see a show, visit a museum, or tour ellis island.

CONNECTING Writing & Grammar

Add specific nouns, vivid verbs, and colorful modifiers to help readers envision the place(s) you are describing.

Exercise 2 Writing a Paragraph

Write a description of a memorable trip, a trip you dream of taking, or a real or imaginary place. In a paragraph, include the name of at least one city, one body of water, a country or region, and a park, building, or monument.

Copyright © 2014 by William H. Sadlier, Inc. All rights reserved.

LESSON 12.3

Quotations, Organizations, and Titles

Capital letters are used with quotations, the names of organizations, and in titles.

Capitalize the first word of a **direct quotation** if it begins a complete sentence.

Noah yelled, "**T**urn the music down right now!"

In a **divided quotation,** a speech tag divides the quotation into two parts. Do not capitalize the first word of the second part unless it starts a new sentence.

"I didn't hear what you said," Patti called back. "**S**ay it again."

"Do you realize," asked Larry, "**w**hat time it is?"

Capitalize all of the important words in the names of organizations, institutions, teams, government bodies, and companies.

Peace **C**orps	**G**lenbrook **H**ospital	**R**iley's **B**akery
Atlanta **B**raves	**D**epartment of **D**efense	**D**rake **U**niversity

Capitalize the abbreviations of names of organizations and institutions.

NFL (National Football League)

FBI (Federal Bureau of Investigation)

Capitalize the first and last words and all other important words in a title or subtitle. Do not capitalize articles (*a, an, the*), coordinating conjunctions (such as *and* or *or*), or prepositions of fewer than five letters (such as *of* and *with*).

"**C**asey at the **B**at"	"**G**one: **S**tories from **C**hina"
***J**ulie of the **W**olves*	***T**o **K**ill a **M**ockingbird*

See **Lessons 11.6** and **11.7** for more about punctuating quotations and titles.

Remember

Capitalize an article at the beginning of a title only if it is part of the official title.

He subscribes to ***T**he Sporting News*, not to **t**he *Orlando Sentinel*.

ONLINE PRACTICE
www.grammarforwriting.com

Exercise 1 Adding Capital Letters

HINT

Do not capitalize (or italicize) the word *magazine* unless it is part of the title.

Time **M**agazine

People **m**agazine

Write the items below, adding capital letters where necessary. Remember to underline items that are shown in italics.

1. *lost in space*
2. house of representatives
3. san francisco giants
4. "the man with two faces"
5. first bank of sun city
6. *anne of green gables*
7. *flowers for algernon*
8. *into the wild*
9. "the ransom of red chief"
10. *newsweek* magazine

Exercise 2 Proofreading Sentences

Add or delete capital letters in the following sentences as needed. If a sentence is correct, write *C*.

1. Denny asked, "who wrote *the westing game*?"
2. "I finished my paper," Julia said, "But I forgot to bring it."
3. Mr. Sanchez described the play as "not one bit funny."
4. "Dee And Sons Hardware will close at noon," Paul said.
5. "I just found out," Sapna announced, "That I got a raise."

Exercise 3 Writing About a Chart

Work with a partner to write six sentences based on information given in the chart below. Use at least one direct quotation. Check that you have used capital letters correctly.

HINT

If you're not sure what to write, try comparing statistics, asking questions about the information, or reacting to it.

Selected Universities

University of Arizona	Tucson, AZ	29,100 students
University of Connecticut	Storrs, CT	16,350 students
University of Florida	Gainesville, FL	35,200 students
University of Michigan	Ann Arbor, MI	26,100 students

Copyright © 2014 by William H. Sadlier, Inc. All rights reserved.

LESSON 12.4

Other Capitalization Rules

The chart below lists several kinds of words that should (and should not) be capitalized. (See Lessons 12.1, 12.2, and 12.3 for other rules of capitalization.)

Type of Word	Examples
Proper adjectives	**J**apanese language, **B**ritish accent, **M**ozart concertos
Languages, races, and nationalities	**S**panish, **N**ative **A**mericans, **L**atin, **G**erman, **S**wedes
Religions and religious writings	**C**hristianity, **J**udaism, **I**slam, **H**induism, the **B**ible, the **T**orah
Historical events, documents, and periods	**W**orld **W**ar I, **B**ill of **R**ights, **B**attle of **I**wo **J**ima, the **R**enaissance
Days of the week, months, holidays, and special events (but not seasons)	**T**uesday, **J**anuary, **M**emorial **D**ay, **H**anukkah, **S**uper **B**owl, **s**pring, **f**all
Particular school courses (but not general subjects except for languages)	**G**eography I, **W**orld **L**iterature, **B**asic **A**lgebra, **F**rench, **h**istory, **c**hemistry
Ships, planes, trains, and spacecraft	the ***M****onitor*, the ***C****oncorde*, the ***O****rient* ***E****xpress*, the ***C****hallenger*
Awards and brand names	**P**ulitzer **P**rize, an **O**scar, **C**runch-ee **C**hips
Most abbreviations	**A.M.**, **P.M.**, **B.C.**, **A.D.**, **S**t., **I**nc., **G**en. Grant, **P**.**O**. Box

When you write letters, remember to capitalize the first word in the greeting and the closing.

Dear Keith, **Y**ours truly,

Also avoid capitalizing entire words in e-mail messages.

USING CAPITALS IN YOUR WRITING IS ANNOYING. It is similar to shouting.

Remember

Proper adjectives are formed from proper nouns. See **Lessons 7.1** and **9.1** for more about proper nouns and adjectives.

Exercise 1 Proofreading Sentences

Insert capital letters where they belong in the sentences below. To indicate a capital letter, use the proofreading symbol (≡). If a sentence is correct, write *C*.

1. Over 90 percent of China's population is chinese han.
2. Other nationalities include tibetan and korean.
3. In school, I am taking a class in chinese history and learning to speak mandarin.
4. We learned that Buddhism was introduced many centuries ago.
5. The treaty of nanking turned Hong Kong over to british rule.
6. Mr. Mehta returned from his asian trip last friday.
7. He left India on a national holiday, republic day.
8. India was a british colony until the mid-twentieth century.
9. Last fall in our language arts class, we read a speech by Mohandas K. Gandhi, a well-known Indian leader.
10. Many indian people practice hinduism, islam, sikhism, or christianity.

Exercise 2 Writing a Paragraph

Work with a partner to write a paragraph about a historical event or document.

1. Explain the event or document and its importance to an audience of younger children who know little about the topic.
2. Keep your vocabulary and sentences simple.
3. Proofread your draft carefully. Be sure to correct any errors in capitalization.

Remember

Capitalize names of specific historical periods but not general measurements of time.

Industrial **R**evolution
twentieth **c**entury

Copyright © 2014 by William H. Sadlier, Inc. All rights reserved.

LESSON 12.5

Spelling Rules

Misspelled words are major errors that can distract or confuse your readers. Learn the basic spelling rules below, and make it a habit to proofread your writing carefully for spelling errors. (See Lesson 12.6 for rules about adding prefixes and suffixes.)

Rule	Examples		
Use *i* before *e* for most words when the sound is a long *e*.	bel**ie**ve br**ie**f ch**ie**f	f**ie**ld hyg**ie**ne n**ie**ce	p**ie**ce rel**ie**f sh**ie**ld
Use *e* before *i* after *c* or when the sound is not pronounced as a long *e*.	**cei**ling de**cei**t per**cei**ve	**ei**ght fr**ei**ght n**ei**ghbor	the**ir** h**ei**ght w**ei**ghs
Watch for words that end with the sound *seed*. Only one word is spelled with *-sede*. Three words end with *-ceed*. Most other words end in *-cede*.	super**sede**	ex**ceed** pro**ceed** suc**ceed**	pre**cede** con**cede** re**cede**

Some words are easily confused with others. **Homophones** share the same pronunciation but have different meanings and spellings. Below are several examples. For others, see pages 325–328.

I gave each child a **piece** of cake, and everyone was finally at **peace.**

In the **past** week, Larry **passed** his driving test.

Check the Web **site,** and **cite** your information carefully.

To improve your spelling, create a spelling notebook in which you list words that you frequently misspell. Look at the word, and say it aloud, pronouncing each syllable. Write the word several times until you have memorized the correct spelling.

Remember

There are often exceptions to spelling rules. Below, for example, are a few words that don't follow the rules for *ie* and *ei*.

ancient	mischief
anxiety	neither
caffeine	patience
conscience	protein
either	science
friend	seize
leisure	weird

If you're unsure how to spell a word, check an online dictionary. See page 323 for a list of frequently misspelled words.

Exercise 1 Proofreading Sentences

If a sentence contains a misspelled word, underline it, and write the correct spelling. If a sentence has no spelling errors, write *C*. **Hint:** Two sentences have more than one error.

Remember

Be alert for silent letters. Look for letter combinations that often contain silent letters.

com**b** **k**nick
crum**b** **k**night
gnarled **k**nuckle
gnome si**g**n

1. The teacher siezed the opportunity to read the textbook.
2. Neither of us has any anxiety about succeeding on the test.
3. I believe my friend will concede the election for class president.
4. Principal Martinez announced with patience, "This form I past out should superseed all previous copies."
5. Please sight your sources when you summarize that wierd science article.

Exercise 2 Analyzing Your Writing

Find a paper you are currently writing or have written recently.

1. Use a print or online dictionary to check it for any errors in spelling or with homophones.
2. List any words you misused or misspelled, and identify which, if any, of the rules in this lesson apply.

Write What You Think

On a separate sheet of paper, write a paragraph of at least six sentences in which you explain your answer to the question below.

Should schools pay students for getting good grades and high test scores?

1. Use at least two words that demonstrate a spelling rule listed on the previous page.
2. When you have finished writing, ask a classmate to help you proofread your paragraph for spelling errors.

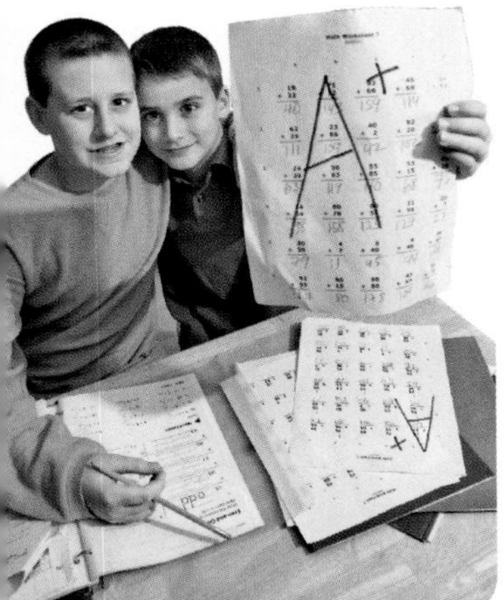

Copyright © 2014 by William H. Sadlier, Inc. All rights reserved.

Adding Prefixes and Suffixes

LESSON 12.6

A **prefix** is added to the beginning of a word to change its meaning. A **suffix** is added to the end of a word to change its meaning. Follow these rules to avoid spelling mistakes when you add prefixes and suffixes.

Rule	Examples
When adding a prefix to a word, do not change the spelling of the original word.	*mis-* + spelled = **mis**spelled *un-* + necessary = **un**necessary
Drop a word's final silent *-e* before adding a suffix that begins with a vowel. **Note:** Keep the final silent *-e* if the word ends in *-ge* or *-ce* and the suffix begins with *a* or *o*.	describe + *-ing* = describ**ing** create + *-ive* = creat**ive** courage + *-ous* = courage**ous**
Keep the final silent *-e* before adding a suffix that begins with a consonant.	hope + *-ful* = hope**ful** state + *-ment* = state**ment**
If a word ends in *-y* preceded by a consonant, change the *-y* to *i* before adding any suffix that does not begin with *i*.	lazy + *-er* = laz**ier** easy + *-ly* = eas**ily** carry + *-ing* = carr**ying**
If a word ends in *-y* preceded by a vowel, keep the *-y*.	joy + *-ous* = jo**yous** employ + *-ment* = emplo**yment**
Double the final consonant in some one-syllable words when the suffix begins with a vowel. These words end in a single consonant preceded by a single vowel.	cram + *-ing* = cra**mming** drip + *-ed* = dri**pped** win + *-er* = wi**nner** dim + *-est* = di**mmest**
Double the final consonant in some words of more than one syllable. These words end in a single consonant preceded by a single vowel, and the new word is accented on the second syllable.	prefer + *-ed* = prefe**rred** omit + *-ing* = omi**tting** begin + *-er* = begi**nner** admit + *-ed* = admi**tted**

Common Prefixes and Their Meanings

il-, im-, in-, ir-	(not)
mis-	(bad)
pre-	(before)
re-	(again)
sub-	(below)
super-	(above)

Common Suffixes and Their Meanings

-able	(capable of being)
-ate, -fy	(make, become)
-dom, -hood	(state of being)
-er, -or	(a person who)
-less	(without)
-ous, -ful	(full of)

ONLINE PRACTICE
www.grammarforwriting.com

Remember

Do not change the spelling of the original word when you add *-ness* or *-ly* to most words.

dark + *-ness* = **dark**ness

quiet + *-ly* = **quiet**ly

EXERCISE 1 Adding Prefixes and Suffixes

On a separate sheet of paper, spell each of the following words, adding the prefix or suffix given. Choose ten words, and write sentences with them. You may use a dictionary.

EXAMPLE forbid + *-en* *forbidden*

We were forbidden to explore the cave.

1. approve + *-ing*
2. *un-* + interested
3. amuse + *-ment*
4. usual + *-ly*
5. *semi-* + circle
6. outrage + *-ous*
7. bright + *-ness*
8. control + *-ed*
9. empty + *-ing*
10. defy + *-ed*
11. obey + *-ed*
12. quit + *-ing*
13. *im-* + migrate
14. noise + *-y*
15. child + *-ish*

EXERCISE 2 Proofreading an Article

As you read the article below, find ten spelling errors. Underline each misspelled word. Write the sentence number and correct spelling on a separate sheet of paper.

[1]Her knees shakeing and her hands trembling, Marian Johnson quietly smiled as she openned the front door of her house in Elmwood Heights last night. [2]The ninety-year-old woman had been waiting for this moment for a long time. [3]Fourteen months ago, Mrs. Johnson's old home had been completely destroyed by the fire that also damaged two other homes on First Street. [4]However, thanks to her careing neighbors and a dozen volunteers from Habitat for Humanity, Johnson once again has a home, a brand-new, spacious one. [5]Mrs. Johnson prefered to avoid reporters as she and her family hurryiedly carryed in two boxes of treasures she had been keeping in storeage after the fire. [6]Grining from ear to ear, her great-grandson sumed up her feelings. [7]"Granny thinks everything is amazeing," the nine-year-old yelled to the crowd that had gathered.

Copyright © 2014 by William H. Sadlier, Inc. All rights reserved.

Forming Plurals

LESSON 12.7

Follow the rules in the chart below to form the **plural** of many nouns.

Noun	Rule	Examples
Most nouns	Add *-s.*	crystal – crystal**s** fossil – fossil**s**
Nouns that end in *-s, -sh, -ch, -x,* or *-z*	Add *-es.*	church – church**es** Mr. Fox – the Fox**es**
Nouns that end in *-y* preceded by a consonant	Change the *-y* to *i,* and add *-es.*	pony – pon**ies** reply – repl**ies**
Nouns that end in *-y* preceded by a vowel	Add *-s.*	valley – valley**s** boy – boy**s** alley – alley**s**
Most nouns that end in *-f* or *-fe*	Change the *-f* to *v,* and add *-s* or *-es.*	thief – thie**ves** leaf – lea**ves** knife – kni**ves**
A few nouns that end in *-f*	Add *-s.*	roof – roof**s** belief – belief**s**
Most nouns that end in *-o* preceded by a consonant	Add *-es.*	hero – hero**es** echo – echo**es**
Nouns that end in *-o* preceded by a vowel	Add *-s.*	patio – patio**s** video – video**s**
Compound nouns	Make the most important word plural.	sister-in-law – sister**s**-in-law
Irregular nouns	Memorize these forms. No rules apply.	person – people sheep – sheep series – series

HINT

If you're not sure of a word's plural form, check a dictionary. It will list irregular plurals or alternate plurals. (Note that a few nouns have two acceptable forms: *hoofs* or *hooves.*) If no plural form is listed, refer to the rules in the chart.

Exercise 1 Forming Plurals

On a separate sheet of paper, write the plural form of each noun. Then use it in a sentence.

1. daisy
2. ratio
3. torpedo
4. half
5. loaf
6. ambush
7. bill of sale
8. mouse
9. tooth
10. child
11. species
12. toothbrush
13. Smith
14. galaxy
15. chief
16. raspberry
17. vice-president
18. Thursday
19. half-dollar
20. bookshelf

Exercise 2 Choosing Plural Forms

Underline the correct plural form in parentheses.

1. (Radios, radioes) will be on the spaceship.
2. The astronaut made several (discoverys, discoveries).
3. Two letter (*m, m*'s) are visible on the space suits.
4. All (watches, watchs) are synchronized.
5. Two (monkies, monkeys) went on board.
6. This shuttle has three (womans, women) in the crew.
7. All the astronauts are true (hero's, heroes).
8. Quiet time is followed by (flurries, flurrys) of activity.
9. This and other (journies, journeys) into space are worthwhile.
10. There are many space exploration (by-products, bys-product).

Remember

Do not use an apostrophe to form the plural of most nouns. However, to form the plural of numbers, letters, and words referred to as words, add an apostrophe and -*s*. See **Lessons 7.6** and **11.8.**

SINGULAR	*q*	*the*
PLURAL	*q*'s	*the*'s

Copyright © 2014 by William H. Sadlier, Inc. All rights reserved.

Timed Essay

Nearly all standardized tests include a timed essay. **Timed essays** require that you respond to a prompt in a limited amount of time. Prompts typically require one of the following from you:

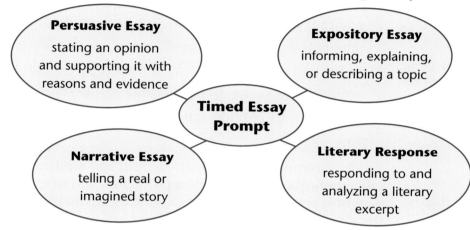

Timed Essay Prompt

- **Persuasive Essay** stating an opinion and supporting it with reasons and evidence
- **Expository Essay** informing, explaining, or describing a topic
- **Narrative Essay** telling a real or imagined story
- **Literary Response** responding to and analyzing a literary excerpt

When you write a timed essay, include the features below.

Key Features

- concise introduction with clearly stated thesis, or claim
- clear and logical organization
- relevant supporting details, facts, examples, or quotations
- complete answer to the prompt and fulfillment of all requirements
- strong conclusion

ASSIGNMENT

TASK: Write a two- to three-page **problem-solution essay** about an issue that you have studied that affects the environment.

PURPOSE: to explain the problem

AUDIENCE: your teacher or others interested in this topic

KEY INSTRUCTIONS: Include at least two possible solutions.

Understand the Prompt First, read the prompt carefully. Watch for key words that specify the task you are being asked to perform.

Length requirements Topic Purpose and format: problem-solution essay Requirements	**PROMPT:** Write a two- to three-page essay about an environmental problem that you have studied, such as unnecessary garbage caused by the use of plastic bags or bottled water. Your essay should fully explain the problem and suggest two possible solutions for correcting it. Be sure to provide specific supporting details.

In this prompt, the key words *problem* and *solutions* indicate that you are being asked to write a problem-solution essay. Problem-solution essays are a kind of expository writing that explain a specific problem and offer solutions for it.

Make a Plan Next, spend a few minutes planning your response. Follow these tips:

See **Lesson 5.2** for more about developing your **thesis,** or the main idea of your essay.

1. **Narrow your topic.** Make a list of environmental problems with which you are familiar. Choose the topic about which you have the most knowledge.
2. **Form a thesis, or claim.** State two possible solutions clearly, and use key words from the prompt. List your solutions in your thesis. Remember to make your thesis, or claim, neither too broad nor too narrow for a two- to three-page paper.

TOO BROAD	There are dozens of ways to recycle.
TOO NARROW	My sister never recycles her plastic sandwich bags.
STRONG	Unnecessary garbage caused by plastic grocery bags is an environmental problem that could be solved by requiring shoppers to bring their own reusable bags or by offering only paper bags.

Copyright © 2014 by William H. Sadlier, Inc. All rights reserved.

Support Your Claim Next, you will need to support your thesis with details. Brainstorm a list of different kinds of support.

- **Facts** Include statistics, dates, or any other relevant facts.
- **Personal observations** Describe your own experiences.
- **Examples** Include instances or details that illustrate the point you are trying to make.

Write a Complete Essay Then, write the introduction, body, and conclusion.

1. Your **introduction** presents your topic and states your thesis, or claim. Begin your essay with a question or an intriguing fact that will catch your audience's attention.
2. Your **body** presents supporting details in a consistent and logically ordered way. Each paragraph in the body should begin with a **topic sentence,** which states the main idea of the paragraph. The rest of the sentences in that paragraph must support the topic sentence.
3. Your **conclusion** restates your thesis, or claim, and all of your essay's major points. Leave your audience with something to think about. The model below shows one writer's conclusion.

For more about writing complete essays, see **Chapter 5.**

Writing Model

[1]All over the world, plastic grocery bags litter streets, hang from tree branches, and cling to beaches. [2]These bags are unnecessary and harmful. [3]Reusable and paper bags would significantly reduce this problem. [4]As consumers, we must work with our businesses to fix this dangerous environmental problem.

CONNECTING Writing & Grammar

Remember basic spelling rules such as the one below. See **Lesson 12.5** for more rules.

Put *i* before *e* except when it comes after *c*, or when it sounds like *a* as in *neighbor* or *weigh*.

(bel**ie**ve, rec**ei**ve, **ei**ght)

Check Your Essay Use the checklist to review your essay. The model below shows the beginning of one writer's essay.

WRITING CHECKLIST

Did you...

- ✔ write a clear thesis and include key words from the prompt?
- ✔ write a complete answer and fulfill all requirements?
- ✔ include relevant supporting details, an introduction, a body, and a conclusion?

Writing Model

Attention-grabbing introduction

Interesting facts

Clear thesis, or claim

[1]Plastic litter has invaded almost every corner of the globe. [2]Besides the plastic bags littering our streets, bits of toxic plastic can be found as far north as the Arctic. [3]Plastic trash floats in heaps in the Pacific Ocean, choking marine life and blocking waterways. [4]Unnecessary garbage could be reduced by requiring shoppers to bring their own reusable bags or by offering only paper bags.

Topic sentence of first body paragraph

[5]The first solution is to use reusable bags. [6]Customers must be the first to take responsibility for the way they contribute to this environmental problem. [7]Once more customers use reusable bags, stores will be less inclined to spend money on plastic bags.

Copyright © 2014 by William H. Sadlier, Inc. All rights reserved.

Chapter Review

A. Practice Test

Read the draft and questions below carefully. The questions ask you to choose the best revision for sentences or parts of the draft. Fill in the corresponding circle for your answer choice.

(1) Roald dahl was born in Llandaff, wales, in the fall of 1916. **(2)** As a child, he had a difficult time at school. **(3)** However, one School he attended was located near the offices of a famous Chocolate Company, and students were often asked to test new flavors. **(4)** This experience likely helped Dahl create the plot of *Charlie And the Chocolate Factory*. **(5)** With this book, Dahl acheived worldwide success. **(6)** The novel was published in many languages, and the chinese edition alone sold over two million copys. **(7)** The book was followed by more best seller's, including *Matilda* and *The Witches*.
(8) Generations upon generations of kids everywhere love Dahl's books, and the following quotation by the author may illustrate why. **(9)** "I only write about things," said mr. Dahl, "That are exciteing or funny. Children know I'm on there side."

Ⓐ Ⓑ Ⓒ Ⓓ Ⓔ **1.** Which of the following is the best revision of sentence 1?

(A) Roald Dahl was born in Llandaff, Wales, in the Fall of 1916.
(B) Roald Dahl was born in Llandaff, wales, in the Fall of 1916.
(C) Roald Dahl was born in Llandaff, Wales, in the Fall season of 1916.
(D) Roald Dahl was born in llandaff, wales, in the fall of 1916.
(E) Roald Dahl was born in Llandaff, Wales, in the fall of 1916.

Chapter Review

ⒶⒷⒸⒹⒺ **2.** Which of the following words should not be capitalized in sentences 3 and 4?
(A) Chocolate, Company
(B) Chocolate, Company, *Factory*
(C) School, Chocolate, *And*
(D) School, Chocolate, Company, *And*
(E) School, *And*

ⒶⒷⒸⒹⒺ **3.** Which of the following corrections need to be made to sentences 5 and 6?
(A) Correct spelling of *acheived*, *languages*, and *worldwide*.
(B) Capitalize *chinese* and *copys*.
(C) Correct spelling of *acheived* and *copys*, and capitalize *chinese*.
(D) Correct spelling of *acheived*, and capitalize *chinese* and *edition*.
(E) Correct spelling of *acheived* and *edition*, and capitalize *chinese*.

ⒶⒷⒸⒹⒺ **4.** Which of the following words or phrases in sentences 7 and 8 contain a spelling or plural form error?
(A) generations
(B) *Witches*
(C) followed
(D) best seller's
(E) There is no error.

ⒶⒷⒸⒹⒺ **5.** Which of the following is the best revision of sentence 9?
(A) "I only write about things," said Mr. Dahl, "that are exciteing or funny. Children know I'm on there side."
(B) "I only write about things," said Mr. Dahl, "that are exciting or funny. Children know I'm on their side."
(C) "I only write about things," said Mr Dahl, "That are exciting or funny. Children know I'm on their side."
(D) "I only write about things," said Mr. Dahl, "that are exciting or funny. Children know I'm on there side."
(E) "I only write about things," said Mr. Dahl, "that are exciteing or funny. Children know I'm on their side."

Copyright © 2014 by William H. Sadlier, Inc. All rights reserved.

B. Correcting Capitalization and Spelling Errors

Rewrite the following sentences on a separate sheet of paper, correcting any errors in spelling, plural forms, or capitalization.

1. Last year, my whole family went on a cruise to alaska.
2. Uncle todd, aunt Susan, and the cousins came, too.
3. We went over independence day weekend because we thought it would be a good time to visit a part of north america we hadn't seen before.
4. Reading jack London's unforgettable book *Call of The Wild* helped get me in the mood for our trip.
5. We stoped breifly in several ports; two of the citys we visited were ketchikan and skagway.
6. We took many videos of ancient Inuit costume's.
7. "I can't beleive this," I said. "it's just like the book!"
8. The gorgeous scenery exceded my expectations.
9. Uncle Todd prefered the pieceful sound of the waves.
10. We came home with a lot of great storys and are planing to take another trip next july!

C. Proofreading and Evaluating a Timed Essay

Read the essay prompt and the following draft a student wrote in response to it. Use proofreading symbols to correct any errors in spelling or capitalization. Then answer the questions that follow.

PROMPT: Write a short essay about a time you had a conflict with someone who is close to you. First, describe your relationship with this person. Then, describe the problem, and tell how you resolved the conflict in detail.

Chapter Review

Chapter Review

Proofreading Symbols

Delete.	Capitalize.
Add.	Switch order.
Make lowercase.	

[1]My freind lucy and I got into a big fight once because I felt she was being irresponseible with my things. [2]It all started when I lent her my dvd of <u>Raiders Of The Lost Ark.</u>

[3]About two Weeks after giving it to her, I asked her to return it. [4]"Well," said Lucy, "My brother has it." [5]As it turned out, her Brother Mike broke it! [6]I still wanted to beleive it wasn't Lucy's fault, so when she asked to borrow my mp3 player, I said, "Yes, please treat it carefuly." [7]That time, Lucy said she had lost it. [8]After a few more trys, I said, "I can't lend you anything anymore." [9]she got realy mad, but eventually she conceded she had been iresponsible.

1. What are the main strengths and weaknesses of this draft?
2. What test-taking tips would you give to this student about writing timed essays?

Copyright © 2014 by William H. Sadlier, Inc. All rights reserved.

Frequently Misspelled Words

abbreviate
accidentally
accommodate
achievement
analyze
anonymous
answer
apologize
appearance
appreciate
appropriate
argument
attendance
awkward
beautiful
because
beginning
believe
bicycle
brief
bulletin
business
calendar
campaign
candidate
canoe
cemetery
certain
changeable
characteristic
chorus
colonel
column
commercial
committee
courageous
criticize
curiosity
decision
definite
dependent
descend
description
desirable
despair
development
dictionary
different
disappear
disappoint
discipline
dissatisfied
eighth
eligible
embarrass
enthusiastic
environment
especially
essential
exaggerate
exceed
existence
experience
familiar
fascinating
favorite
February
foreign
forty
fragile
generally
genius
government
grammar
guarantee
height
humorous
hygiene
immediately
incidentally

independent
judgment
knowledge
laboratory
leisure
library
license
lightning
literature
loneliness
mathematics
minimum
mischievous
misspell
muscle
necessary
neighbor
niece
ninety
noticeable

nuclear
nuisance
obstacle
occasionally
opinion
opportunity
original
outrageous
parallel
particularly
people
permanent
persuade
pneumonia
possess
possibility
prejudice
privilege
probably
psychology

realize
receipt
receive
recognize
recommend
repetition
restaurant
rhythm
ridiculous
sandwich
schedule
scissors
separate
similar
sincerely
souvenir
specifically
success
surprise
syllable

sympathy
symptom
temperature
thorough
throughout
tomorrow
traffic
tragedy
truly
Tuesday
unanimous
unnecessary
usable
vacuum
variety
various
vicinity
Wednesday
weird

Commonly Confused Words

accept, except The verb *accept* means "to receive" or "to agree to something." *Except* is a preposition that means "not including."

Malcolm decided to **accept** a higher-paying job elsewhere.

He liked his job **except** for the low pay.

affect, effect *Affect* usually acts as a verb that means "to influence." When *effect* is used as a noun, it means "the result of an action."

The storm will **affect** the baseball game.

The **effects** will likely be a cancellation and upset fans.

all ready, already *All ready* is a phrase that means "completely ready." *Already*, an adverb, means "before now."

We packed the last bag and were **all ready** for vacation.

Liza is not coming to the restaurant because she **already** had dinner.

all right *All right* is always spelled as two words.

Is everything **all right**?

a lot *A lot* is always spelled as two words.

I like pizza with **a lot** of toppings.

borrow, lend The verbs *borrow* and *lend* mean opposite things. To *borrow* is "to take something on loan." To *lend* is "to loan something."

My sister asked to **borrow** my blue sweater.

I will **lend** it to her for the night.

bring, take These verbs have opposite meanings. *Bring* refers to an action toward or with the speaker. *Take* refers to an action away from the speaker.

Would you please **bring** me my glasses?

The teacher had to **take** some toys away from the misbehaving children.

capital, capitol *Capital* is usually a noun that refers to a city. The noun *capitol* refers to a building where the state government meets.

Jefferson City is the **capital** of Missouri.

The **capitol** building in Jefferson City has a large dome.

desert, dessert *Desert* can be a noun that refers to "a hot, dry area of land." It can also be a verb that means "to abandon." The noun *dessert* is a sweet treat.

The tourists must **desert** the **desert** if a sandstorm is predicted.

My favorite **dessert** is raspberry-flavored ice cream.

fewer, less Use *fewer* to refer to nouns that can be counted. Use *less* to refer to nouns that can't be counted.

The state fair had **less** publicity than the previous year, so **fewer** people came.

good, well *Good* is always an adjective. *Well* is usually an adverb that means "done in a satisfactory way." *Well* can also be an adjective meaning "in good health."

Megan is a **good** runner, but she did not run **well** in the last race.

She had a cold and did not feel **well**.

it's, its *It's* is a contraction for "it is." *Its* is a possessive pronoun.

It's time to get the door fixed.

Its creaking hinges are annoying.

lay, lie *Lay* means "to place." *Lie* means "to recline."

Before you **lie** down in a tent, remember to **lay** a tarp under your sleeping bag in case water comes in.

lead, led *Lead* (pronounced with a short *e* as in *fed*) is a noun that refers to a heavy metal. *Lead* is also a verb (pronounced with a long *e* as in *seed*) that means "to guide." *Led* is the past tense of the verb *lead*.

Pencils have graphite in them, not **lead** as some people think.

This week I will **lead** the class discussion. Maria **led** it last week.

loose, lose, loss *Loose* is usually an adjective that means "free or not tied up." *Lose,* a verb, means "to misplace." *Loss* is a noun that means "something or someone that was lost."

Jim's dog keeps getting **loose**.

He hopes to not **lose** his pet. It would be a sad **loss** for him.

passed, past *Passed* is the past tense of the verb *pass,* and it means "went by" or "succeeded." *Past* can be an adjective that means "of a previous time" or a noun that means "a previous time."

After I **passed** my science exam, the **past** year of hard work seemed long in the **past**.

The year had **passed** so quickly!

peace, piece *Peace* means "a state of calm or stillness." *Piece* means "a part of something."

Even though he loves New York, a **piece** of Andrew misses the **peace** of the countryside.

principal, principle A *principal* is a person in charge of a school. A *principle* is a belief.

Our **principal** is always trying to improve the school.

She says that hard work is a **principle.**

raise, rise *Raise* is a verb that means "to lift up." *Rise,* also a verb, means "to go up."

If you **raise** your kite high up and run, the wind will take it and make it **rise** into the sky.

their, there, they're *Their* is a possessive pronoun. *There* is a pronoun used to introduce a sentence. *They're* is a contraction for "they are."

There are lots of sports fans at the stadium.

They're hoping that **their** favorite team will win.

to, too, two *To,* a preposition, means "in the direction of." *Too,* an adverb, means "also" or "very." *Two* is the number 2.

Are you going **to** the assembly?

My class is going, **too**.

I hope it isn't **too** long.

Two presenters will speak.

whose, who's *Whose* is an interrogative pronoun. *Who's* is a contraction for "who is."

Do you know **whose** jacket this is?

Yes, it belongs to the girl **who's** standing by Juliet.

your, you're *Your* is a possessive pronoun. *You're* is a contraction for "you are."

The way **your** foot is tapping makes it seem like **you're** nervous.

Index

Q

R

S

T

U

V

W

Y